A SEVERE MERCY

*The National Religious Book Award
for Best Popular Book*

*The Evangelical Christian Publishers Association's
Gold Medallion Award*

The Campus Life Merit of Excellence

A SEVERE MERCY "touched me so deeply
that the book, finally, was like an essay in
self-understanding."
—Paul L. Holmer, author of
*C. S. Lewis: The Shape of
His Faith and Thought*

"I wept as I read. What Vanauken has written
makes all the books on marriage and
courtship seem shoddy."
—Clyde Kilby, author of
C. S. Lewis: Images of His World

"Presents the unusual experience of being taken
so utterly into a tale that one loses any distance.
The story is overwhelming. One is caught,
overwhelmed."
—Tom Howard, author of *Christ the Tiger*

A SEVERE MERCY

SHELDON VANAUKEN

BANTAM BOOKS
TORONTO · NEW YORK · LONDON

*This low-priced Bantam Book
has been completely reset in a type face
designed for easy reading, and was printed
from new plates. It contains the complete
text of the original hard-cover edition.*
NOT ONE WORD HAS BEEN OMITTED.

A SEVERE MERCY

*A Bantam Book / published by arrangement with
Harper & Row, Publishers, Inc.*

PRINTING HISTORY

Harper & Row edition published November 1977

*A selection of the Word Book Club, May 1978,
the Catholic Digest Book Club, June 1978,
the Christian Book Club for Today's Woman, June 1978,
and the Evangelical Book Club, July 1978.*

*Excerpts appeared in Christianity Today, Evangelical
Ministries (Eternity Magazine), The Dallas Morning News,
Youth in Action-South Baptist Convention, Bookshorts,
and the Canadian C. S. Lewis Journal.*

Bantam edition / July 1979

Drawings appearing throughout the book are by the author.

ISBN 0-553-12963-5

Published simultaneously in the United States and Canada

For Davy

Ah Studio! We'll meet again.
It won't be gaslight in the lane,
But just as gentle, only brighter.
And Jack on Aslan's back.
We'll sing His glory
Around those two: One Love-truth.
Old world will give one final 'crack!'
Our hearts could not be lighter.

Dom Julian, O.S.B.
(*Upon reading the Oxford
chapters of this book
in manuscript.*)

The Shining Barrier

Author's Note

The C. S. Lewis letters to me that appear in this book have been given to the Bodleian Library at Oxford. Except for salutation and closing, the latter being invariably, "Yours, C. S. Lewis," with a single exception which is shown, the letters are complete unless otherwise noted. Any ellipsis is Lewis's. An appendix at the end of the book gives the dates and places of origin of the letters. The two letters in Chapter IV and the first (welcoming) letter in Chapter V appeared in my booklet "Encounter with Light" (see below) with C. S. Lewis's permission and are not copyrighted. The Trustees of the C. S. Lewis Estate have granted a non-exclusive permission to me to publish here the remainder of C. S. Lewis's letters to me; and my thanks are tendered to them. C. S. Lewis normally but not invariably used such contractions as shd., wd., and cd. for should, would, and could; v. for very, and wh. for which—all common words—and the letters are printed as he wrote them.

The booklet, "Encounter with Light," by me was written about 1960 and is drawn upon or paraphrased for some of the material in Chapters IV and V. Copies of "Encounter" may be obtained from Wheaton College, Illinois, or the Church of the Covenant, Lynchburg, Virginia, in America.

The poems by Julian are published with the consent of the author, Dom Julian, O.S.B., Portsmouth Abbey, Portsmouth, Rhode Island.

All of the events in this story happened, the people are real people, the conversations are reconstructed —or quoted—from diaries and are very close to what was actually said. It is a true story.

Contents

Contents

A Severe Mercy

—❈{ I }❈—

Prologue: Glenmerle Revisited

The country road stretched ahead white in the moonlight and deserted. A single car, an MG-TD two-seater, was creeping along with its lights off and its top down. The driver looked intently at every tree and contour. The few houses were dark and silent, for it was long past midnight. The moon was full, high in the dome of heaven, and the June air was mild, carrying the scent of flowers and growing things.

Ahead on the right appeared a white board fence set back a ways from the road, the long x's, formed by the diagonal boards, running parallel to the road and disappearing over a low hill. The car came to a momentary halt, then moved on a few yards and crept off the road beneath a big oak. The driver uncoiled his long frame and climbed out.

The night was very still, only the faintest rustle of leaves above him betrayed some stir in the air. Somewhere in the distance a lonesome dog barked in a patient and leisurely way.

The traveller, a tall man in the late thirties, stood looking up into the branches of the oak and then began to walk with an easy stride along the road with the white fence on his right. Behind it he could see an old cherry tree: he remembered suddenly the sharp sweetness of sun-warmed red cherries and birds chirping crossly at a boy in their tree. A few hundred yards farther on, over the hill, he came to massive stone gateposts. The gates of Glenmerle. A brief smile touched his lips as he looked at the left-hand gatepost and remembered his small brother on top of it—it was easy to climb from the fence —waving frantically and unnecessarily at the fire engine that had come to put out a minor fire in a servant's room. Between the gateposts the driveway lay white and still in the moonlight, running straight in to where it curved down a hill into the trees of the park. The house itself, up a further hill, was hidden.

He stood there in the stillness, looking. A tiny breeze touched his face like a brief caress. He closed his eyes for a second or two, fancying as always that she was in the wind. "Davy?" he murmured. "Dearling?" Then he walked in through the gates, the gravel crunching where he trod. On either side beyond the poplars that began the avenue lay the gate meadows where the wild strawberries grew. An image leaped into his mind of a sunny white tablecloth and a blue and white bowl heaped with small exquisite red strawberries and flaky shortcake in the thick yellow Jersey cream from the near-by Glenmerle Farm. He swallowed and walked on.

Past the meadows the drive curved steeply down into big trees where the blackbirds lived, and the gravel became dappled with light and shadow. Now, as he descended, he could hear a ripple of water on the left where the stream flowed, and he could see gleams of silver where the moonlight fell upon it. In the shadows fireflies danced. At the bottom of the hill a little glade opened on the right, and—yes, there it was, the round lily pond: but dry now with grass bending over its edge. He looked at it, and suddenly it was full of water, and children stood around it in the sunlight. On its surface sailed a tiny frigate—a present from far-away England— with all sails set and flying the white ensign, followed by a beautifully sailing sloop; he waded in to rescue the frigate when she drove into the lilies. He looked again, and the pool was dry. He went on in the moonlight.

At length he came to a sturdy wooden bridge. Here, long ago, he had said goodbye to his brother and Davy— Davy laughing with sunbeams filtering through the trees upon her brown hair—when he left to join the fleet.

Davy, though, a few months later had come eagerly across the blue Pacific to be near him. The real farewell, not even dreamt of then, had been farewell to Glenmerle; for in the war years that were approaching, his youthful vigorous father had died and the estate had had to go. Now, more than a decade later, he stood again upon the old bridge; and Davy, unbelievably—especially here—was dead, too. And Glenmerle, unchanged as far as he could see, save for the dry lily pond, lay serene and lovely under the moon.

Across the bridge the driveway swept up another, gentler hill to the house. He could see it plainly now in the flood of moonlight, long and white and spacious. Once, in the years that were gone, there would have been lights whatever the hour, if only a dim glow from his mother's room; but tonight all was dark. He could of course have come in the daytime and been welcomed by the present owner, but he would not see others in this place. Indeed, he would go no farther than the bridge. He looked up the hill at the big comfortable country house with the dark woods behind and the lawns sweeping away in front, first down from the house and then up to South Hill, where he had so often lain as a boy, tracing the stars with his father's shooting telescope. Below the hill in the far lawn stood one willow tree. It seemed bigger than he remembered it. Now that he thought of it, so did the elm in the driveway circle and the cone of shadow that was the blue spruce in the near lawn: it looked more than twice as tall as his tall father. Beyond the spruce the ground sloped down, except for Sycamore Point, a peninsula in a sea of grass where his father had loved to sit beneath the many-trunked sycamore. Beyond the house, towering far above its three storeys, was the mighty beech that he, to his mother's suppressed alarm, had loved to climb; perched twice as high as the house, he would feel the great tree sway in the wind. Far beyond the house and the cottage and the other outbuildings came the grape arbour and then the orchard, stretching back to the tall forest trees. The far corner of the orchard, with woods on two sides, had been called "his acre." On it there had been a tiny cabin with two bunks, one above the other, where he could "sleep out." Because of his love for apples, his acre had contained ten varieties of apple tree—the crisp Jonathans had become his favourite. He wished he had one now or a bunch of purple grapes from the arbour. He remembered coming out of the cabin in summer dawns, the grass wet with dew and cold on his bare feet, and eating grapes to stay his hunger till the cook came down to cook eggs and bacon and sausage.

He pictured the interior of the house as he had known it: the drawing-room with his mother half-reclining on the graceful old Duncan Phyfe sofa, the carved Chippendale chair that a great-aunt had brought from England, the oriental rugs glowing on the floor, the white columns of the mantelpiece. Past the fireplace, at the other end of the long room where the door opened into the study, was the piano: he could see his mother seated there with her auburn hair piled high on her head and hear her clear soprano singing the light-opera songs she loved. Or he might glance out a window and see her in the flower-garden cutting flowers or conferring with the ancient gardener.

The gardener's grandson had been his playmate when he was a child. Together they had fished in the stream with bent pins and swum and prowled about the woods, sometimes with his little brother trailing along. Sometimes the two of them had gone out in the night from his cabin to steal a watermelon or two from some farmer—stolen watermelons are sweeter—and brought them back where, on top of the haystack beside the cabin, they would eat the dripping hearts while bats flitted across the stars.

His mind returned to the house. Through the study door, sitting under the "gothic" lamp with its strange leaded shade, would be his father in the deep leather chair with books and pipes all around and casement windows opening towards the wood. Other images of his father came into his mind: his father with a book and a lawn chair on Sycamore Point or his father and himself out with the guns on a frosty morning. He thought of the curious excitement of waiting for birds to burst upwards or even a rabbit's white scut bounding across a field. Once he had merely winged a crow and had brought it home to add to the white rabbits and other creatures, including a snake, that he fed and watched.

Other people came and went through his mind, the aunts and cousins who had stayed at Glenmerle. The house was always merry with people. He thought of his Kentucky aunt with her soft voice and the round tins of home-made chocolates and other sweets she would bring, especially the melt-in-your-mouth white ones that could only be made on a marble-topped table, and the beaten biscuits, too, and the country hams. She and his cousin had been much at Glenmerle, and he had been much at her house in the Bluegrass. Then he thought of his father's boyhood home, the great farm called Magic Grove, a grove planted in a mathematical figure by his grandfather's father, who was a mathematician. He remembered sitting on his grandfather's knee and being given a tiny gold dollar. Then he travelled to his other grandfather's house: the many-veranda'd Victorian house set in its ample shady lawns. In it there were marvels, the staircase window with squares of deep-red stained glass, and a bedroom-sized bathroom with an immensely long tin bathtub and a wonderful grating in the floor to bring heat up from the kitchen: whilst having your bath you could hear people chattering in the kitchen and smell the savoury odours of bacon cooking to hurry you. Or maybe his grandfather's deep voice calling you to hurry. He could see his grandfather now, white-bearded and jovial and, apparently, the permanent mayor of his town.

Somewhere along the stream a bird awoke and twittered sleepily for a moment. The ghostly watcher in the night returned to Glenmerle and in his mind ascended own domain, an odd L-shaped room with windows on the curving staircase and went along the corridor to his three sides, since part of it was a stubby wing of the house. The other arm, even when he was a boy, contained bookcases to the ceiling: his parents gave him any book he, or they, could think of. He remembered his *Treasure Island,* bound in yellow with Long John on the cover and inscribed by his father: "To my dear son on his tenth birthday." Where the bookcases made a corner, rifles and shotguns leaned, and on a shelf there were what he deemed collector's items: a discarded snakeskin, a piece of petrified wood, and actual snake in alcohol, and other treasures. Above were pictures of boys at his school: one boy, mounted, wore a helmet and held a polo stick, looking proud; and there was one of himself sitting a glossy bay. Behind the photographs, pinned to the wall, there was a tiny Confederate battleflag. The other wing of the room contained a desk and a chest of drawers, both of glowing old cherry; and above the chest was a painting of a square-rigger with a radiant sunrise or sunset astern. But he had never doubted that it was dawn and the vessel westward bound: "Leaning across the bosom of the urgent West." He wondered whether that picture had influenced his life: certainly there had been much of the sea in it, the ships of the Navy and liners and yachts under sail.

But there had been other influences as deep or deeper. The books of course had shaped his mind in a hundred ways, especially perhaps the poetry. He thought of the master at his school who had awakened him to the glory of Shakespeare, and his own discovery of Shelley. So many of the books, the best-loved ones, had been about England, and of course the poems were England itself. As a child England had seemed much nearer than New York or the cowboy west. Partly, he supposed, it was because of the year in Kensington when he was very small: Kensington and the Round Pond and tea in the nursery and "Here comes a chopper to chop off your head." And being taken out to the shires to visit country friends. That year had given England reality—perhaps that was why it lived in the books. And even as a boy he had wanted to go to Oxford. When in the end he had gone up, it had seemed both right and inevitable.

His bed had been drawn up to the east window where he could see the moonrise over the orchard and sometimes be wakened by the dawn. Across a short stretch of lawn to the north was the giant beech at the edge of the wood. At night when he went to sleep, often with his pillow on the window-sill, his last sight of the world would be the dark trees and the bright stars overhead. What was the line? "We have loved the stars too fondly to be fearful of the night." A thousand times he had imagined himself a small animal, like Mole or Rat, stealing to the edge of that familiar, friendly wood and peering out of the sheltering shadows. No, he thought, for anyone brought up like that, the woods and the night would hold no terrors, only safety.

And of course beauty: the beauty that was for him the link between the ships and the woods and the poems. He remembered as though it were but a few days ago that winter night, himself too young even to know the meaning of beauty, when he had looked up at a delicate tracery of bare black branches against the icy glittering stars: suddenly something that was, all at once, pain and longing and adoring had welled up in him, almost choking him. He had wanted to tell someone, but he had no words, inarticulate in the pain and glory. It was long afterwards that he realised that it had been his first aesthetic experience. That nameless something that had stopped his heart was Beauty. Even now, for him, "bare branches against the stars" was a synonym for beauty.

He went back up to his room, imagining himself there on a rainy day, lying comfortably on his bed and reading a book. Kipling maybe or Sherlock Holmes—or, more properly, Watson—or Rider Haggard. Or perhaps Olaf Stapledon: he had loved stories of remote futures. Then there might be a rustle outside the door, and it would be a maid with the lunch he had decided to have in his room—lunches at Glenmerle were solitary affairs—a lunch that would invariably be lemonade, fresh-squeezed, and buttery beef sandwiches. Ah, that bread! The thought of it conjured up another image of his mother, one with floury arms: only she could make the bread; that task was never entrusted to the cook. And the whole house would soon be filled with the delicious smell. The aroma of baking bread, the faint scent of lavender, and the fragrance of the cut flowers his mother was always arranging: those were the smells of Glenmerle. And perhaps the smell of his father's pipe tobacco. And the smell of guns and gun oil. He could almost smell them now, even down at the bridge in the night; and they almost persuaded him that all was as it had been. He had but to stroll up the driveway and go in through the never-locked door and go up to his room and climb into bed. He grinned in the darkness: there might be some surprises if he did. Anyhow, if it were the past, there would long since have been a quick patter of paws and Polly's nose thrust into his hand. He thought of her, a collie red-gold in the sunlight, and of all the other Glenmerle dogs, running through the grass. Dear old Polly!

He remembered suddenly a particular summer morning, wandering about the woodlands with Polly. Far from home they had come out into a lush meadow with a little hill in the centre crowned with a spreading oak. There he had sat, leaning against the bark, with Polly lying daintily at his side. He must have been, he supposed, about fifteen. He couldn't recall what it was in his reading that had begun the train of thought—yes, he could: it had been the great brains in their towers in Stapledon's splendid *Last and First Men*. He had been wont to despise emotions: girls were emotional, girls were weak, emotions—tears—were weakness. But this morning he was thinking that being a great brain on a tower, nothing but a brain, wouldn't be much fun. No excitement, no dog to love, no joy in the blue sky—no feelings at all. But feelings—feelings are emotions! He was suddenly overwhelmed by the revelation that what makes life worth living is, precisely, the emotions. But, then—this was awful!—maybe girls with their tears and laughter were getting *more* out of life. Shattering! He checked himself: showing one's emotions was not the thing: *having* them was. Still, he was dizzy with the revelation. What is beauty but something that is responded to with emotion? Courage, at least partly, is emotional. All the splendour of life. But if the best of life is, in fact, emotional, then one wanted the highest, purest emotions: and that meant joy. Joy was the highest. How did one find joy? In books it seemed to be found in love—a great love—though maybe for the saints there was joy in the love of God. He didn't aspire to that, though; he didn't even believe in God. Certainly not! So, if he wanted the heights of joy, he must have, if he could find it, a great love. But in the books again, great joy through love seemed always to go hand in hand with frightful pain. Still, he thought, looking out across the meadow, still, the joy would be worth the pain—if, indeed, they went together. If there were a choice—and he suspected there was—a choice between, on the one hand, the heights *and* the depths and, on the other hand, some sort of safe, cautious middle way, he, for one, here and now chose the heights and the depths.

Since then the years had gone by, and he—had he not had what he chose that day in the meadow? He had had the love. And the joy—what joy it had been! And the sorrow. He had had—was having—all the sorrow there was. And yet, the joy *was* worth the pain. Even now he reaffirmed that long-past choice.

Leaning there against the bridge railing in the deep still night, made only the more still by the faint murmurs and gurglings of the water beneath the bridge and the silent flashes of the fireflies, he thought of his childhood and youth in this place that was part of him, this place that lay about him so serene and lovely in the moonlight. It had been, beyond doubt, a place of accepted security. And a house of peace, peaceful and gay at the same time. His mother had gone through her days, cheerful and loving, a bit unworldly, one thought, until she suddenly and shrewdly and gently pointed out something that no one else had seen. His father, when he was home from the great world, was quiet and relaxed and amused—though capable of fearful sternness. His mother had always been quick to praise and admire; his father's rare "Well done!" had been a thing to treasure for days. A house of peace—now in the hushed night he could feel the immemorial peace that lay upon Glenmerle.

It had been a house of honour, too. In those days one was not embarrassed—that strangest of embarrassments!—at the word, the word that had to be spelled in the English way with a "u" to look right. Nor was there any embarrassment in the idea of being a gentleman. In these matters his mother and father had been completely at one; and, somehow, it seemed that they instilled what was honourable almost without speaking of it. He remembered his own code that he had made up when he was about twelve, a code of three points only: "Never betray a friend. Never betray beauty. Never betray the sword." By that last he had meant being brave when he was afraid. His father had had an old dress sword from army days in the study, and sometimes as a boy he had drawn it, just to hold it in his hand and see the long bright blade, his mind perhaps full of pictures from his reading of Sir Lancelot or Montrose. It came to him now in the night that his father, lawyer, soldier, and lover of his land, had been a very honourable gentleman. From where he stood he could see the windows of his father's room as well as his mother's, and he felt a surge of gratitude to them both, just for being what they were.

Glenmerle, he thought, had been a place to come home to, home from Kentucky or Florida or England, home from schools and home from college. He pictured coming home from boarding school, perhaps for the Christmas holidays, perhaps with snow all about—the woods full of snow. It would be a winter dusk with the big blue spruce a-twinkle with tiny white lights like stars, the big car sweeping up the hill to the house. Then his mother's cries of welcome and her kiss, his father's handshake, and his brother grinning in the background. And of course, as always, the cheery fire in the drawing-room, and through the french doors the dining-room alight with preparations. Upstairs, waiting, would be his own room, just as he had left it. Heaven itself, he thought, would be—*must* be—a coming home.

He sat down on the edge of the bridge, his legs dangling towards the silver-glinting water. All these thoughts and memories, so long in the telling, had, in fact, crowded through his mind with incredible swiftness. And even as he remembered his childhood, what was really filling his mind was Davy, Davy so loved, so dear, and now a sixmonth dead. It was she—she alone—that had brought him back to Glenmerle in the night, the girl he had loved here, the girl he had married and continued to love for a decade and a half until that winter dawn when she had blindly touched his face a last time and died with her hand in his. Since then grief, the immensity of loss, had filled his life. And yet, amidst the tears and the pain, there was a curious hint of consolation in one thought: the thought that nothing now could mar the years of their love. As he had written to his friend, C. S. Lewis in England, the manuscript of their love had gone safe to the Printer.

He wished for a moment that Lewis were here with him, just for an hour, here at Glenmerle sitting on the bridge above the stream. Lewis, he thought, would like Glenmerle; it was not, perhaps, so different from the house of the Wardrobe that led to Narnia. And Lewis understood so well, somehow, the nature of loss. Although he was so far away across the sea, Lewis had been his mainstay in this half-year of sounding the depths of grief. He it was who had said that Davy's death was a severe mercy. A severe mercy—the phrase haunted him: a mercy that was as severe as death, a death that was as merciful as love. For it had been death in love, not death of love. Love can die in many ways, most of them far more terrible than physical death; and if all natural love must die in one way or another, Davy's death—he and she in love—was the death that hinted at springtime and rebirth. Sitting there on the rough wood of the bridge, he remembered his absolute knowing—something beyond faith or belief—in the moments after her death, in that suddenly empty room, that she still was. She had not ceased with that last light breath. She and he would meet again: "And with God be the rest!" He prayed for a moment in the silent night, prayed for her wherever she might be; and for Lewis, too. In another year he would be sailing for England. That would be a coming home, also.

England and Oxford. And he and Lewis would talk
deeply and drink some beer and perhaps, as Lewis had
written, get high.

He looked up at the house on the hill and thought
again of Narnia. But Glenmerle itself, especially in the
white pour of moonlight, was a place of magic, unearthly
in its serene beauty. He remembered suddenly another
summer night in this place, a night like this one. He and
Davy, alone in the house, had put Mendelssohn's *Mid-
summer Night's Dream* on the record player at high
volume, and, with all the casements of the study flung
wide, they had gone out onto the lawn at the edge of
the wood. Everything was blanched white in the moonlight except for deep pools of shadow, and there was the
scent of roses in the air. They had held each other's
hands and danced and chased each other, smiling in the
moonlight, and at last flung themselves down laughing
beneath the great beech while the music sang around
them. He chuckled at the memory, and then, in the instant, tears were burning in his eyes and rolling down
his cheeks. That was always the way of grief: laughter
and tears, joy and sorrow.

Almost from their first meeting they had been in love,
deeply in love, and somehow sure of each other, too.
They had been secretly married before the year was out,
both of them still in their colleges. And he had brought
her to Glenmerle from the first, her own family being
far away. Glenmerle and love and springtime, the orchard
a sea of blossoms and the lilacs massed near the house.
Young love in springtime—banal perhaps to those who
had never known it or whose love had failed, not to him.
Nor to her. In those last days they had talked of Glenmerle, talked, indeed, of this very bridge where now he
sat: they had often sat here together, wrapped at times
in each other's arms. And they had talked, there in the
hospital, of dogs and trees and poems and adventures,
and of how it had all been.

From where he sat he could see the swimming pool in
the hollow below the house. A breeze must have stirred
its surface, for there were ripples in the moonpath that

ran across its surface towards him. There by the pool one
night, dreaming of the beckoning future, their special
dream had been born: the dream of a rakish schooner
sailing among far islands. The schooner was to be named
Grey Goose—for the grey goose, if its mate is killed, flies
on alone and never takes another. For a moment the
wood of the bridge became a deck, heeling slightly in a
sea-breeze, and the glint of the stream became the cold
fire of phosphorescent waves.

He and she had been much at Glenmerle: he had
always been welcome to bring home whomever he would,
bring them to a welcome and acceptance. And so on
weekends and long vacations she had been there. She
was utterly part of it. He remembered the summer when
they had got up every morning in the dark in order to
be, by the early summer dawn, out and walking with
Laddie—he of the sad eyes and adventurous heart—following country roads and paths wherever they led, patting
horses and making friends with dogs and stealing the odd
apple from a roadside tree. Sometimes they would walk
as much as twenty miles, or ride even further, and then
come home to dive into the pool, not bothering with
suits, and eat an enormous breakfast. And there were
the lazy afternoons of reading aloud and talking and
maybe going out in the night to walk down to the bridge
or the lily pond. Then they would come back to the
house and say their goodnights and go to their rooms—
but, later, when the house was all asleep, Davy would
slip into his room, between the blue sheets.

He imagined her in the house now, going softly into
his room, only to find him gone. But she would know
that he was out in the night, so she would steal down
the stairs and across the drawing-room and out into the
soft darkness, still in her nightgown. My God! was that—
had he really seen a white figure whisk down the steps?
Was she, this minute, walking soundlessly in the grass
along the borders, down towards the bridge? He stood
up, looking amongst the shrubbery for a flutter of white.
For an instant he thought he smelled the fragrance of
lilacs, and perhaps the delicate scent of the lilies-of-the-

valley she loved. Then a little breeze touched his face, and he remembered that she was in the wind now. It was too late in the year for lilacs and lilies-of-the-valley anyway. And too late, always now, for her to come to him in the night.

Once more he looked up the hill at the big comfortable house and the mighty beech above it, knowing that it was for the last time. Here at the bridge, where they had said those goodbyes so long ago, he was merely a ghost in the night. He picked up a pebble and chunked it into the bright water. Stepping off the bridge, he knelt and patted the grass, as he might have patted Laddie. Then he stood up and turned away and went back across the bridge, following the avenue past the dry lily pond and up the hill and out between the gateposts.

·{ II }·

The Shining Barrier
(the Pagan Love)

We met angrily in the dead of winter. I wanted my money back. Her job was to keep me from getting it. The scene was the photographic studio of a department store. I was probably cold and polite. She was charming but annoyed with me. She, in fact, won. On the counter between us lay a tinted miniature that had been badly done, though not by her. She, indeed, was an expert and would do it right. I left it with her and, quite possibly, stalked away.

I was then in my third year of college, home for the Christmas holidays. The miniature was of a roommate at my school, years before, who had been drowned. I wondered why I had let myself be persuaded by her. Without perceiving that I was answering the question, I remembered her quite beautiful, wide-spaced eyes, snapping with anger.

She was the daughter of a Methodist Episcopal clergyman in a small New Jersey town. She was of good family and had been to a good school in Vermont. But then the Reverend Staley Davis had died; and she, though able to finish school, had had to give up college plans. Sadly, she had gone to work in the studio of a big New York department store. But, hating New York, she had saved towards getting away from it and going to college. Now, though she was ten days my elder, she was a freshman, along with part-time work, in a small university far from New York.

15

I drove home, about twenty miles, still thinking of her, sometimes crossly, sometimes not. That afternoon a friend, Don, who lived a few miles away at Beech Hill, rang up. We were old friends and, since his return from school in Switzerland, we had both gone to the same small, academically excellent men's college, forty or fifty miles away. At the moment Don was having an idea. One of our close friends, Bob, was over at college, working and alone in the House. Why didn't we, with some girls, including Bob's girl, Mary, drive over? If Don had rung up a day later—or of course a day earlier—my sudden inspiration might not have come: now I thought rapidly of that girl's lovely if angry eyes. And I had her name on a receipt somewhere, didn't I? Yes, here it was: Jean Davis. And Don would be taking Margery, who just happened to be the personnel manager of that store, wouldn't he? Ah, good. Listen, Don: something I'd like you to do. Ring up Margery like a good chap and ask her to arrange . . .

Thus it came about that on a mid-December night, with Don and Margery and an effervescent Mary in the back seat of Mother's enormous car, I arrived in front of the white-columned House at the university where dwelt the lady of the angry eyes. An hour and a half later we reached our college town, where Bob, alerted to our coming, had made a fire in the big fireplace and welcomed us with enthusiasm. We had a drink or two, talked, danced a bit. And I discovered that Jean was called "Davy" from her surname; it seemed, somehow, to fit her, now that her eyes were no longer angry.

Then Davy and I found ourselves alone in front of the fire. Her eyes, I had not failed to observe, were indeed beautiful: long eyes, grey eyes with a hint of sea-green in certain lights. A wide brow and a small determined chin—a heart-shaped face. Rather suddenly, without previous reflection on the matter, it began to appear to me that heart-shaped faces were perhaps the best kind. She was not very tall, and I was; but now I wondered whether, after all, small girls were not more—well, more adorable, sort of. Especially when they had shining brown hair and low lovely voices and beauteous eyes.

We talked and looked at each other by firelight, for I had switched out the lamps. She told me about a coasting voyage she had taken all by herself, just because she wanted to be on a ship and the sea. No girl who liked ships and the sea could be all bad. There had been a storm, and the passengers had run or been shoo'd below; but Jean had crept forward into the bows and crouched in a coil of line, wet and loving the spray and the plunging bow. This story appealed to me beyond words. Then we discovered that we both loved poetry; she capped one of my quotations. We grinned at each other, and were linked by metre. She wasn't exactly a countrywoman, but she liked dogs; and her family had a stone cottage, built by her father, at a lake in western New Jersey. Davy liked to paddle in a canoe along the wooded shores at night, listening to the owls. A girl who liked the sea and owls and dogs and poetry: Good heavens! a girl of girls! Then—then she said something about how beauty hurts. "What! You, too?" I exclaimed, in effect. "You know *that*? The pain of beauty? I thought I was the only one." Whether love was born that night, I cannot certainly say: friendship was.

For once, at least, I listened more than I talked. And yet we both knew that everything—the sea and the owls, poems and beauty, and a sort of humour that was more a grin than a laugh—was making links between us. There was a growing excitement of discovery. I expect I talked about flying a bit, for I was very keen. And she was eager to fly. She was, indeed, an eager spirit. If any single word captures the essence of her—the *mot juste* for her, always—it is that: eager. Gay and sweet and eager. Straight, too. And valiant. That night, when very late we drove back to the city, the others sleeping in the back and she and I still eagerly talking, we had found a real closeness. Earlier I had said I would never kiss a girl unless it would really mean something. This was a bit of a challenge to Davy. Anyhow, it would have meant something.

So the next time I did. But not, as she might have
expected, in a scene of soft lights and music. Rather,
when she proved that she was not one of the screechy
girls I detested. The streets were icy. Perhaps I was
driving a bit too fast. A major intersection as the lights
changed against us—and a sheet of ice. We slid help-
lessly into the traffic. Buses thundered down upon us.
Cars all but reared up on their hind wheels to avoid us.
I snapped a glance at Davy. She caught it and grinned.
I grinned happily back. We came gently up against the
diagonally opposite kerb. A policeman with an old-
fashioned look on his face strode towards us. I leaned
quickly over and kissed her. Later, the ice being broken
as it were, I kissed her lots more.

Thus, rather improbably, began what I must call,
judging by all others I've known of, a rather remarkable
love. Its remarkableness lay, *not* in our falling quite
desperately in love—many have experienced that glory—
but in what we made of that love. The pagan love made
invulnerable by means of the Shining Barrier.

We were together three times in that December. Sadly,
a month-old commitment prevented her from coming with
me to Don's New Year's Eve party. On the morning after
that party, well after daybreak, Bob and I climbed out
of Don's car at the Glenmerle gate. We had gone somewhere else from Beech Hill and we were all sloshing with
champagne. Bob, Don's houseguest, was refusing to drive
further with Don who had thrice gone to sleep at the
wheel. Don drove obstinately off. Bob and I stood there
talking a few minutes, cars looking curiously at us—
white tie and tails in the bright morning; and then he,
refusing breakfast, set off on foot for Beech Hill. Incidentally, he met Don's mother rushing off to the scene
of the wreck; they found Don, the silly owl, sitting
gloomily on a fence waiting for the car to blow up, he
having seen a wisp of steam from the smashed radiator.
Meanwhile I trudged along the driveway, a few winter
birds chirping in the park, thinking of Davy as I had
all night. After a short sleep I rang her up just when

she was hoping hard that I might; and I drove in to get her.

On New Year's Day she came to Glenmerle. The pattern of the coming year was set: she and I together, and together at Glenmerle, which was to be the main setting for the deepening of our love. From that day forward there was to be no one else for either of us, although each of us was confronted with one difficult choice. Her moment of choice, a month later, was posed by a West Pointer who had taken her to Academy dances: he was flying in on the night we were to go to a college dance. My first impulse was to be generous—what was one evening? Then I had second thoughts. "Listen, Davy," I said. "If you go out with him instead of us going to the dance, mightn't we be sorry later? Not because you went out with him—that's not important—but because, well, because that chapter of *us* wouldn't happen. Like the New Year's Eve we didn't have. Still, you decide." We went to the dance. Much later, my very different choice came when my old flying comrade—we called ourselves the "Squadron" and had won some fame among friends for reckless deeds in the air—urged me to go with him upon a very appealing aerial adventure in Arizona. It would have meant staying out of college for a year—and no Davy. I chose her. We later referred to these choices as the "Air Force Defeat" and the "Squadron Defeat."

Not long after the New Year's Day, I had to return to college: our times together must now be weekends and an occasional midweek evening. At the college Bob and Don spread the tidings of my involvement, supported by the appearance on my desk of a quite lovely photograph of Davy. In the House whenever anyone became engaged or parted with his pin, they sang a traditional song that went: "There stood little Johnny (or Dicky)/ With his hands tied behind him . . ." After that dance— the one that was, after all, a chapter of us—they sang it for me. But long before that, just after the holidays, I worked my own ruin in the House. I was writing to

Davy one night, despite the babble of several chaps in the room, and I was saying something about how, even in cities, glimpses of beauty were precious. But that last word, though correct, didn't look right. "Bob," I said. "How do you spell 'precious'?" I should have spelled it "preshus" or even cut my tongue off. Instantly the hounds were in full cry. Did I know how to spell "adorable"? How about "angel" or "cutie"? It took awhile to live that down. Years later people would gently inquire whether I were quite sure of the spelling of "precious."

All the same, though I hadn't said so, she *was* indeed precious to me. The truth is, we were in love almost from the first, falling into love if not fallen on that first night: and I must try to tell how it was. We were hesitant to admit our love even to ourselves at first: it was too soon; one must be cool; one must be wary. The question was: could it be believed? It was like a letter announcing one's inheritance of a fortune from an unknown great-uncle. Some things take a good deal of believing. There was in both of us a kind of hesitant, incredulous wonder. Could this really be happening—this marvel? And yet in January one of us found something on falling in love that, with the appropriate pronouns, was just the way it was for both of us. A bit sentimental, perhaps, but then lovers are. It is quoted from memory, perhaps inaccurately, with thanks to the unknown author:

> To hold her in my arms against the twilight and be her comrade for ever—this was all I wanted so long as my life should last . . . And this, I told myself with a kind of wonder, this was what love was: this consecration, this curious uplifting, this sudden inexplicable joy, and this intolerable pain.

What was happening was happening to us both. I believe it is always so, mutual and, at least at first, equally intense, if it is genuine inloveness. The actual thing— inloveness—requires something like a spark leaping back and forth from one to the other becoming more intense every moment, love building up like voltage in a coil.

Here there is no sound of one hand clapping. Unreciprocated love is something else, not genuine inloveness, I think: perhaps it is infatuation and passion or, perhaps, potential inloveness. I believe that genuine inloveness is rather less common than the romantic novelists suggest. One who has never been in love might mistake either infatuation or a mixture of affection and sexual attraction for being in love. But when the "real thing" happens, there is no doubt. A man in the jungle at night, as someone said, may suppose a hyena's growl to be a lion's; but when he hears the lion's growl, he knows damn' well it's a lion. So with the genuine inloveness. So with Davy and me. A sudden glory.

We were too overwhelmed by the glory—and we had too few evenings together—to spend much time with others. In town, when I got over from college, we had quiet little dinners in restaurants with small tables and shaded lamps. In one of them a gypsy girl played her violin among the tables. I arranged for her to come to ours when I signalled and play the "Humoresque." When the moment came and she played it, I said to Davy in a low voice: "Now and always: The Humoresque means I love you." All our days whenever we chanced to hear it I said those words. Its meaning fixed, I had but to hum a few notes or whistle them for her to know.

The place we most frequented in town, though, was my father's club. There we could dine in moderate splendour. More important, one of its bars, open to ladies, was an utterly charming little wood-panelled room with a noble stone fireplace and lofty mantelpiece. On it was carved the words:

Fires, Friends, and Books Decree
Wisdom, Strength, and Covrtesy.

The fire was there, in the colder months; we were friends as well as lovers; and there were even books, in cases set into the walls. In front of the fire two short red-leather sofas faced each other, and somehow they were always waiting for us. We must have spent hundreds of hours in that quiet pleasant room, sipping a whisky-and-soda, looking into the fire or each other's eyes, talking about poetry and life and love. Talking, above all, about how love should endure: "O! how shall summer's honey breath hold out/Against the wrackful siege of battering days . . . ?" We were to raise the Shining Barrier to make it endure. The first time we came to the club we were so happy that we spoke of the evening as a "moment made eternity"—changing Browning's "instant" to the timeless "moment" of infinite duration. We were to speak of a thousand happy days and hours as moments made eternity.

As winter yielded to early spring, we came again and again to Glenmerle. There was something tender and gentle about our love, something a little shy, that was like early spring. It was as though we couldn't quite believe that it wouldn't be snatched away. The time of the crocus. Pussywillow spring. In a letter she spoke of "the gentle awkward yearning I feel for you, just to touch your face." Our love of course seemed to us a miracle. First love always does, the old, old story sung by the poets and sneered at by the wrinkled of heart. And yet it *is* a miracle, an unbelievable miracle, just as every springtime of the earth is a miracle. Here and now, in us and around us, the glory. So we wandered about Glenmerle, hand in hand, sensing the stir in the earth and in our hearts. One damp and misty day I came back from the house to meet her by the lily pond and heard her singing to herself the song from "Maytime":

> Sweetheart, sweetheart, sweetheart,
> Will you love me ever? . . .

In my room we read poetry, poems by Yeats and Shelley and Browning. We were touched by William Morris's "April" and Richard Le Gallienne's "A Ballade-Catalogue of Lovely Things." More often than not I was the one that said the poems, for anything metrical burned into my mind; and she played for me on the drawing-room piano.

If we were caught up in love, we were no less caught up in beauty, the mystery of beauty. Essentially we were pagan, but it was a high paganism. We worshipped the spirits of earth and sky; we adored the mysteries of beauty and love. Early spring became full spring. The orchard was a sea of white blossoms where we drifted enraptured in starlight and sunlight. Sometimes we walked in the rain, and we pressed our faces into masses of damp cool lilacs. I picked little posies of lily-of-the-valley to pin on to her blouse. However often it has happened to other lovers, it was to us the greatest glory we had ever known.

Long before the month it celebrates, I wrote for her the first poem of our endearing. It was as true as a poem could be. It said how it was and how it would be:

MAYTIME

The agèd winter fled away
Before the bugles of the May,—
   And love, dear love, arose.
   But when spring's glory goes
The lilacs of our love shall stay,
For ever Maytime sweet and gay,—
   Until the lilacs close
   Beneath the deathly snows.

The second time we were together we began to talk of how we should do things if we should, just conceivably, marry. We had already discovered shared values the first night by the fire at the college. Now, a little while after the perilous skid to a kiss, I said with great casualness: "You know, Davy, when two people sort of, well, like each other, it's always possible that—well, that, um, something might come of it. Like, um, getting married. So why don't we sort of talk about it? I mean, how we might do things?" Davy gulped slightly and said with barely suppressed enthusiasm: "I think that would be very interesting. And we'd learn a lot about each other, too." So, half as a game, we did so.

We considered what we supposed to be the standard problems of marriage: and solved the lot. In-laws, money, decision-making, children, jealousy. About in-laws, we said, the only possible thing was a completely united front, politely and firmly rejecting any sort of interference. And, of course, any "going home to mother"—something that women were supposed to do rather a lot of—or, indeed, going to anybody with troubles must be, for us, unthinkable: it would be a confession of failure and, therefore, the end. Firm agreement. What next? Oh, money. Well, all money, wherever it comes from, must belong equally to both of us—ours. As to spending it—and this brought us to decision-making—we should decide everything of importance by discussion, discussion until agreement is reached. No laying down the law by any-body, ever. Now, children. How do you, um, feel about that? There were, we agreed—even then we saw it—too many people everywhere. Tentatively we said: no chil-dren. What else? Jealousy? That's the worst wrecker of all. We agreed first that the only sort of marriage we should even be interested in would be one of such love that unfaithfulness would be impossible. Whether that sort of love would always be present we weren't yet asking. What we did see was that jealousy is fear: it can corrode even if quite baseless. There was only one answer: *total* trust. And, we said, if that trust were ever violated, even the least bit, then a quick end; for trust could never be restored. But until then, however risky, the trust had to be total. By the end of the evening we felt we had been very wise, very penetrating. In a way we had been, though of course we didn't appreciate the full complexity of the problems we settled so blithely. Still, most of those half-playful decisions were to hold through all the years, above all total trust, given and honoured.

One night we left the club for our car, a nondescript coupé known as the Green Duck. We drove into the country in drumming rain, imagining the snug little car to be the cabin of an aircraft. Eventually we parked, or came in for a landing, in order to kiss each other a few hundred times before I took her back to the university. In an interlude we spoke further of that which might divide lover from lover. On that earlier occasion we had thought that children might. Now we considered possessions as divisive. We knew a woman who loved her house so much that her husband could never put his feet up or smoke in his own house. We condemned her to wander the earth homeless. Over-valued possessions, we decided, were a burden, possessing their owners. We decided to own nothing that we couldn't be comfortable with—reproductions not originals, cheap bindings not rare editions. This idea of the burden of possessions we held to—and years later when we got our first glossy new car, we hit it severely with a hammer to make it comfortably dented.

Quite early on, a few weeks after we met, we had our first quarrel. My mother was in hospital for a few days, and I took Davy to see her, leaving them for awhile so that they might get better acquainted. In due course I returned for her. As I got the Green Duck underway, I said lightly, "Well, who said what?"

"Oh, secrets!" she said, also lightly. "Women's secrets. I'll never tell."

I knew quite well of course that nothing of the slightest importance had been said. But I felt obscurely that even trivial secrets were a wedge between us. Still lightly but with a hint of seriousness, I said:

"Come on! You've got to tell me! That's part of the united front."

"No," she said. "We didn't say one word about secrets." Her little chin was firm.

"Davy!" I said. "You *know* we meant no secrets. Tell me!"

"No!" she said. "We also said nobody was to lay down the law, didn't we?"

"I'm *not* laying down the law." I said. "It's a law we agreed to. Tell me."

"No," she said. "I'm not going to do it, and that's all there is to it."

"You *are* going to do it!" I said grimly. "We are *not* going to have secrets from each other." I paused. "Mind you," I added virtuously, "*I'd* tell *you*. Come on!"

Silence.

"All right!" I said, swinging the Duck violently around a corner. "I'm heading for the university. If . . . you . . . don't . . . tell . . . me . . . by the time we get there, I'll drop you and go. And I will NOT be back—ever!"

I grew pale. She grew pale.

Out of the corner of my eye I could see a stony profile. Out of the corner of her (beautiful) eye she could see a stony profile. We drove on in frightful silence.

I thought of her heart-shaped face, now forsworn, almost. I slowed the car.

Still, the car was moving. It was creeping into the university. I heard a little sound from her, like a small suppressed yelp. I gave her a hurried glance. There were tears on her cheek. Oh, God!

In a rather broken voice I croaked a few notes of the Humoresque. She uttered a loud sob. I stopped the car. A young man went by on a bicycle.

Davy said in a small voice: "All right, I'll tell you (sob). It's nothing anyway." She told it, and of course it was nothing. As she did I got the Duck moving and headed it towards Glenmerle. She finished by saying: "I wouldn't have told you, no matter what, if a little voice inside me hadn't kept saying that you were right: we really shouldn't have secrets from each other. But—would you have done it? Left? For ever?"

I thought for a moment, then said: "I meant to, you know. At least, till you sort of yelped. But—if I *had* gone, I'd have come back. Probably tonight. To ask you if you wanted to talk about it. Because it was something we had to decide."

At Glenmerle I pulled the car off the drive in the park, and we went over to the bench by the lily pond. We looked at each other with wry grins. Then we kissed each other, a kiss that was pure bliss because of the peril and pain that had torn us. There would be other fights in future years—we were both strong-willed (and both Leo, for what that's worth)—but always the reconciliation in each other's arms would be such heaven that we wondered whether the joy wasn't worth the agony. The heights and depths.

It was a mild winter afternoon, this day of the crisis. A crow cawed in the distance. Encircling the glade were the trees of the park, their bare branches reaching upwards. In front of us was the round placid lily pond where once my little ships had sailed. We talked deeply, not about the already-settled matter of secrets but about justice between lovers and about how to make love endure. What emerged from our talk was nothing less, we believed, than the central "secret" of enduring love: sharing.

"Look," we said, "what is it that draws two people into closeness and love? Of course there's the mystery of physical attraction, but beyond that it's the things they share. We both love strawberries and ships and collies and poems and all beauty, and all those things bind us together. Those sharings just happened to be; but what we must do now is share *everything*. Everything! If one of us likes *anything*, there must be something to like in it—and the other one must find it. Every single thing that either of us likes. That way we shall create a thousand strands, great and small, that will link us together. Then we shall be so close that it would be impossible—unthinkable—for either of us to suppose that we could ever recreate such closeness with anyone else. And our trust in each other will not only be based on love and loyalty but on the *fact* of a thousand sharings—a thousand strands twisted into something unbreakable."

Our enthusiasm grew as we talked. Total sharing, we felt, was the ultimate secret of a love that would last for ever. And of course we *could* learn to like anything if we wanted to. Through sharing we would not only make a bond of incredible friendship, but through sharing we would keep the magic of inloveness. And with every year, more and more depth. We would become as close as two human beings *could* become—closer perhaps than any two people had ever been. Whatever storms might come, whatever changes the years might bring, there would be the bedrock closeness of all our sharing. So we saw our way, horizon beyond horizon, ahead. And so it was to be. Gaily and seriously we sealed our compact with a handshake and then, suddenly, kissed each other.

Now I reached into my pocket and brought forth a poem. In the awful silence of our crisis I had pictured it burning with a sad blue flame, but now the time was right for it. It embodied something she had written about bare branches and so was particularly *ours*, though in truth all I have ever written has grown out of the marriage of our minds and spirits. Now by the lily pond I read it to her:

SPRING (blue)

We two shall wear the blue of spring, through all
  The years the lilac and the singing;
No drowsy summer hiding hints of fall,
  But April always, blossoms clinging.

And as night falls, before we've lost the leaven
  Of spring—bare branches, reaching, budding,
Melt quietly in dove-grey fields of heaven—
  One April kiss as dark comes flooding.

To conclude that memorable day—the devastating crisis, the master idea that was to shape our love, and the poem—my father invited us to dine with him at his club, and he called Davy "a good feller" for going to call on Mother in hospital. Davy glowed at that accolade for days. At the club we discussed large steaks and burgundy.

Later we looked back upon that day when sharing was born as the day when, earnestly, hopefully, gaily, we began to raise the Shining Barrier.

The Shining Barrier—the shield of our love. A walled garden. A fence around a young tree to keep the deer from nibbling it. A fortified place with the walls and watchtowers gleaming white like the cliffs of England. The Shining Barrier—we called it so from the first—

protecting the green tree of our love. And yet in another sense it was our love itself, made strong within, that was the Shining Barrier.

But why does love need to be guarded? Against what enemies? We looked about us and saw the world as having become a hostile and threatening place where standards of decency and courtesy were perishing and war loomed gigantic. A world where love did not endure. The smile of inloveness seemed to promise for ever, but friends who had been in love last year were parting this year. The divorce rate was in the news. Where were any older people in love? It must be that, whatever its promise, love does not by itself endure. But why? What was the failure behind the failure of love?

On a day in early spring we thought we saw the answer. The killer of love is creeping separateness. Inloveness is a gift of the gods, but then it is up to the lovers to cherish or to ruin. Taking love for granted, especially after marriage. Ceasing to do things together. Finding separate interests. "We" turning into "I." Self. Self-regard: what *I* want to do. Actual selfishness only a hop away. This was the way of creeping separateness. And in the modern world, especially in the cities, everything favoured it. The man going off to his office; the woman staying home with the children—*her* children—or perhaps having a different job. The failure of love might seem to be caused by hate or boredom or unfaithfulness with a lover; but those were results. First came the creeping separateness: the failure behind the failure.

We raised the Shining Barrier against creeping separateness, which was, in the last analysis, self. We also raised it against a world of indecencies and decaying standards, the decline of courtesy, the whispering mockers of love. We would have our own standards. And, above all, we would be *us*-centred, not self-centred. Against creeping separateness we would oppose the great principle of sharing. We saw self as the ultimate danger to love, which it is; we didn't see it as the ultimate evil of hell, which it also is. We saw only the danger to our

love. Still, we turned away from it, turned away because
we loved our love. And we were determined that it
should endure.

Creeping separateness and sharing were opposite sides
of one coin. We rejected separate activities, whether
bridge or shooting or sailing, because they would lead to
creeping separateness; on the other hand, if one of us
liked anything, the other, in the name of sharing, must
learn to like it, too. It was now that we re-examined
our doubts about children. If children could be raised
by a nanny, we sharing them for a few hours each
day, or even if we were farmers, children might be a
good. But in the pattern of modern life, where they
became the centre for the woman, they were separating.
We would not have children. Nor would we allow any
career, unless we pursued it together, to become domi-
nating.

We began immediately, with enthusiasm and thor-
oughness, to live by the principle of sharing. We decided
that each of us must read every book, even children's
books, the other had read; and we did so. Even as I was
more at home in the world of literature, so she was in the
world of music; and I began to study in the music room
of the college, letting the symphonies and quartets flow
into my being. I might remain our maker of poems and
she our maker of music—she was a talented organist and
pianist—but we became at home in both worlds. Specially
loved music she played for me and specially loved books
—and of course all poems—we read aloud. One such
book that I knew and loved was George du Maurier's
Peter Ibbetson, the story of a deathless love. We read it
together with delight; and, unable to find the film of it,
old when I'd seen it, we arranged a private showing—in
the name of sharing. In a quiet little park near the club
where we often met, there was a small bronze fairy on a
stone tree stump: she became "la fée Tarapatapoum";
and "Mimsey" became a secret, endearing name for Davy.
But that beloved book was one of hundreds; and every
book, like every poem or concerto or string quartet, became a dear bond between us. We read new books to-

gether or one right after the other. We went to plays and concerts together; and if one couldn't go, neither did. It seemed to us that one of the great separating things was the gender points of view: girls brought up to think like women, boys like men. We therefore commenced an immense effort, which we continued over the years, to see and understand the very different points of view: it is not too much to say that I learnt to think like a woman and she like a man. Inevitably our closeness was deepened, incredibly deepened, by our doing so. Our thesis that if one of us liked something there must be something to like about it which the other could find was proved again and again. And sharing was union. More and more, as I read her books and knew her music, she was in me and I in her; and so for her: the co-inherence of lovers.

The Shining Barrier was, above all, sharing and the defence against creeping separateness; but we developed other principles. One of these of course was total trust. Another that I have mentioned was our insight that possessions could become a burden. Somewhat later— I'm looking a bit beyond that first spring—we developed what might be called a principle of spontaneity: if one of us had an impulse—to stop and listen to a bird, to go for a walk in the night, to cut classes, to do anything— we both followed it always. Another, not quite the same, was the principle of the affirmative: if one of us arrived at a belief, we both accepted it unless it could be disproved; we considered that any affirmative was more to be trusted than the negative. If one of us had seen a ghost, not that either did, the other would accept, not scoff. And there was a principle of courtesy: whatever one of us asked the other to do—it was assumed the asker would weigh all consequences—the other would do. Thus one might wake the other in the night and ask for a cup of water; and the other would peacefully (and sleepily) fetch it. We, in fact, *defined* courtesy as "a cup of water in the night." And we considered it a very great courtesy to *ask* for the cup as well as to fetch it.

We sought closeness through sharing in order to keep

inloveness; but such closeness was simply true union. In an early talk at the club, we saw the process of achieving union as like two stones becoming one by grinding together, the hard bits of one wearing away the soft bits of the other, until at last the fit is perfect: one stone. Pagans that we were, we were not reminded of Christ's "one flesh" for marriage; if we had been, we might have felt a faint alliance with Him. We of course realised that our initial "fit" had been quite close—particularly in response to beauty and in sense of humour—but still the process of becoming one stone was not unattended by squeaks and howls, especially since we were both strong and combative. But we could laugh at ourselves. Another blessing—though we took it for granted—was that we could always *talk* together. We were both highly articulate, using words in the same way, and both willing and eager to talk about anything. Finally, we both believed—again we took it for granted—that we could, of *course*, alter ourselves if we once saw good reason to do so: our minds and wills were in control. The statement, so common in these days of mass psychologising, "This is the way I am and you'll just have to accept it," would have been quite impossible for either of us. We may have been over-confident, but I can't help feeling that our willingness to tackle anything was altogether preferable to the passive acceptance of known faults. In Tschaikovsky's Fifth Symphony there is a motto running through all four movements, sometimes melancholy, sometimes ominous, becoming finally a paean of triumph. We identified our love—the Shining Barrier—with it: it sang our love.

Sometimes we had fights: we were human and had tempers. Usually the fights were over nothing: we would be tired or a bit out of touch from being out in the world and apart. Our very closeness was a danger in that we were instantly aware of the slightest disharmony: a grain of dust that would not affect an alarm clock may throw off a fine watch. A hint of anger or coldness in a voice would shock the other. Outrage would be politely expressed. Love had been betrayed. Unbelievable disaster had come upon us. Hope was gone, eyes would be averted, and an awful silence would ensue. And yet, in the depths, we *knew* that if we caught each other's eye we would laugh and it would be over. But we were not going to forgive that betrayer. We also knew that one loving word or even putting a record on—especially the humorous music of "The Love for the Three Oranges"— would restore us. Sometimes one of us would act. Once a bird landed on the sill of the open window and looked out of one bright eye at us, silent and motionless, within; and we burst into laughter. Sometimes the silence would become ridiculous and we would both be suppressing a desire to laugh; finally one of us would, uncontrollably, grin; laughter would follow and we would be lovers again. Heaven would follow: reconciliation, tenderness, joy. Depths and heights.

We learned one thing from these rare quarrels, and that was that separation was a danger. Fights always came when we had got a little bit out of harmony with each other. In later navy days when my ship would be at sea for a fortnight, we found that it took about twenty-four hours for us to recover the reality of each other, even though we would have been thinking constantly of each other. What happened, we decided, was that, apart, we would slightly idealise each other, and to that extent lose the real person. Similarly, if we went out with other people several nights running, we would get a little bit out of touch. We must have days or evenings just to be with each other, playing music, reading poems, and being outdoors. "Outdoors alone"—alone together—expressed something we needed: the wind and sky, the earth and the sea.

To be the watch upon the walls of the Shining Barrier, we early established what, later, we called the Navigators' Council. It was in part a "truth session" but, more significantly, it was an inquiry into the "state of the union." Were we fully sharing? Was there any sign of creeping separateness? These Councils would occur fortnightly or monthly. In them we would pour out sherry and begin with a burst of music from some noble symphony, perhaps the singing motto of the "Fifth," and then we would talk. Often there were decisions to make. Whatever the decision, it would be made upon the single basis of what we called the "Appeal to Love."

The "Appeal to Love" was an essential part of the very structure of the Shining Barrier. What it meant was simply this question: what will be best for our love? Should one of us change a pattern of behaviour that bothered the other, or should the other learn to accept? Well, which would be better for our love? Which way would be better, in any choice or decision, in the light of our single goal: to be in love as long as life might last? No argument could prevail against it. The Appeal to Love was like a trumpet call from the battlements of the Shining Barrier, causing us to lift our eyes from immediate desires to what was truly important.

The Appeal to Love, with its declaration that inloveness was for us *first*, and the very name of the Shining Barrier, with its image of walls, might together suggest the exclusion of friendship and family love. The suggestion would be false. One of the three points of my childhood code—which is something of a key to this book—was "Never betray a friend." That might imply that friendship was important to me: and so it was, to me and to Davy, too. We believed in deep and genuine friendship, and we held our friends and our families very dear and were intensely loyal to them. The Shining Barrier—it is necessary to remember what it was—did not exclude anything that was good and beautiful, as all the loves appeared to us to be; and the Appeal to Love was simply an ordering of values: first things first. Conflicts between inloveness and friendship rarely or never arose. Conflicts were almost always between the wilful self and love.

It might be mentioned here that the most spirited feminist of later years could not easily fault a union based on sharing and the Appeal to Love in decision-making, a union where no one exercised authority. We did what was necessary to do—housework or sail-mending—together as a part of sharing: not in the name of women's rights but in the great name of love.

Signals for use in the outer world or in company were a useful and practical means of maintaining our connections. There was a "recognition signal," a gentle four-note whistle with a slightly different response, that was useful in a hundred situations; and a sharp "Alert" or "Emergency" that would, and often did, bring one of us out of sleep with a bound. For use in company we had a whole range of signals that didn't depend on catching each other's eye or contorted faces. They were, in fact, mostly innocent questions, such as asking, "Did you bring those English Ovals?" And they meant such things as "This person is boring me out of my mind: do something!" or "Let's get out of here!" or "Keep your eye on the one I shall glance towards" or "The one that just spoke is lying" or "When we go, let's ask the person (or couple) I shall glance at to come with us." These and many others, some more subtle and complex, along with the appropriate responses, in all of which we were well drilled, enabled us to carry on fairly elaborate conversations with privacy in a roomful of people.

Apart from the signals, we were often thought to be able to read each other's mind. Regrettably, this wasn't true with respect to actual telepathy, though not for want of trying, with rare but startling successes that were, maybe, coincidence. But we were, in truth, so close, so familiar with the way each other's mind worked, so much in the co-inherence of lovers, that we usually knew by a glance or tone of voice what the other was thinking and, especially, feeling. We sometimes startled our more observant friends by acting upon such knowledge, hardly aware that we were doing so; but it would seem uncanny to the observer. Once a friend saw Davy glance fleetingly at the candles on our mantelpiece but not at me; and then a moment later I got up and lighted them. "It almost scared me," the friend concluded later. "It was too perfect."

The Shining Barrier was all of these elements, centred

in sharing and absolute trust, that we built into our love, making it invulnerable, we believed, to the destroyers of love, such as creeping separateness. We fell in love—a springtime first love—and we swore it should endure. Whatever might happen to other people's loves, ours should endure. And it *did* endure, though it was to encounter, long years later, something we never reckoned on. What was remarkable, if not unique, about our love— our inloveness—was all we built into it, giving to it all our minds and devotion. But beneath all the hard thought was the loveliness of the love itself, love so deep and clear that it almost broke our hearts with its passion and tenderness. The passion, the sexual element, was there: and sexual harmony like sexual playfulness was an important dimension of our love. But it wasn't itself the whole thing; and we knew that to make it the whole or even the most important element was to court disaster. Those who see love as only sex or mainly sex do not, quite simply, know what love is. They are the blind man assuming that the trunk of the elephant—or perhaps the phallus—is the whole creature. Sex is merely part of a greater thing. To be in love, as to see beauty, is a kind of adoring that turns the lover away from self. Just seeing Davy asleep, defenceless and trusting and innocent, could tear my heart, then in that first spring or a dozen years later. When we first fell in love in the dead of winter, we said, "If we aren't more in love in lilactime, we shall be finished." But we *were* more in love: for love must grow or die. Every year on our anniversary we said, "If we're not more deeply in love next year, we shall have failed." But we were: a deeper inloveness, more close, more dear. She in me and I in her: the co-inherence of lovers. And every year we would drink to the future in the old toast: "If it's half as good as the half we've known, here's *Hail!* to the rest of the road."

But the Shining Barrier, however invulnerable to the separating forces of life, was not invulnerable to death. We were aware of death: those who love life most always are. We reminded ourselves in Walter de la Mare's words

to "Look thy last on all things lovely/Every hour . . ."
And we said, meaning it, that if death came tomorrow,
after only a year of such a love, or after only five years
or ten, it would *not* be defeat. However brief, a mortal
splendour!

No defeat, that is, if death came for us both at once.
But death is no respecter of love. If we so perfected our
love, if we were so much one, we were running a ghastly
risk. How could one of us ever bear the death of the
other? We were haunted by the thought; we dreamt of
it with terror. It was in that first spring that I first dreamt
of her death. In the dream we were improbably skylark-
ing about on the top of a ten-storey building, Davy
laughing on the parapet . . . falling . . . I racing down
all those flights of stairs in such anguish I wonder I
didn't perish in my sleep . . . she in the deserted street,
every bone broken . . . giving me one tiny kiss and dying.
That dream was the single most awful agony of my whole
life; and she was haunted by such dreams. It was not
to be borne.

And so we completed the Shining Barrier: we would
die together. We were pagans, not compelled by any
religion, expecting only the dark. We had only each
other and our lovely love. "Until the lilacs close/Beneath
the deathly snows." If we shared this love, should we not
share this death? We resolved—deeply and intensely
resolved—that, be our days long or as brief as a shooting
star, we would go together. If one were killed by sudden
chance, the other would instantly follow. Or if one were
mortally ill or when both became too old and frail to
enjoy life (perhaps about thirty, we may have thought
initially), then we would go. We would take a plane up,
up into the high pure sky, and put the nose down,
thundering straight downwards, a bright arrow in the
sunlight, in the last long dive. A bit later, when we
began to plan our schooner yacht, the "last long dive"
(as we still called it) changed: we would take our little
ship to sea; and then one night, with the stars shining
upon the heaving waters, we would open the seacocks

and go down together. Our resolution to do this thing
was like steel: this we *would* do. Now the Shining
Barrier was truly invulnerable. I wrote a poem of the
last long dive, a way to die:

IF THIS BE ALL
(Rondeau)

If this be all to glorify
The end of love and to deny
The parting that alone we fear—
When wasted days for one draw near,
Surrender them without a sigh—

We'll sail, then, seawards, you and I,
And sink our ship and so we'll die
Still, *still* together, oh my dear!
If this be all.

In light we loved in days gone by;
As darkness shudders down the sky
We'll plight again, and death—austere
Dark minister—shall wed us here,
Together under night to lie,
If this be all.

On a May morning, long before the dawn had begun
to lighten the sky, I drove into the university. Under
Davy's window I whistled the "Alert." She, already
dressed, came down, and we drove through the night.
At an abandoned airfield I left her, warmly bundled up
against the pre-dawn chill, and drove away. Davy stood
in the lee of a derelict hangar. A faint light appeared in
the east, and she could see patches of mist on the empty
field. Then she heard the sound of an aircraft. She
shivered, as much from excitement as from cold. A
moment later she could see the plane coming through
the skies, an open-cockpit biplane, swooping down across
the field. Beyond the field it banked steeply around and
descended, shouldering through the patches of mist. The
nose came up and it landed lightly. The helmeted pilot
pushed up his goggles and waved.

Davy came running up. I hugged her and gave her a helmet and goggles. Then I put her in the forward cockpit, making sure that the seatbelt was tight. In the cockpit with her was a mass of lilacs. I climbed back into the after cockpit and taxied to the edge of the field, turning into the wind. The east was brighter now, but the sun had not yet risen. Davy turned and grinned.

I pushed the throttle all the way forward. The engine roared and the plane ran down the field. It lifted, was airborne. The earth fell away. We climbed into the sky, into the dawn. Suddenly we were bathed in sunlight, though the earth below was still dark. Higher and higher: we were above the scattered clouds, rose-coloured in the sunrise. The air was cold and pure. I pulled the throttle back till the engine was just turning over. Davy was singing loudly. She held up a lilac and the blossoms drifted back. I put the nose down. The ship rushed earthwards, and lilac blossoms streamed back in our wake. Just below was a rosy cloud. I dived straight into it. A moment of damp greyness, then we burst forth into sunbright air and swooped upwards again under full throttle. Davy waved and twisted round to grin, meaning that she loved it: it was her first flight. The plane banked steeply, rushed downwards under power, and then swooped upwards—up and over in a loop. In the moment that we hung upside down, Davy laughed and shouted. So we played in the sky in that beautiful and splendid Maytime dawn. Flight in lilactime.

After the descent to earth, back at her House, we said goodbye, for I must return to college. It was still morning, and we were alone in one of the reception rooms. Davy, sitting on a sofa, was telling me what she had thought during the flight and how she was looking forward to learning to fly, as of course in sharing she must do. I was standing, about to depart, standing across the room by the door, still in my leather flight jacket with helmet and goggles dangling from my hand. A beam of sunlight slanting through one of the tall windows fell upon my head and shoulders, turning my light-brown hair to gold. I was smiling at her. She paused in what she was

saying, then she said in a low voice: "My golden one!"
She never quite forgot the image of me standing there
in the morning light, an image linked to the dawn and
flight. When she lay dying after the years, she murmured
"My golden one!" and I knew all she was remembering:
lilacs and flight into the mystery of the dawning and
me standing there in the light.

In that same lovely Maytime we took to the river in
a canoe. Here she was the skilled one and I the crew. At
night we would paddle far upriver, and then, sitting
together, leaning against the rack, we would drift down,
talking in low voices so as not to offend the peace of the
night. Remembering, I think of her face, a pale heart-
shaped blur in the starlight, and the bright stars themselves above the dark trees.

As May moved into June a shadow hung over us. A
week or two after the term was done, I should have to
leave—it had all been arranged before we had even met—
to be a ranger at Grand Canyon. We were together at
Glenmerle on the last day—a perfect June day—down by
the lily pond; but Davy was sad and gloomy. We were
both sad at parting; but for me it was adventure, at least,
while she, poor little thing, must work indoors at that
studio. Still, we had today. We talked: talked of throwing away golden hours, of love heightened under the
sword, of how what must be borne ought to be borne
gallantly and gaily. As we talked, Davy made valiant
efforts to throw off her gloom. She made wry jokes at
herself and then fell into a vein of dark crazy humour,
and finally, amused at herself, she recovered joy. I ran
up to the house and fetched beef sandwiches and lemonade, and we merrily picnicked under the June sky.

And then, after all, the separation was not so absolute,
for she prevailed upon her mother and brother to go
a-journeying—with her of course—to the westward; and
the grandeur of the Canyon, in the day and in the night,
became part of our sharing. She became the Assistant
Rim Patrol when I was on duty; and off duty we explored
and wandered far out along the rim, the moon filling the
upside-down mountain, as the Red Indians call it, with

mystery. One night in the woods behind us, something—whether catamount or bear we never knew—gave a horrible hoarse cough, midway between a consumptive cow and an amplified mosquito, that froze our blood; and we tip-toed very rapidly away from there.

In September as the new term began, we were secretly married—secretly because of my father's forbidding views on early marriage, especially of people still *in statu pupillari*. Why, then, marry? Not, certainly, as a sanction for sex: we had known each other in the spring without guilt. There was no great reason: there might be in some emergency a legal value in our being wed. And I thought Davy would be pleased—which she was. It was not, assuredly, a desire to feel "married," for we thought of marital attitudes and jokes as destructive of love; and we never did overcome our distaste for the words "husband" and "wife": we said we were "comrade-lovers." Perhaps we had a sense that there ought to be a confirmation by ritual of our deep vows.

At all events, one Saturday morning, licence in hand, we set forth to find a clergyman in some village far from our usual haunts. We drove into a village and found the Rectory. Despite ourselves we felt a small wave of excitement. But we had reckoned without football: the Rector was on his way to watch and cheer. Village after village, hundreds of villages: not one gentle old man writing his sermon and meditating. Amazed at the faithlessness of the cloth, we became hot and tired and discouraged. On the point of giving up, we tried a last Rectory; and there we found a white-haired old gentleman who had doubtless been meditating. Perhaps a saint. Thunder rumbled as we went in. He talked to us kindly for a few minutes. Then, as thunder crashed and rain poured down, we were wed. A bed-ridden sister upstairs signed as witness, which she wasn't; so perhaps it wasn't legal. As we left, the sun was striking through. The air was rain-washed and cool, and there were bright puddles by the walk. As we drove away, a rainbow appeared. Heaven approved. When we got to the wooded park where we would have a two-day honeymoon—the only guests in the small hotel

—we discovered that each of us had a different idea of which village we had finally married in. In later years, whenever there was some unresolvable difference about a fact, we would chant the names of the two villages at each other.

In time the secret marriage became rather an open secret. Mother knew and was conspiratorially delighted. Even my father must have had the odd suspicion, but he chose not to inquire. Actually, he liked Davy a lot. She was a gay, bright, mischievous spirit, and she would always play chess with him, a game much played at Glenmerle. "Miss Jean," as the servants called Davy, became part of the family, and in the following summer she came to Glenmerle to stay all summer.

That was the summer when Davy and I rode or walked for miles every morning. Even walking we would usually do ten miles and once twenty. On one such walk we found a puppy, mostly collie, with perhaps a bit of wolf, at a farmhouse. We chose him over the brothers and sisters because he was the stubbornest and yet had sad eyes; and we named him Laddie. Subsequently he was a blithe and venturesome companion on all our walks or rides. Once he crept through a fence to bark at a huge and dangerous sow. She grunted and heaved herself up to lunge at him. He danced about and then seized her tail, causing her to squeal with pain and rage while, despite his spread paws, she dragged him along. He decided, apparently, that he didn't dare let go, though he rolled his eyes at us. We were laughing so hard that we couldn't have helped, even if we had known what to do. At last he did let go, and fled, soaring over the fence like a hunter.

The walks, especially as the sun got up and began to warm us, were leisurely, full of pauses to talk to a farmer or farmwife. Sometimes they would have us in for a glass of fresh milk. Or sometimes we would stop and sit on a wall, eating a sun-warmed tomato, talking or peacefully silent. Often we talked of the sad and somehow outrageous fact that in most lives, perhaps our own before long, there isn't time for long walks and sitting on walls.

We quoted a poem by W. H. Davies to the effect that it is a poor life if we have no time "to stop and stare" as sheep and cows do. We agreed. Nor were we cheered by the prospect of an occasional day off from an office, for with only one day there would be a sense of time at one's back, a time too limited to "waste" sitting on walls. How were we to contrive a life full of time—a timeful life—where we could be quiet and leisurely, where we could stop and stare?

One day when we had walked as usual and then come back to Glenmerle to swim and eat a mighty breakfast and nap, we were sitting down by the swimming pool in the long June evening, reading a Chinese gentleman, Lin Yutang, on the good life—which to him as to us required leisure. As dusk came down, we shut the book and dived into the pool. Dressed again, we resumed our chairs, looking down towards the park where there were a million "fireflies dancing in a netted maze/Woven of twilight and tranquillity," in Richard Le Gallienne's lines. We talked about the good life, the life without the pressure of time. A life we could lead *together*, even if we had to sell apples along the road. How were we to have such a life?

Perhaps the little waves in the pool, still astir and glinting with starlight, had something to do with it. Anyhow, someone, perhaps Davy, said meditatively:

"It would be nice to live by the sea. It's beautiful. And we could have a boat."

"If we had a cabin boat," I said, "we could live on that. Go where we pleased. No rent. Good lord, Davy! Do you realise that if we had a boat, living would hardly cost *anything*? No rent; fish and crabs to eat?"

"I like fish," said Davy. "Except for the bones. Just think of the wild, beautiful coves to anchor in! Or if we wanted to be in a city, we could go into its harbour and be right in the centre of it. But—well, don't cabin boats—cruisers—use enormous amounts of fuel? All the money we saved on rent would go for that."

"Um, that's true," I said. "That's no good. Oh, I know! A sailboat! With a cabin. The wind is free. A sailing yacht is more seaworthy anyhow. We're on to something, Davy!"

"Oh, yes!" she said excitedly. "Oh, dearling!" And then, more doubtfully, "But we don't know how. Yachts are terribly complicated—all those ropes! And navigation..."

"We can learn, can't we?" I said. "Actually, I did sail a little, at school. Anyhow we can learn. And, Davy, *think* of it! Anywhere! England, Hawaii—all the most interesting places are on the sea. And we'd have our books and music with us."

"Our *home* with us!" she said. "Like turtles. Or one turtle for two. Never mind! We could get jobs wherever we were, and then sail away. And Laddie could be a seadog!"

"And we could write books," I said. "Oh, dearling, I think this is our answer—the way to freedom! Beauty and time to live. If we can just get the boat..."

So the sea-dream was born, born by the quiet waters of a swimming pool. By the time we went up to bed, just as a great misshapen golden moon was rising, we were practically sailors. A slight roll in our gait perhaps. And the painting of the square-rigger on my wall had a new meaning.

The next day we bought yachting magazines and books and plunged straightaway into them. We read immensely, not only books on yacht design and handling but books on the far places of the world, including the fascinating tales of Tahiti by Nordhoff and Hall. Indeed, we became particularly enchanted with Polynesia: Hawaii, New Zealand, Tahiti, and the wild Tuamotu, the cloud of islands under the wind. It was not long before we had a real grasp of the considerations involved in choosing a vessel: she would be, we decided, a schooner, a blue-water yacht with a long straight keel, about forty or forty-five feet overall. We debated gaff versus jib-headed rigs and whether the galley should be amidships or aft. We knew what shrouds and strakes were, bilges and baggywrinkles; and we shouldn't have dreamt of calling a line a rope. As unthinkable as shooting a fox. On the basis of some moderate military experience at school, I applied for and got a naval-reserve probationary commission in order to learn navigation: we did correspondence-course assignments together in seamanship, piloting, navigation, and even gunnery. But salty though we were, our life on the ocean wave was still limited to the canoe, when we ought to have been setting topsails, clawing off lee shores, keel-hauling people, and the like. All we needed was a yacht and of course an ocean. But the necessary thousands seemed as remote as the moon: my father would never give them to us, for he had firm ideas about my winning my own goals.

From the first our ship was named *Grey Goose*. Not only wild nature and a water bird, but a lover: the grey goose, if its mate is killed, flies on alone for ever. We designed and had a jeweller make grey-goose signet rings in gold like a coat-of-arms: the grey goose, fess, flying over stylised waves at the base, and above it and ahead, dexter, a tiny sapphire star.

The *Grey Goose* was initially only a means to an end: the good life. The timeful life. But our imaginations were more and more caught up in the grace and beauty of the ships and the sea. We would sail the seas in storm and sunshine to far islands, carrying with us our beloved books and our few possessions—our earlier thoughts on the burden of possessions fitted in neatly—and we would be free, free to be, free from schedules. And, with time, we would write: which of course we *could* do if we chose—had I not just got a First in English?—just as we could become seamen if we chose. Or make love endure.

We wrote a huge poem of a hundred and fifty lines called "Anchor Watch," beginning with the moment when we should row out to *Grey Goose*: "And from our deck we scorn the land." Then, through "all that bright exultant afternoon," we stow our kit below: "The books and music in the main saloon," and food and guns. At twilight we sit on our deck, ready to sail with the morning tide, dreaming of all that lies ahead: storms and southern nights with the moonpath stretching across the moving waters "where the ghosts of galleons sail." We see the yacht entering some far lagoon, where "the anchor splashes and the bow swings round," and we stow the sails, hearing "the sound of breakers on the barrier reef." We play music that floats "across the darkening lagoon" and then sleep while the tall masts are "pencilling across the stars." That was the dream, born by the pool at Glenmerle, that had caught us up. It caught up more than one of our friends, too. The combination of our bright and adventurous dream and our evident love for one another half-persuaded some of our friends that we had discovered some special secret of existence. So perhaps we had: the quality of joy. Someone—was it Byron?—spoke of having known but three genuinely happy hours in his whole life. Thinking of that remark, we hugged to ourselves the knowledge of literally hundreds of joyous hours. As I had seen under the tree in the meadow long before, a great love is the way to joy. But how should it be paid for?

We were having the heights but maybe the depths were drawing near. Europe was at war. True, not much was happening—except the quite incredible defeat of a German battleship by three valiant cruisers of the Royal Navy—and perhaps it would end soon. But perhaps it wouldn't: perhaps it would turn into real war, drawing America in, and then years might pass: youth and the dream lost.

Then the Blitz thundered across France, and the British army was taken off from Dunkirk by anything that would float: we longed to be there with *Grey Goose*. France surrendered. England, everybody said, would be next. We refused to believe it, and we betted every penny we had on England. We listened to "Rule, Britannia" with our hair standing on end.

We decided in the following winter to announce our marriage. Mother approved and generously offered us a fortnight in Florida for "a proper honeymoon": we planned to spend it looking at boats. In a rather cowardly way we got Mother to tell my father of our marriage on the night before the announcement appeared in the

papers. If everything was peaceful, she would put a lamp
in a certain window that we could see from the park. If
no lamp, we would be off for Florida that night. But the
lamp was lit. When we went in, I glanced into the
study: "Hello, Dad," I said. He looked up with a half-
smile. "Good evening, Son," he said. Some day he would
say something more, but everything was all right. Next
morning we drove off on a roundabout course for Florida,
roundabout because we were going to visit my aunt and
uncle in the Bluegrass of Kentucky.

We got no farther. Mother rang up next evening: the
Navy, despite its being more or less peacetime, was
ordering me to sea. A destroyer. As I later found out, at
Pearl Harbor. A chapter in our life was ending, and the
future was veiled.

But we had shaped our love, and it would endure,
whatever came: that we believed. If worst came to worst
and one was gone, the other would follow after: "whither
thou goest . . ." Somehow we were able to face this
separation with less of agony—or anguish better concealed—than our parting for the Grand Canyon. We were
rather optimistic by nature, and we had a sort of faith
in the future. So we approached parting almost gaily.

All this year we had been working together on a poem
that would express what we believed about love: a poem
that would tell what we chose:

THE SHINING BARRIER

This present glory, love, once-given grace,
The sum of blessing in a sure embrace,
Must not in creeping separateness decline
But be the centre of our whole design.

We know it's love that keeps a love secure,
And only by love of love can love endure,
For self's a killer, reckless of the cost,
And loves of lilactime unloved are lost.

We build our altar, then, to love and keep
The holy flame alight and never sleep:
This darling love shall deepen year by year,
And dearer shall we grow who are so dear.

The magic word is *sharing*: every stream
Of beauty, every faith and grief and dream;
Go hand in hand in gay companionship—
In sober death no sundering of the grip.

And into love all other loveliness
That we can tease from time we shall impress:
Slow dawns and lilacs, traceries of the trees,
The spring and poems, stars and ancient seas.

This splendour is upon us, high and pure
As heaven: and we swear it shall endure:
Swear fortitude for pain and faith for tears
To hold our shining barrier down the years.

We said goodbyes, Davy and my brother and I, on the bridge at Glenmerle. Laddie was not with us: he had been killed a month before, and we missed him. Then Dad drove down to the bridge and I got in. He was proud of me, though he didn't say so, and a little envious. Later he would move heaven and earth to get back into the army. As the train drew out after our last handclasp, I saw him standing there on the railway platform, tall and bronzed and young-looking. He gave me a wave and a grin. I was never to see him again, nor ever to see Glenmerle as a living house; but of course I did not know.

A few minutes later the train was flagged down at our village station by special arrangement, and Davy climbed aboard. For two hundred miles we drank sherry and talked about my sending for her as soon as possible. Then there was a quick hug and exchanged smiles and she was gone. She took another train back to Glenmerle, and I went on.

Before I sailed from the west coast for Pearl Harbor, a letter from her came, a letter written late in the night. She described how she and my brother had walked in from the gates in mist and moonlight "with the impudent loyal wraith of Laddie at our side," pausing on the bridge and "seeing the big blue spruce a dark mystery on the lawn with the mist creeping about it." Now, later in the night, "as I write, the moonlight makes a ghostly glimmer through the strangely empty rooms of Glenmerle and makes the windows silver—here where your ghost and the ghosts of all of us in our happy times haunt me." Perhaps across the years to come she sensed me in my deep-night return to Glenmerle, standing on the bridge when she passed and wandering about the rooms of the house in my imagination.

A day later my ship sailed, westward-bound, and it seemed to me that the long, tumbled-white wake stretched back to Glenmerle—and Davy.

⊰ III ⊱

The Shadow of a Tree

On a May morning, the last morning of the month, a long, narrow destroyer of the generation known as "four-stackers" was steaming slowly just off the white beaches and coconut palms of an island. The deep-blue sea was calm, and great tumbled white clouds, driven by the trade-wind, ambled across the blue sky. A young officer in an immaculate white uniform suddenly came bounding up on deck and ran up the ladder to the bridge. There he snatched up binoculars and from the starboard bridge wing scanned the shoreline ahead. If an emergency existed, no one else appeared to be affected. No bosun's pipes twittered, and other officers and men went calmly about their duties while the ship steamed slowly on. And yet the young officer still stood tensely on the bridge wing, the morning sun striking glints of gold from his buttons and cap, staring intently at the same spot on the coast, now slowly drawing astern. The island was Molokai in the Hawaiian group, and his binoculars were fixed upon the harbour channel of the town of Kaunakakai. Minutes passed. The channel was now off the starboard quarter. From it a small white cabin cruiser emerged. "Sir!" he said to another officer who had joined him on the bridge wing. "There she is, sir! The *Ebbtide*."

Half an hour earlier a message had come by voice radio from the squadron flagship, presumably at the town, that Davy—Davy!—would shortly be coming out of Kaunakakai in the cruiser *Ebbtide*, and the message had been relayed from bridge to wardroom by speaking tube. Davy! How *could* she be there? He hadn't even known she was in the Islands, though there had been a cable last week before the destroyer sailed that she was coming. But still, Kaunakakai on a motorboat! He raised the glasses. Was that small figure in the bows . . . ?

Davy was, in fact, in the cruiser's bows, and she was at that instant filled with gloom as she watched the destroyer steaming away. One minute later the gloom turned to joy. The destroyer was turning. She was coming back. There was a stir of excitement among the dozen or so people on the little cruiser; and some sympathetic smiles were directed towards Davy. The cruiser steered to meet the destroyer. Davy saw the young officer on the bridge, "looking handsome, brown, and pleased," as she wrote in our diary. But "pleased" was an understatement.

The destroyer was dead in the water. The cruiser came around in a wide circle. For an instant the shadow of the destroyer's mast and yardarm fell across the white motorboat and then she was alongside. The young officer looked down at the girl and she looked at him. Everybody else was watching them both with smiles. It was impossible for them to speak of love and joy; they muttered inanities like "Good morning," and they looked at each other with speaking eyes. Love and joy crossed from vessel to vessel in their gaze, and both faces were wreathed in smiles. Davy wrote: "People kept prompting me to say something, but I didn't need to. We were close for five minutes, looking our happiness to the delight of all on board the two vessels. We must have seemed like storybook lovers, or maybe a symbol, to some; for people afterwards came to me to say how touched they were by our evident joy and love. So we had our Maytime after all—Maytime at sea, loving each other just as much, and more if possible, than in the lilac-and-blossom-time Mays of the past."

An order was given on the destroyer's bridge; the engines went to slow ahead; the ship gathered way. She went to standard speed and then to full, swinging round to her former course. Davy watched till she was hull down and then gone.

Thus we met after the longest separation of our lives —almost three whole months. In the midst of debate by letter whether she should come out yet—it was uncertain whether the destroyer would stay in the area—Davy simply sent a cable that she was coming, and came. Since I was going to sea, I hastily arranged for some army air force friends, Allene and Jack—Allene was an old friend of ours—to meet her if she came; and they, with other army people, had laid on the cruise among the islands. Davy's meeting the destroyer-squadron commodore in Kaunakakai and my ship's being at hand were merely our Maytime luck.

A chapter in our lives had ended when we left Glenmerle, and a new chapter had begun when we met, appropriately, at sea on a May morning—appropriately because in the oncoming years, almost a decade, a decade that might be called midmorning in our lives, there was to be much of the sea, both ships and yachts. In these colourful and adventurous years, years that were to include, besides the navy and the yachts, a great university, Yale, and a Virginian farmhouse, the single most important fact is that the Shining Barrier held. This book is, after all, the spiritual autobiography of a love rather than of the lovers. And we had built well when we raised the Shining Barrier. We had that special loveliness that lovers have—inloveness—when we looked into each other's eyes as our two vessels lay alongside one another in that bright May morning and we had it still, years later, on the eve of a new chapter in our lives set in England.

After our Maytime meeting, the destroyer kept the sea for another week. One night I had the midwatch from twelve to four in the morning as junior Officer of the Deck. The ship was steaming south at standard speed, out of sight of land, at the head of a column of four destroyers. I stood on the bridge wing, occasionally sweeping the horizon with my glasses or looking aft to make sure the other ships were keeping station. It was a mild night with a yellow half-moon low in the sky, the moonpath glittering across the waves. The long, narrow destroyer rolled in the big Pacific swell, but I was too used to that to notice. The familiar sound of the blowers and the occasional smash of the bow meeting a wave were equally unremarked. I was thinking, not for the first time, of the meeting with Davy at sea.

I saw again the white motorboat curving round to come alongside, with Davy practically hopping up and down on her decks, and I remembered suddenly how the shadow of our mast and signal yardarm had for an instant been sharp and black against *Ebbtide*'s white hull, making an X. I felt this to be faintly ominous. Maybe at this very moment the motorboat, stove in by a rock, was sinking, Davy swimming along in the sea, looking about for help. Then it occurred to me that the mast and yard had thrown a shadow that was really more like the Christian sign of the cross. This was better, though not much. Christianity was something I wanted nothing to do with. How could anybody believe such rubbish? A mere local religion of earth, quite inadequate for the immensities of the farflung galaxies. Inadequate, at least, to anyone who had read Stapledon and the other science-fiction greats. I, indeed, had seen through the pretences of Christianity in my teens, and forthwith abandoned it. How could any intelligent person actually believe it, believe that an obscure crucified Jew was God! What was so odd was that quite a lot of people, not just sheep but highly intelligent people, *did* apparently believe it. T. S. Eliot, for instance. Or Eddington—in fact, quite a few physicists, the very last people one would expect to be taken in by it. Philosophers, too. Was it possible—was there any chance—that there was more to it than I had thought? No, certainly not. Of course not! Still, it *was* odd. Damned odd. And it wasn't just a matter of keeping their childhood faith without examination, either. Some of them—intelligent people, too—were actually converts from atheism or agnosticism. *Could* there be more to it? Something I missed? After all, I was pretty young when I rejected Christianity. Oh, but there can't be! Everybody knows what Christianity is. But then, those converts? Maybe I ought to have another look at it. Some day. Just to be—well, intellectually honest. Not that it could possibly be true of course. Still, fair play. Hear both sides. Yes, I'll do it. Some day.

This train of thought did not appear next morning to be of much importance. The aberrations of a midwatch. One thinks strange thoughts in the deep night. Of *course* Christianity wasn't true. And Davy was amused, amused and a bit mocking, when I told her about it. We laughed together, and I put it out of mind. There wasn't much I could do about it, anyway: a destroyer's library usually runs to three old copies of *Time* magazine. Besides, it all looked like rather a lot of work. But what was odd about it was that I didn't quite forget it. Didn't quite forget that, some day, I really ought to have that second look. For years I kept remembering it every now and then, remembering it, indeed, with moderate loathing, and always finding good reason not to do anything about it at the moment. Not now but some day.

Davy and I called ourselves agnostics, but we were really theists. A creator seemed necessary, a creator with an immense intelligence embracing order. Apart from reason, the one quality that we attributed to this creative power was awareness of beauty. Everything in nature, in creation, was beautiful, except where marred by man. But we could not, or at least did not, similarly attribute goodness to it, for good was in man, not in wild nature, and was balanced by evil, also in man. So there was a power—a god—of beauty with a high and inscrutable purpose quite unknowable to man except for such inklings as might come through the contemplation of beauty. Beauty was somehow at the very centre of meaning. For us, love was an aspect of beauty, though that might not be true of the power, which perhaps cared nothing for man. We might acknowledge a creating power, but our religion, if it could be called that, was really an adoring of love and beauty. It was the domain of Aphrodite, and, as I have said, we were really pagans. Many an ancient philosopher and, even more, many a Hellenic lyric poet would have approved, or at least sympathised with, our dedication to love and beauty, our trust in reason, and our goal of the good life.

One Saturday afternoon several happy months later, Davy and I drove round the island of Oahu in our incredibly ancient, hundred-dollar Ford roadster. We swam at various windward beaches, white sand and the intense blue of the sea, usually without another person even in sight; and we scrambled up a mountain trail. The weather was perfect, neither too hot nor too cold, rather like mid-May. And we, sun-tanned and lithe, plunging through the breakers or lying in the sunlight on bright beaches below the cloud-hung green wall of the mountains, were being pagans in the commoner sense of the word: just loving life. In the late afternoon, salty and sun-soaked, we came back to our flat in Waikiki. We paused briefly to talk to a brother officer from my ship and his wife and then went in to shower and dress, after which we drove out to Hickam Field, the army air force base near the harbour, to dine with Jack and Allene. A flying fortress thundered overhead as the sentry snapped to rigid salute.

We had a pleasant evening, not without its own little inner drama. Allene had asked us to bring our recording of Tschaikovsky's "Sixth," and we knew why: she was still haunted by the memory of the man she had listened to that music with, George, our old friend and fellow-adventurer. During dinner Jack proposed that he and I go flying in the morning—Sunday—in a trainer, but I had some navy business to do. After dinner, we talked a bit and Jack played his violin. Then Allene wanted to hear the "Pathétique." The symphony filled the darkened room. When the last sombre notes died away, we were all silent, deep in our thoughts. At last Allene said slowly, "It sounds like the dirge of a dying world." Not long after, we said our goodnights and drove back to Honolulu, looking at the jewelled lights cascading down the hills.

Early in the morning, standing on a low hill above Pearl Harbor, I watched the destruction of the Pacific Fleet by Imperial Japan. Farther away the hangars at Hickam burned. A few months earlier my destroyer division had screened the battleship *Arizona* back to the west coast. On a misty early morning off Point Loma, the task force had encountered a flotilla of Japanese sampans fishing. They had scuttled out of the way as the battleship, dark and gigantic on the flat sea, had borne down upon them. This morning at Pearl Harbor I remembered that scene off Point Loma as, my glasses fixed upon *Arizona* just as her magazines blew up, I momentarily and for ever saw, just on the edge of that immense explosion, a sailor's body like a little white rag doll, floating, it seemed, quite gently and casually in the air. I saw five Jap aircraft in flames at once from the fire of the fleet. I saw my own ship streaking for the harbour channel with the duty ensign in command. I emptied a pistol at a low-flying Jap plane without, regrettably, noticeable results. A rainbow arched over the burning ships.

The Pacific war had come, and the great battleships were sunk at their moorings. We expected invasion momentarily. That night Davy and a dozen other navy wives huddled in the one blacked-out room of the flats. But, though there was no invasion, all the news in the next days and weeks was bad. The Japanese task force escaped. The captain of one of our heavy cruisers entering Pearl Harbor wept as he saw the battle fleet destroyed without a chance to fight back in the sneak attack. Guam was gone and Wake was falling. The Royal Navy's *Prince of Wales* and *Repulse* went down fighting in Malayan waters. Unbelievably, Singapore, the Lion City, fell. Jack, our host on the last night the lights were on, went down at the controls of his bomber somewhere out towards Midway.

Davy and I had snatched hours together—hours under the sword. At any minute we might be parted for years; but we were not parted. She was not evacuated with the other navy wives, for she had got a sensitive naval job. I was at sea for brief periods in Hawaiian waters. After the battle of Midway, which I was on the remote fringes of in a graceful converted motor yacht armed with popguns, the war moved off to the west. We were not separated, and we knew ourselves to be incredibly fortunate. We had dreamt of sailing to Hawaii in *Grey Goose*, and the fortunes of war brought us here—both of us—and kept us here. One almost feels a bit guilty about it, but there it was: nobody could have had a happier war, even under the sword.

During the war years we kept our dream of *Grey Goose* intact. We read our poems and listened to our music, and we came to love the Islands, sun and sea and tangled green mountains. A saddening cablegram announced my father's sudden death—in his last letter from Glenmerle, where he was staying alone, my mother being at the town house, he had said that he expected to be back on active service in a few months, and he had finished by saying: "I just made myself a whisky and soda, and I raised it high in the direction of the Pacific and drank to two good fellows, you and Davy." Now, by a doctor's blunder, he was dead; and I flew briefly home, returning from 'Frisco in a magnificent heavy cruiser.

In the last year of the war—four years after the lights of Honolulu went out—the yachts of the Honolulu yacht basin, mainly through my efforts, were allowed to resume ocean racing; and we were rewarded with membership in the Yacht Club. We knew most of the people, for we had hung wistfully about the yachts, and all yachtsmen love people that love their boats. We had already bought a tiny sloop, a forerunner—an egg, as it were—of *Grey Goose*; and now we began to crew on the big yachts, learning a great deal. Once, crewing aboard a forty-foot sloop, I went forward to back the jib as she came about. A flap of the sail knocked my expensive uniform cap over the side. The sloop, up in the wind, was barely moving, and as the cap drifted back along the side Davy reached far out for it, then farther, then—whether she reached too far or jumped we were never certain—she was overboard. At that instant the great mainsail filled with a bang, and the sloop began to move. We were several miles off Diamond Head, not, fortunately, in a race. At first I laughed, knowing Davy could swim like a fish. She laughed, too, and waved the cap. But, then, the skipper tried to come about without enough way on, and the boat was in irons. Suddenly I realised that Davy's

head was very far away in a big ocean. I kicked off my
shoes and dived in and swam fast towards her. She was
glad to see me, and I, her. I took the cap and put it on
my head, and, as the sloop seemed to be getting farther
away, we contemplated the long swim to shore. I wasn't
at all sure we could make it—at least four miles—but
said, "We'll get there in time for dinner, I think." And
Davy said, "I don't think I'll want any salt on my steak,
but, at least, we can see the sunset going in." They picked
us up though. Aboard, everybody took the whole thing
lightly; but that night in bed, to our amazement, we
shuddered with a delayed terror at the thought that we
might have lost each other.

In this same year, the last year of the war, we had our
first—indeed, our only—leave from the navy: ten whole
days. We decided to begin it with an extended Navigators' Council, a review of all our years together, where
we had been and where we were going. For three long
mornings in a row, mugs of coffee laced with cream
beside us, we talked about it, and we concluded that we
were still "on course." Our goal in that long-past Glenmerle springtime had been, simply, to keep our love—to
keep the magical quality of springtime inloveness. We
knew that we had kept it. The Shining Barrier stood.
Next morning at dawn we walked up a deep cool valley
where we had never been before. Great blue morning
glories grew on a wall, and we came at last to a fresh-
water pool where we bathed. Sunlight filtered through
branches, dappling the water and Davy's smiling face,
and we kissed each other in the fresh morning. Somehow
that morning—one of those moments made eternity—
seems in its clear and lovely "morningness" to represent
our lives at that point in time.

A few months later came orders to report to Great
Lakes pending reassignment. Perhaps the sword was beginning to fall. But, shortly after we arrived, the Bomb
was dropped and Japan surrendered. Soon afterwards I,
by now a lieutenant-commander, was released from the
navy. Picking up precisely where we'd left off, we headed
for Florida.

Ten days later, in Miami, we were masters of a sturdy, teak-built, gaff-rigged sloop named *Gull*. Only eighteen feet on the waterline, she had two long bunks and a tiny galley below. She was the second stage in our progress towards *Grey Goose*. We lived aboard and sailed the waters off the southern tip of Florida, exploring the keys and inlets, eating fish and lobsters and sand sharks we caught with hook and line or speared. Sometimes we would spend two months at a stretch wandering among the islands, brown and half-naked, our hair long and wild. Then we would come back to a mooring in the filthy Miami River, and I would take my typewriter out under a palm tree in the small adjacent park and knock out a story of cruising and send it off to *Yachting* magazine, which would send back some money. With it we would buy the odd fitting for the boat and tins of food and be off again.

Scenes flicker through my mind from those carefree days: *Gull* wing and wing before a fresh breeze. The two of us, brown as nuts with spears in hand, wading in waist-deep shallows, peering down through the clear water for the feelers of the wily lobster sticking out from beneath a rock or sunken log, and later discussing a huge lobster salad in the cockpit as the sun went down. Or the two of us lying in warm shallows with only our heads, crowned with immense straw hats, and our hands, holding books, out of water—one of us smacking the water now and then to drive away the tiny dorsal fins of little sharks that might fancy a toe or two. And I hear the sounds of the keys: the flap of a sail, the hum of mosquitoes, the wind in the rigging, the wild lost cry of a seabird.

One night, after sailing all day with an old sailor named Cap, who was teaching us out of the kindness of his heart all his sea-lore, we made fast to the stern of his *Beachcomber*, both boats swinging from Cap's anchor. Dinner with him over, I stayed there talking awhile after Davy went back to *Gull*. Then I said goodnight, too. On his deck I hauled *Gull* up and stepped soundlessly aboard in my bare feet and went aft. Standing there in the cockpit I looked down the companionway. Davy's head, her hair shining in the light of the tiny oil lamp, was bent over an array of bright seashells on the cabin table. Over my head arched the vast and tonight-mysterious darkness of the wild keys with no light anywhere, not even on Cap's boat, and, below, that bright warm little world of the cabin in which Davy, unconscious of my gaze, arranged her shells.

Life in *Gull*, though expansive on deck—the islands and ocean for our garden—was rather like living in a packing case below. But we did not mean to continue it indefinitely—it was only a stage on the way to the blue-water schooner. We were expecting a small post-war depression and drop in boat prices, at which time we would buy *Grey Goose*. But it hadn't happened yet. One night we had a long discussion in the cabin, the sloop anchored in the lee of an island. We decided that, while waiting for that drop in boat prices, we would not stay longer in *Gull*, since we had learnt what she had to teach us, but would turn for a bit to books, a university, Oxford we hoped, where we would gain a further education that would help us in getting the occasional job when we were wandering the world in *Grey Goose*. But Oxford proved at that moment impossible because of all the men returning from the forces, and we looked elsewhere.

When autumn came, we were at Yale, immersed in a sea of books, fifty-six of which had got to be read by next Thursday. We felt our minds expanding, and we chalked up a thousand intriguing intellectual byways to return to some day. Among the things we studied in the graduate-school seminars, in a broad programme that we could shape as we chose, were the history of ideas, aspects of both American and English literature, and English history and historians. When we wanted to get away from New Haven, especially in the summer, we went to Davy's mother's stone cottage at Culver Lake in New Jersey. There we could read peacefully, and walk, and take a canoe along the shores and hear the owls at night.

In New Haven we lived in a single, large, handsome room, originally the dining-room or drawing-room, in an old house full of graduate students. We cooked, mostly, on a hot plate; sometimes in the kitchen. In our room there was a small elegant fireplace, and in it we burned, not coal but beautiful walnut gun-stocks—rejects from an arms factory that we could get for a song. A wheat-coloured, black-muzzled bitch named Gypsy, part collie, part husky, we thought, was abandoned by her owners, and we adopted her.

But, although our minds were stimulated and expanded, although we were impressed by Yale, although we had a houseful of friends, and although—as I wrote in our Journal—"we rediscovered leafless northern trees in all their bare grace," we did not ever forget *Grey Goose*. In that Journal I also wrote: "Somewhere, beyond the buildings that loom against this lowering winter sky, the trade-winds blow, the long blue rollers crash upon the reef in white foam, and a rakish schooner swings, tugging at her anchor. God! what are we doing here?" Moved as we were by the great library, by that "quiet disrespect of libraries" of E. B. White's line, we sometimes suspected that the little bespectacled scholars who crawled about in the stacks of that splendid aspiring library, writing the learned commentaries and the footnotes upon the footnotes, had forgotten what the poem *meant*. I wrote a disrespectful poem about them, and I wrote in the Journal of scholars who "forget in a world of grey stone and parchment that stars shine on a tree in the quad, that the poem sings. And we, Davy and I—if we don't stay close to the wind and the stars, we shall be lost in a cloud of ambiguities." We, too, of course were writing learned papers, and publishing them, also, but we were not forgetting the poem and the wind on the sea.

One evening after a seminar I walked home through the snow and icy air thinking that I'd get everything ready or cooking for dinner before Davy came home from the library, but I found that she had got there first. A bright gun-stock fire blazed in the fireplace, candles burned on the mantelpiece, and the table was drawn up to the fire with a grand dinner upon it—and the first notes of the Bruch violin concerto were softly sounding.

Davy smiled at my pleased look. Suddenly it was—the whole scene—the innermost heart of love. I snatched her into my arms, staggered by my love for her, aware of joy and the brief lovely warmth of life, with all the freezing darkness, the endless night, of death beyond. I murmured something of this in her ear, still holding her while the concerto sang on. We both had tears, tears of joy, in our eyes: whatever the darkness beyond, now, now the candle of our love held back the dark.

In the spring Davy decided one afternoon to take her book into the city park. She read peacefully, looking up now and then to watch children at play. They went away after awhile. She read on. She heard a hoarse cry somewhere behind her. It was repeated, and she twisted round to look. A man exposing himself. The loose lips smirked. Awareness of dusk and an empty park but for him swept over her. The man ran towards her. Although I had taught her some methods of defence, Davy sprang up and ran like a hare out of the park, the man pounding along behind her till she proved faster. She leaped out into the street, sobbing a little and filled with loathing, and came home. That was all—a man whose whole being was a monstrous ego, consumed in self. It would have given me a terrible pleasure to exterminate him. Davy was able to smile at herself later that night, but she did not forget the feeling of being prey.

In our time at Yale we had read immensely; and we had heard the poets' cries of despair, all the way from Blake's "The Sick Rose" to Auden's "Faces along the bar." And we had been reflecting upon Hawthorne and his theme of the stain of guilt upon the soul. Perhaps that had something to do with it, and perhaps the man in the park, all but consumed in the evil of self, had something to do with it. At all events, on this night, a couple of months after the man in the park, I had gone to the library to hunt something up, leaving Davy cheerfully curled up with a book.

I came home to find her face streaked with tears, and she clung to me desperately and wept. It was some time before she could try to tell me what had happened. The

two lines she wrote next day of a poem that was never
completed are the beginning point:

> All the world fell away last night,
> Leaving you, only you, and fright.

Her sins, she said, had come out and paraded before
her, ghastly in appearance and mocking in demeanour.
What sins? What sins could this eager, loving creature
have committed? Not sins as the world counts sins. Not
one person had she murdered, nor one gold ingot stolen.
No unfaithfulness, no secret drinking, no dishonesty,
no sloth, no kicking dogs. But sometimes she had been
grouchy or snappish. She had said cruel things to people,
perhaps to her mother or brother. Once in the war, when
a young officer—a friend who had been brought up a
Catholic—had said that, some day, he would no doubt
return to the Church, Davy had said with mocking
scorn: "Whatever for? Not brave enough to stand alone?"
And he had changed the subject. Now her words haunted
her. Sin: she knew there was such a thing as plain sin,
not something any psychiatrist could absolve or explain
away. Even worse, the sins of omission. She quoted some
poet whose name she did not know: "O unattempted
loveliness!/O costly valour never won!" She was shaken
to the depths, shaken as I had never known her to be.
I knew that. I knew it had been a huge and dreadful
experience. But how could I understand—I who had
never known the like? I held her and soothed her and
gave her my love. But, I told myself, a strange mood, a
result of the man in the park, some curious aberration
of mind and heart like our strange terror the night after
we had been in the sea off Diamond Head. For she was
clearly *not* a sinner, merely human and the dearer for it.
What she needed, what we both needed was the sea and
the sky, nature, to soothe our souls. So I held her and
comforted her, up against something I could not com-
prehend; but something I would help her fight.

I know now, of course, that she had experienced the
classical conviction of sin. Christianity knows all about

it, but I didn't know all about Christianity. If I had actually understood what was happening, understood it as spiritual process, I should have been wildly alarmed. Or, again, if I had deeply *understood*, perhaps I shouldn't have been alarmed—but for deep understanding I'd have had to be a Christian. For the Hound of Heaven was after her, following after with unwearied pace. But I did not understand. Neither did she of course; but then, when "all the world falls away" one night, one doesn't quite forget the experience.

Now it was time to leave Yale, M.A. in hand, and move towards *Grey Goose*. I would take a job teaching in a small Virginian college whilst a schooner was a-building. We found an old farmhouse near the college, which, since the farm's friendly white horse had gently nipped Davy the first day, we christened Horsebite Hall. There we and our New Haven street dog, Gypsy, were ensconced.

And a builder on the Eastern Shore of Maryland laid down the keel of a thirty-six-foot schooner. Slender she was with a lovely clipper bow, designed by Howard Chapelle, with whom we had long talks. Later I should write more articles for *Yachting* about these talks, about the building and launching of the ship, and about cruising in her. She was a centre-boarder, gaff-rigged, and very fast. We travelled often to the Eastern Shore to see her taking shape. From a drawing Davy made, a sculptor friend was carving a block of mahogany into a figurehead: a girl breasting the wind, valiant and graceful. Under the tall, raked mainmast was a sliver of wood, liberated by me from a northern museum, from the Confederate ironclad *Virginia* that fought the *Monitor* in Hampton Roads. Still, we said, this ship would be the last forerunner of the deep-keel ocean-keeping schooner that is to be; this ship is not *Grey Goose*. But she was *Grey Goose*, and so I shall call her. When she was launched, Davy christened her, breaking a bottle of wine against the lovely-curving bow, and crying as the schooner slipped into the water: "Keep us out of the set ways of life!"

We camped ashore while the schooner, anchored in a pool of a tidal creek, was being rigged and fitted. One soft dark night we were seized by a desire to row out to her. The only problem was that we couldn't see her at all from the shore; there wasn't even starlight. Still, the pool was small; we should find her eventually. So we rowed out into the darkness in our dinghy, a tiny double-ender surfboat that we had brought from the Islands and towed after *Gull* in the Keys. We quested about the pool but no schooner. After a bit I stopped rowing to light a cigarette. The brief flare of the match pushed back the darkness; and there within arm's reach was the graceful bow soaring up, and high above us the figurehead with the long white bowsprit shooting out over her. The match burned my fingers, and I lighted another. We were strangely thrilled by this unexpected glimpse of the pride of the schooner's bow—she was, not a boat but a ship. Then we drifted back along her side and climbed aboard further aft: "And from our deck we scorned the land." It was an unplanned moment that was a dream come true, the dream we had written about in that old poem of Glenmerle days, rowing out to *Grey Goose*. We sat there long in the soft darkness, feeling the schooner move a little at her anchor, talking of the old dream, of Glenmerle and the Islands.

While the schooner was being built for her spring launching, I of course taught my classes and we lived in our farmhouse, Horsebite Hall. We drank pure springwater and we kept chickens. A big collie came courting, and Gypsy, to her apparent amazement, produced puppies that we gave sailor names to: Jib and Tops'l, Spinnaker and Flurry—a flurry of wind over the waters. It was Flurry that we kept and loved through the years, Flurry swift and graceful and intelligent. Once while she was still a puppy we went out in a hurry after dinner, leaving everything, including a whole country ham, on the table. Out of Flurry's reach—we supposed. She gave the thing a bit of thought. She seized the corner of the tablecloth in her sharp little teeth and braced her small paws and tugged. And tugged. We came home and gasped: a ruin of broken crockery. And the whole ham inside Flurry who could scarcely walk. She heard our horrified gasp and my sharp invocation of my God. Perhaps she had been wondering in any case about all those smashing dishes. Anyhow, she raised her small muzzle and roared—the queerest, most mournful, most guiltily repentant roar ever emitted by any creature, possibly excepting a guilty lion. We broke up in laughter, unable to punish her.

We enjoyed Horsebite Hall, stoking the stoves with wood till they glowed red-hot, tending our chickens, riding the white horse bareback, and walking. Being out of doors—outdoors alone—climbing the blue Virginian hills. We sang folksongs about the fox that went out on a chilly night and the Scotchman who turned robber all on the salt seas, and we sang that we knew where we were going. We also went to church a few times, not out of any accession of belief but just to hear the beautiful and ancient Anglican liturgy. Once we even made a communion, just because it was the going thing. It didn't mean anything. Unless, of course, it did mean something. One church that we sometimes went to was a tiny 150-year-old church, St. Stephen's, set in lovely rolling country with a few noble old houses here and there and the Blueridge glowing in the distance.

Davy was painting. She had always been deft with a pencil or brush; now she was painting in earnest, getting steadily better. She painted Virginia: scenes along the St. Stephen's road and on our own farm. A big black walnut tree stood alone in our meadow, distinguished by an especially massive branch that angled upwards from low on the trunk. Davy did a fine picture of tree and meadow and stream. Then she did another of the tree—recognisably the same tree, black and bare of leaves—but the meadow had given way to a dream landscape of rocks and earth and cliffs. In the cliffs were caves out of which grotesque and even fiendish faces leered. In the foreground was the tree and, near it, a wraithlike female figure—the soul beyond doubt—groped, as though unable to see clearly, towards the tree: the tree whose massive branch cast upon the bare earth the shadow of the crucified Messiah. The Shadow of a Tree. The picture grew of course out of that Yale experience of all the world falling away, and we called it, lightly, her "Sin Picture." All the same, I regarded it somewhat uneasily, though it was certain that Davy was not a Christian. And, after all, many an unbeliever has used the symbolism of the Cross in art. Surely that was all it was. I was the one who—because of another shadow cross, oddly, the shadow of the destroyer's yardarm—was some day, maybe, going to have another look at Christianity, not Davy. But the truth was that I was far too remote from Christianity to judge anyone else's distance from it. I knew Davy almost as well as I knew myself. But I did not know the place from which all distances are measured.

We discovered that we could, now, go to Oxford if we chose. We had wanted to do that when we went to Yale. Now we could. There were several reasons, we thought, to support our deferring the ultimate *Grey Goose* voyaging for another two or even three years. Apart from Oxford itself which might be worth deferring anything for, we had all along planned a somewhat larger deep-keel schooner; and we might, perhaps, better find it in England. Moreover, at Yale, Davy had been thought to have an obscure and undangerous ailment for which a restful life for a few years had been suggested. She didn't, in fact, have it; but it played a part in our deferring—only deferring—the off-soundings voyaging and the far islands for Oxford.

We had been exploring the Chesapeake, exploring islands and little Eastern Shore ports and, with our shallow draft, the lovely tidal creeks. We had experienced the fierce white squalls of that body of water and been becalmed. Sometimes we took friends along, but more often it was just the two of us with Flurry and Gypsy for crew, until Gypsy, true to her name, ran away and was lost. The schooner sailed like a dream, fast, able to windward, and swift to come about. On hot summer days there was usually shade from the great mainsail, and there was a canopy that, at anchor, could be rigged over the cockpit. One of the most attractive features was a long after deck, abaft the cockpit, where even I could stretch out.

One day, virtually on the eve of Oxford, began with a fine fresh breeze in the morning as we left our anchorage. We were on a broad reach to the southwards, going like a clipper, and we actually overhauled a motor cruiser, passing her like a whirlwind. But then in the afternoon the breeze died completely and we were becalmed. We couldn't have cared less, though. We rigged the canopy and stretched out with books on the after deck with a pitcher of iced lemonade. Towards evening a tiny breeze got up, and the ship began to move as we took down the canopy: she moved; the sails were asleep; but it was movement in a dream. The water was still mirror smooth; the breeze was aloft and so light that our movement was barely perceptible and altogether soundless—what is called ghosting. The mainsail shaded us from the afternoon sun: I was in the cockpit, keeping a finger on the tiller, and Davy was still lying on her stomach aft with her chin in her hands. The crew—Flurry—was asleep on the deckhouse. I went forward for a moment and could hear the faintest little chuckle of water under the forefoot, but it couldn't be heard aft. Under a blue sky, darkening in the east as the sun set in splendour in the west, across calm water turned to flame by the setting sun, we sailed in a dream. Ahead, dead ahead, where the coastline curved out, a cove opened to the north. I steered for it, expecting the tiny breeze to die any minute. But it held, and as dusk came on we ghosted straight in and rounded up and the anchor splashed over. We had a swim and a light dinner. The evening seemed to grow more sultry. Perhaps a storm was brewing, but when we sought our bunks it had not materialised.

Some time in the night I awoke, feeling the yacht swinging at her anchor. A stream of lovely cool air was pouring down the forward hatch. I got up soundlessly and emerged from the hatch as far as my waist. At the same instant Davy popped out of the after hatch and crept forward along the deck to where I stood, half out of the hatch. The breeze had sprung up and back to north so that it was coming straight in the mouth of the cove, though not strongly enough to cause any worry about the anchor holding. It had blown every bit of humidity and sultriness away. The air was cool and fresh. Ten thousand brilliant stars arched across the sky. But what transfixed us was phosphorescence. Every little wave rolling into the cove was crested with cold fire. The anchor rode was a line of fire going down into the depths, and fish moving about left trails of fire. The night of the sea-fire. Davy had crept near to me, still crouching, and I put my arm about her, and she snuggled close. Neither of us spoke, not so much as a whispered word. We were together, we were close, we were overwhelmed by a great beauty. I know that it seemed to us both that we were completely one: we had no *need* to speak. We remained so in timeless loveliness—was it hours? We never knew. All about us was the extraordinary beauty of the sea-fire and the glittering stars overhead. We were full of wonder —and joy. *Grey Goose* was alive, lifting to the little waves, and the tall dark masts were pencilling across the stars. The moment was utterly timeless: we didn't know that time existed; and it contained, therefore, some foretaste, it may be, of eternity. At last, still with no word spoken, we went below again and, in comfort and a great peace, slept.

Next day we did not know at all whether that time-less moment—that moment made eternity—had been hours long or minutes long. But the question was, of course, of no importance.

What is important, perhaps, is that the moment was a culmination of all we had ever dreamt: not just *Grey Goose*, not just the good life—the timeful life without the pressure of time—but also the green tree of the pagan love flourishing within the Shining Barrier. Still in love, still outward bound. We were leaving this *Grey Goose* way for a little while, but only for awhile. The far islands waited. Life stretched ahead.

In the late summer the P. & O. liner, *Stratheden*, pressed into the Atlantic run, went astern from her berth in New York harbour with huge blasts of her whistle, and then went ahead, standing out to sea bound for London. We were aboard.

·¤{ IV }¤·

Encounter with Light

The soft, green grass of early June, dotted here and there
with little blue flowers, spread to the very edge of the
small river. On the other side of the grassy place stood
an ancient beech, and the landscape contained many
other trees, both near and far. A gentle blue sky with a
few scattered clouds arched above. From somewhere up
there, near the zenith, fell the piercing sweetness of a
skylark's song. A faint haze softened the outlines of the
more remote trees; and in the distance, also hazy, rose a
splendour of towers and spires. Oxford in Summer Term
along the River Cherwell. Here in the lush grass lay
Davy and I reading aloud from *The Wind in the
Willows*, one of the wonderful books of the world, the
part about Rat and Mole on the river bank. We had just
finished laughing at Rat's response to Mole's admission
of his having never been in a boat: " 'What?' cried the
Rat, open-mouthed. 'Never been in a—you never—well,
I—what have you been doing, then?' " Now the book had
slipped to the ground, and with still-smiling faces we
listened lazily to the skylark. Two young men poling a
punt passed on the river. A moment later there was the
sound of distant bells, the bells of Oxford.

We had come up to the university for Michaelmas
Term in the previous autumn, and by now we were to
be numbered for ever amongst the lovers of Oxford. And
amongst the lovers of England, too, especially rural England. On our crossing of the Atlantic in the P. & O. Line's
Stratheden, eating mighty Indian curries every day, talk-

71

ing to English people aboard, already beginning to think in pounds, shillings, and pence, we had wondered how it would be to come to the England that we knew so well in books and that I, at least, had known as a small child: would it be, essentially, a foreign country, or—well, not foreign? But by the time the ship was coasting along the white cliffs and then proceeding up the Thames, we had begun to think what we later found to be true: that coming to England was like coming home, coming to a home half-remembered—but home.

A curious incident had occurred aboard the liner. Reading a notice outside the Purser's office that a woman travelling to Rome for holy year had lost her handbag and her all, four hundred dollars, we were struck by the fact that the ship held just four hundred passengers. Only one dollar apiece and the poor lady would smile again. With our dollars in hand we went in to see the Purser. But he, though quite convinced that the loss was genuine and permanent, could not by Company rules take up a collection. But, he added, why didn't *we* do it? Oh, no! we said with a shudder, we couldn't do that; we're shy types. So we departed. Thought. Looked at each other. Gave each other wry grins. Returned. "We'll do it," we said. The Purser grinned. "Good show!" he said. So, passenger lists in hand, we asked everybody, thereby meeting some fascinating people, ranging from a Shropshire landed baronet to an American communist—both, incidentally, made a contribution and both stood us a drink later. Indeed, everyone contributed except some sulky Germans. New Yorkers, though, were invariably suspicious: what was our racket, bud? But we learned to say very politely: "Do you mind me asking, are you from New York? You are? Well, never mind, then. We're not asking New Yorkers—too suspicious. Forget it. Thank you very much." About an hour later they would sidle up and with a gruff "Here!" hand over twenty dollars. So we collected the lot and gave it to the Purser with the strict injunction not to tell the woman that we collected it. But he or someone betrayed us; and she came over to our table in the saloon and wept rather a lot, which was quite awful, even though she gave the principal credit to the Blessed Virgin.

The curious thing, to us, about the whole affair was the question we were so often asked, seriously asked: Why were we doing this? Were we Christians or something? Naturally we denied it. But we were rather taken aback by the assumption. We had thought we were merely doing the decent thing in the circumstances. Why should so many people think that only Christianity could account for it? Very odd.

After a fortnight in London, we made our way to Paddington and took the train to Oxford. When the train began to slow for what we thought would be it, we were looking out of the right-hand window for the station. There were brick walls. They ended. Suddenly there was a vision of towers and spires reaching up to the summer sky, wheeling round each other with the motion of the train, lovely as a city in a dream. It was only for a moment, and then we were in the station.

We were welcomed to Oxford by one Lew Salter, whose kinswoman I had known in Virginia, and his pretty wife, Mary Ann. Lew, a brilliant theoretical physicist, was in my college, Jesus. He and Mary Ann were, also, we discovered later, keen Christians. Through them we met, almost at once, their English friends, Peter and Bee Campion—Bee, tall and swift, impatient of nonsense; Peter, just out of the Royal Navy, pipe-smoking, nice grin, bright blue eyes. Peter was a physicist, too, in Exeter College. At the same time, we met another friend of theirs, Thad Marsh of Worcester College, lanky, witty, intelligent, who was reading English. These were our first friends, close friends. More to the point, perhaps, all five were keen, deeply committed Christians. But we liked them so much that we forgave them for it. We began, hardly knowing we were doing it, to revise our opinions, not of Christianity but of Christians. Our fundamental assumption, which we had been pleased to regard as an intelligent insight, had been that all Christians were necessarily stuffy, hide-bound, or stupid—people to keep one's distance from. We had kept our distance so successfully, indeed, that we didn't know anything about Christians. Now that assumption soundlessly collapsed. The sheer quality of the Christians we met at Oxford shattered our stereotype, and thenceforward a reference in a book or conversation to someone's being a Christian called up an entirely new image. Moreover, the astonishing fact sank home: our own contemporaries could be at once highly intelligent, civilised, witty, fun to be with—and Christian.

If we had been asked at that time what we meant when we spoke of someone as a Christian, we should have said that we meant someone who called himself a Christian. If pressed, we should have added that he was someone who believed that Jesus was God or one with God, or, at least, said he believed that. But there are people who are so nice in their understanding of the word "Christian" that they don't use it at all. Who are we, they say, to pretend to know who is truly a Christian in God's eyes? This is, indeed, very true, very nice. But a word that cannot be used is not very useful. And we need—we *must* have—a word for believers; and we must, therefore, hold to the age-old, New-Testament use to designate a believer: someone who says he is a believer. Someone we believe when he says it. No doubt there are those well loved of God who are not Christians; no doubt there are false Christians in the churches; God can sort them out as He chooses. In the meantime, we must stick to the plain, definite, original meaning of the word: one who accepts the teachings of the Apostles, one who *believes*.

We, then, were not Christians. Our friends were. But we liked them anyhow.

We found digs in North Oxford and bought bicycles. The three-room flat on the Woodstock Road included a piano that Davy could play to me on. And that Lew Salter could play on: if he hadn't decided on physics, he could have been a concert pianist. He often played for us; and when he played, lost in his music, his sensitive face wore a look of pain that he was unaware of. They would drift in, any or all of the five of them. We would have tea and crumpets by the fire, and we would talk, always talk: talk about the University, talk about books, talk about our work—Peter and Lew explaining He-ions (and perhaps She-ions) in cloud chambers or Thad talking about Spenser. And talk about Christianity. We didn't mind *talking* about it: that's what Oxford is, a place to talk about everything. And there would be, always, music, since we had the piano. Lew would play, or Davy. Sometimes Thad would lift his pleasant voice in song. The "Trout," Schubert's quintet, was one of our special favourites, and it became linked permanently in my mind and Davy's, both with that group of friends and with the pub called the Trout. Even more dear—the song that later would summon up all Oxford for Davy and me and would, for me, be for ever Davy herself—was the lovely little Elizabethan song about the lady passing by:

> There is a lady sweet and kind,
> Was never face so pleased my mind;
> I did but see her passing by,
> And yet I love her till I die.

Meanwhile, we explored Oxford's grey magic, Oxford "that sweet City with her dreaming spires." Oxford and all the country round, sometimes on our bikes, sometimes on foot. There was Marston Ferry—a penny trip across the river and a pub on the other side. And that other country pub, the Perch, with its pleasant garden in the minute village of Binsey, which was across Port Meadow and the humpbacked bridge. Beyond the village, hidden away down a long lane of venerable beeches— one of our earliest and most enchanting walks with a college friend, Edmund—was the ancient and tiny village church, St. Margaret's, with a wishing well beside it into which one cast a penny to make the wish come true. And of course that favourite place of all the university, the Trout, where one lunched and drank brown ale on the terrace and fed the Queen's swans; and then walked back to Oxford along the Isis, sometimes called the Thames by Londoners, watching the college eights flash by.

Coming back to Oxford, we were always, it seemed, greeted by the sound of bells: bells everywhere striking the hour or bells from some tower change-ringing, filling the air with a singing magic. We explored every cranny of this city of enchanting crannies and unexpected breathtaking views of towers and spires. We were conscious all the time of the strong intellectual life of a thousand years. Despite the modern laboratories, Oxford is still "breathing the last enchantments of the middle ages": this wall was part of a great abbey; the Benedictines built the long, lovely buildings that are part of one college quad; the narrow passage where we bought tea things has been called Friars Entry for centuries; the Colleges bear names like Christ Church and Mary Magdalen and Corpus Christi; and the bells with their lovely clamour have rung through the centuries.

Imperceptibly the ages of faith, when men really believed, when the soaring spires carried their eyes and thoughts up to God, became *real* to us, not something in a book. What was happening was that our mind's gaze, almost without our knowing it, was being directed towards the Christian faith that, at once, animated our living contemporary friends *and* had brought this university with its colleges and churches and chapels into being. It was not precisely that we were being called upon to accept that faith but that we were being called upon to acknowledge its existence as an ancient and living force. There was a terrible splendour in these churches with their glorious glowing glass and in the music of the plainsong and in the words of the liturgy. The splendour of course did not mean that the faith was true; but perhaps we felt vaguely that it *did* somehow hint at a validity.

Even as we talked and played with our friends and explored the city, I was discovering Jesus College, dining "on" hall two or three times a week, and making further friends in the Junior Common Room: Trevor and John and Alan, all reading "Greats" (or classics); Edmund Dews, tall and urbane, who had taken us on our first walk to Binsey; and John Dickey, who was reading law and concealed beneath an amiable, easy-going friendliness a mind like a razor. There were conversations with various dons about my work—the matter of choosing a subject for research—and a good deal of exploratory reading amidst the ancient grandeur of the Bodleian Library. Often as I, or Davy and I, pored over the books, there would be in the very background of awareness the persistent sound—almost monotonous and yet, after all, not monotonous, and cheerful, even gay—of change-ringing bells from one of the churches round about. Then, too, there were the college and university societies to look into, societies for every conceivable interest, serious and frivolous, including a yacht club through which we did a bit of sailing on the Isis.

But I was troubled by the things I could do, or had to do like dining in hall, that Davy could not do. We had a long talk about it, she urging me to experience the whole richness of Oxford and come back and tell her—and bring back, as, indeed, I was doing, the friends I made. "I'd rather hear about it than not experience it at all," she said. "Besides, isn't that what Peter Ibbetson and Mimsey did? Showing each other in dreams all they experienced? You can make me see—you're good at that." So it was agreed: we would while we were here seek the whole of the Oxford thing, together when we could, apart when we must. And I did, most faithfully, recount all to her, and in the end what was to prove the deepest part of our Oxford days we shared completely.

One of the societies I, therefore, joined when I was invited to was a college dining society, limited to ten members, called the Antler, which twice a term had a dinner somewhere in the Oxford country, such as the Bear at Woodstock or Studley Priory. The dinner and the wines would be painstakingly selected in advance by one of us, we wore dinner jackets, and for half the dinners we invited a distinguished guest. The conversation ranged from good to brilliant; and what we sought, though we did not of course say so, was civilisation. Lew Salter was a member as was Edmund Dews, one of the most urbane of conversationalists who, in our opinion, outshone

even Sir Maurice Bowra, the Vice-Chancellor, the night
he dined with us.

One most memorable dinner was one Davy and I
gave at the Woodstock flat. We had had Mother send
us a good Virginia country ham, perhaps a Smithfield,
and yams and cornbread. So we had a Lee's Birthday
Dinner amongst the dreaming spires for both our American and English friends, including John Dickey and
Edmund and the "Christian Five" and others. John
lingered afterwards and we talked late.

Always at Oxford there would be in full term literally
an embarrassment of riches: musical productions, including the annual visit of the D'Oyly Carte Gilbert and
Sullivan troupe, plays destined for London opening first
in Oxford, and of course the bump races of the college
eights, which we watched from the handsome Jesus barge,
one of a long line of colourful college barges moored
along the river bank.

While the subject of major research was still being
considered by Davy and me, I did a short paper for
History Today, which paid me twenty guineas. It was
on the English historian, James Anthony Froude, and I
was given some help with it by A. L. Rowse of All Souls,
that beautiful and austere college without undergrad-
uates. Upon completion of my paper, my mentor invited
me to dine at All Souls, black tie and, for some reason,
a long gown.

The vast hall of All Souls was lighted only by candles
—the table was a blaze of candles—but a little ways from
the table and up, up towards the high vaulted roof, there
was darkness. When I followed my host in, as part of
the procession of dons, I was placed next to Warden
Sumner, and, during the dinner, he talked to me with
the most charming courtesy. His face in the candlelight
with the dark behind—all down the table one saw the
scholarly faces and the white of shirt fronts, but the
gowns merged into darkness—his face had the austere
beauty of a medieval saint. All the long centuries of
Oxford came to a focus in that fine-drawn beautiful face.
It is engraved on my mind as one of the great things I

have seen. After the port and the conversation, as I walked out the Woodstock Road with my gown floating about me and the bells near and far announcing midnight, I thought of the words to make Davy see, and I thought that I had begun to know the meaning of Oxford.

One afternoon, having strolled with a friend along the Isis, I was walking alone across Port Meadow into Oxford, hearing change-ringing bells in the distance. It may be that the bells led me to picture a church spire surmounted by a cross. Anyhow, into my mind came, as it had done every now and then through the years, the memory of the shadow of a cross made by the destroyer's mast and yardarm and my subsequent resolve some day to have another look at the case for Christianity. Perhaps now was the time to do it? The idea seemed less revolting than at other times it had recurred. Of course Christianity couldn't possibly be *true*, a thought suggested. Still, another thought pointed out, there was that resolve; and one ought to be *fair*. As I made my way through the streets to Jesus to collect my bicycle, I happened to look up. There against the darkening grey sky was the tremendous soaring uprush of the spire of St. Mary the Virgin. My resolve came to the point: this *was* the time to do it. I swung about, nearly colliding with another Jesus man, and went into Blackwell's, the booksellers.

Somewhile later I arrived at the Woodstock flat with an armload of books on Christianity. Over tea I told Davy of my thoughts and the effect of that thirteenth-century spire of St. Mary's, quite possibly the loveliest spire in Christendom. Davy was pleased.

"I've been thinking that we ought to *know* more," she said. "Oh, good! I see you've got some C. S. Lewis. Thad and the others are always talking about him. Who is he, anyhow?"

"A don," I said. "He's a don in one of the colleges—Magdalen, it says on this book. Not theology, though. English lit. Very brilliant, I think. I read part of a debate he was having with some philosopher. I think I'll read this one first—*Miracles*."

"Okay," said Davy. "I'll read *Screwtape Letters*. Then

we can trade. Mary Ann and Lew, everyone in fact, will be pleased, won't they?"

"They certainly will," I said. "But listen, Davy. We're just having a look, you know. Let's keep our heads. There are enormous arguments against Christianity."

"Oh, I know!" she said. "I don't see how it could be true. But—well, how would you feel if we decided that it *was* true?"

"Um," I said. "I'm not sure. One would know the meaning of things. That would be good. But we'd have to go to church and all that. And, well, pray. Still, it would be great to know meanings and, you know, the purpose of everything. But, dammit! it *couldn't* be true! How could Earth's religion—*one* of Earth's religions—be true for the whole galaxy—millions of planets, maybe? That's what rules it out right in the beginning. It's—it's too little!"

"I know," said Davy. "Look—these three are a sort of science-fiction trilogy: *Out of the Silent Planet, Perelandra,* and *That Hideous Strength.* Did you know that?"

"Good lord!" I said. "No. I'll read those first—unless you want to?"

"No," she said. "I want to read *Screwtape.* Thad says it's funny."

And that's how it all began. The encounter with Light. Only of course it *didn't* begin then. It began when we came to Oxford. Or it began with shadows of masts and trees. Or it began with our abandoning our childhood religion: To believe with certainty, somebody said, one has to begin by doubting. Wherever it began, what it *was* was a coming-together of disparate things—our love for each other and for beauty, our longing for unpressured time and the night of the cold sea-fire on *Grey Goose,* the quality of our Christian friends and the Oxford built by hands and the Oxford that I saw in the face of the Warden of All Souls. They came together into one, into focus, and the Light fell upon them.

There were half a hundred books that first autumn and winter in Oxford. We became interested, absorbed, in the study of Christianity right from the start—though, still, it was only a *study*. It was fortunate that I chose to read that C. S. Lewis science-fiction triology first, for, apart from being beautiful and enthralling, it made me conscious of an alliance with him: what he hated (*That Hideous Strength*) I hated and feared. Much more important, perhaps, the triology showed me that the Christian God might, after all, be quite big enough for the whole galaxy. Nothing was proved except that, quite reasonably, He might be big enough; but, in fact, an insuperable difficulty—that of Christianity's being only a *local* religion—was overcome. Apart from Lewis, we read G. K. Chesterton, who with wit presented in *The Everlasting Man* and other works a brilliant, reasoned case for the faith. And Charles Williams, theologian and novelist, who opened up realms of the spirit we didn't know existed, was tremendously important to us both. Graham Greene showed—terribly—what sin was, and what faith was—also terrible. Dorothy Sayers made Christianity dramatic and exciting, and attacked complacency and dullness like a scorpion. We had read T. S. Eliot for years, but now we began to see what he was really saying in *Ash Wednesday* and the *Four Quartets*—and it scared us, rather. His description of the state of being a Christian lingered in our minds: "A condition of complete simplicity/(Costing not less than everything)." Everything! There were many other books, including Christian classics like St. Augustine, *The Imitation of Christ*, and the *Apologia Pro Vita Sua*. And we read the New Testament, of course, in numerous translations along with commentaries. But there is no doubt that C. S. Lewis was, first to last, overwhelmingly the most important reading for us both. Only someone who has faced the questions—is Christianity false?—can help someone else resolve the counter-question—is it true? We read everything he ever wrote, including *Great Divorce, Miracles, Problem of Pain, Pilgrim's Regress* (which I found very meaningful), and much more, including his scholarly works, such as *The Allegory of Love*. The man's learning was immense, in English literature, in the classics, and, despite his disclaimers, in theology. His was perhaps the most brilliant and certainly the most lucid mind we ever knew: he wrote about Christianity in a style as clear as spring water without a hint of sanctimoniousness or vagueness or double-talk, never suggesting that anything be accepted on other than reasonable grounds. He gave us, simply, straightforward, telling argument laced with wit. And that incredible imagination.

As we read, we talked to our Christian friends, raising our questions and doubts. They answered us very patiently and thoughtfully. By now there were other Christian friends besides the original five, particularly a little Welshman in my college named Geraint Gruffydd, a poet and a reader of poetry. An important insight struck us—Davy and me—one day when we realised that our friends, though Anglican, Baptist, Roman Catholic, and Lutheran, were united by far more—mere Christianity, as Lewis would put it—than divided them. "And they're all so—so happy in their Christianity," said Davy. And I said, "Could it be—that happiness—what's called 'Christian joy,' do you think?" That night I wrote in our Journal:

The best argument for Christianity is Christians: their joy, their certainty, their completeness. But the strongest argument *against* Christianity is also Christians—when they are sombre and joyless, when they are self-righteous and smug in complacent consecration, when they are narrow and repressive, then Christianity dies a thousand deaths. But, though it is just to condemn some Christians for these things, perhaps, after all, it is not just, though very easy, to condemn Christianity itself for them. Indeed, there are impressive indications that the positive quality of joy is in Christianity—and possibly nowhere else. If that were certain, it would be proof of a very high order.

If minds like St. Augustine's and Newman's and Lewis's could wrestle with Christianity and become fortresses of that faith, it had to be taken seriously. I writhed a bit at the thought of my easy know-nothing contempt of other years. Most of the people who reject Christianity know almost nothing of what they are rejecting: those who condemn what they do not understand are, surely, *little* men. Thank God, if there is a God, we said, that we are at least looking seriously and honestly at this thing. If our Christian friends—nuclear physicists, historians, and able scholars in other fields—can believe in Christ, if C. S. Lewis can believe in Christ, we must, at least, weigh it very seriously.

Davy and I, we later decided, were immeasurably helped in our serious look at Christianity by where we considered ourselves to be: we did not at all suppose that we *were* Christians, just because we were more or less nice people who vaguely believed there might be some sort of a god and had been inside a church. We were right outside of the fold. Thus we were perfectly aware that the central claim of Christianity was and always had been that the same God who made the world had lived in the world and been killed by the world; and that the (claimed) proof of this was His Resurrection from the dead. This, in fact, was precisely what we, so far at least, did not believe. But we knew that it was what *had* to be believed if we were to call ourselves Christian. Consequently, we did *not* call ourselves Christian. Later we were to meet people who no more believed in this central claim than in the Easter bunny, yet they called themselves Christians on the basis, apparently, of going to church, being nice and respectable, and accepting some assorted bits of the Sermon on the Mount. I wrote sardonically that such people are proof that there can be smoke without fire. But Davy and I were not too close to Christianity to see it. We didn't mistake the foothills for the mountain. We saw it there only too clearly, solitary, vast, ice-capped, and apparently unscalable, at least by us. For we knew we had to *believe*. Christianity was a *faith*.

And by now we knew that it was important. If true— and we admitted to each other the possibility that it was —it was, very simply, the only really important truth in the world. And if untrue, it was *false*. No halfway house. First or nothing. I wrote:

It is not possible to be "incidentally a Christian." The fact of Christianity must be overwhelmingly *first* or nothing. This suggests a reason for the dislike of Christians by nominal or non-Christians: their lives contain no overwhelming firsts but many balances.

One December night, after Davy and I had been talking about the fact that Christianity claimed to be an *answer* to all the eternal questions—a *consistent* answer, our physicist friends kept murmuring—we admitted to each other that we did, quite desperately, want an answer. The only trouble, I added, was that we couldn't believe the Christian one. Then I suggested that we go out for a walk, but she said she was a bit headachey and wanted to go to bed. I told her to go on, then, and I should just walk up to the corner and back. While I was walking I thought what I should like to ask C. S. Lewis if only he were here. When I returned to the flat, I sat down, on an impulse, and wrote to Lewis, a busy man whom I had never so much as seen. He replied, straight to the point, immediately; and I wrote again.

The correspondence, two letters apiece, now follows with only the salutations and closings omitted:

To C. S. Lewis (I)

I write on an impulse—which in the morning may appear so immodest and presumptuous that I shall destroy this. But a few moments ago I felt that I was embarked for a voyage that would someday lead me to God. Even now, five minutes later, I'm inclined to add a qualifying "maybe." There is a leap I cannot make; it occurs to me that you, having made it, having linked certainty with Christianity, might, *not* do it *for* me, but give me a hint of how it's to be done. Having felt the aesthetic and historical appeal of Christianity, having begun to study it, I have come to awareness of the strength and "possibleness" of the Christian answer. I should *like* to believe it. I *want* to know God—if He is knowable. But I cannot pray with any conviction that Someone hears. I can't *believe*.

Very simply, it seems to me that some intelligent power made this universe and that all men must know it, axiomatically, and must feel awe at the power's infiniteness. It seems to me natural that men, knowing and feeling so, should attempt to elaborate on that simplicity—the prophets, the Prince Buddha, the Lord Jesus, Mohammed, the Brahmins—and so arose the world's religions. But how can just one of them be singled out as true? To an intelligent visitor from Mars, would not Christianity appear to be merely one of a host of religions?

I said at starting that I felt I was treading a long road that would one day lead me to Christianity; I must, then, believe after a fashion that it is the truth. Or is it only that I *want* to believe it? But at the same time, something else in me says: "Wanting to believe is the way to self-deception. Honesty is better than any easy comfort. Have the courage to face the fact that all men may be nothing to the Power that made the suns."

And yet I *would* like to believe that the Lord Jesus is in truth my merciful God. For the apostles who could talk to Jesus, it must have been easy. But I live in a "real world" of red buses and nylon stockings and atomic bombs; I have only the record of *others'* claimed experiences with deity. No angels, no voices, nothing. Or, yes, one thing: living Christians. Somehow you, in this very same world, with the same data as I, are more meaningful to me than the bishops of the faithful past. You accomplished the leap from agnosticism to faith: how? I don't quite know how I dare write this to you, a busy Oxford don, not a priest. Yet I do know: you serve God, not yourself; you *must* do, if you're a Christian. Perhaps, if I had the wit to see it, my answer lies in the fact that I did write.

From C. S. Lewis (I)

My own position at the threshold of Xtianity was exactly the opposite of yours. You wish it were true; I strongly hoped it was *not*. At least, that was my conscious wish: you may suspect that I had unconscious wishes of quite a different sort and that it was these which finally shoved me in. True: but then I may equally suspect that under your conscious wish that it were true, there lurks a strong unconscious wish that it were not. What this works out to is that all that modern stuff about concealed wishes and wishful thinking, however useful it may be for explaining the origin of an error which you already know to be an error, is perfectly useless in deciding which of two beliefs is the error and which is the truth. For (a.) One never knows all one's wishes, and (b.) In very big questions, such as this, even one's conscious wishes are nearly always engaged on both sides. What I think one can say with certainty is this: the notion that everyone *would like* Xtianity to be true, and that therefore all atheists are brave men who have accepted the defeat of all their deepest desires, is simply impudent nonsense. Do you think people like Stalin, Hitler, Haldane, Stapledon (a corking good writer, by the way) wd. be pleased on waking up one morning to find that they were not their own masters, that they had a Master and a Judge, that there was nothing even in the deepest recesses of their thoughts about which they cd. say to Him "Keep out! Private. This is *my* business?" Do you? *Rats!* Their first reaction wd. be (as mine was) rage and terror. And I v. much doubt whether even you wd. find it *simply* pleasant. Isn't the truth this: that it wd. gratify some of our desires (ones we feel in fact pretty seldom) and outrage a great many others? So let's wash out all the wish business. It never helped anyone to solve any problem yet.

I don't agree with your picture of the history of religion—Christ, Buddha, Mohammed and others elaborating an original simplicity. I believe Buddhism to be a simplification of Hinduism and Islam to be a smplification of Xtianity. Clear, lucid, transparent, simple religion (Tao *plus* a shadowy, ethical god in the background) is a late development, usually arising among highly educated people in great cities. What you really start with is ritual, myth, and mystery, the death & return of Balder or Osiris, the dances, the initiations, the sacrifices, the divine kings. Over against that are the Philosophers, Aristotle or Confucious, hardly religious at all. The only two systems in which the mysteries and the philosophies come together are Hinduism & Xtianity: there you get both Metaphysics and Cult (continuous with the primeval cults). That is why my first step was to be sure that one or other of these had the answer. For the reality can't be one that appeals *either* only to savages *or* only to high brows. Real things aren't like that (e.g. *matter* is the first most obvious thing you meet—milk, chocolates, apples, and also the object of quantum physics). There is no question of just a crowd of disconnected religions. The choice is between (a.) The materialist world picture: wh. I *can't* believe. (b.) The real archaic primitive religions: wh. are not moral enough. (c.) The (claimed) fulfilment of these in Hinduism. (d.) The claimed fulfilment of these in Xtianity. But the weakness of Hinduism is that it *doesn't* really join the two strands. Unredeemably savage religion goes on in the village; the Hermit philosophies in the forest: and neither really interferes with the other. It is only Xtianity wh. compels a high brow like me to partake in a ritual blood feast, and also compels a central African convert to attempt an enlightened universal code of ethics.

Have you tried Chesterton's *The Everlasting Man?* the best popular apologetic I know.

Meanwhile, the attempt to practice the *Tao* is certainly the right line. Have you read the *Analects* of Confucius? He ends up by saying "This is the Tao. I do not know if any one has ever kept it." That's significant: one can really go direct from there to the *Epistle to the Romans*.

I don't know if any of this is the least use. Be sure to write again, or call, if you think I can be of any help.

To C. S. Lewis (II)

My fundamental dilemma is this: I can't believe in Christ unless I have faith, but I can't have faith unless I believe in Christ. This is "the leap." If to *be* a Christian is to have faith (and clearly it is), I can put it thus: I must accept Christ to become a Christian, but I must *be* a Christian to accept Him. I don't have faith and I don't as yet believe; but everyone seems to say: "You must have faith to believe." Where do I get it? Or will you tell me something different? Is there a proof? Can Reason carry one over the gulf . . . without faith?

Why does God expect so much of us? Why does He require this effort to believe? If He made it clear that He is—as clear as a sunrise or a rock or a baby's cry—wouldn't we be right joyous to choose Him and His Law? Why should the right exercise of our free will contain this fear of intellectual dishonesty?

I must write further on the subject of "wishing it were true"—although I do agree that I probably have wishes on both sides, and my wish does not help to solve any problem. Your point that Hitler and Stalin (and I) would be horrified at discovering a Master from whom *nothing* could be withheld is very strong. Indeed, there is nothing in Christianity which is so repugnant to me as humility—the bent knee. If I knew beyond hope or despair that Christianity were true, my fight for ever after would have to be against the pride of "the spine may break but it never bends." And yet, Sir, would not I (and even Stalin) accept the humbling of the Master to escape the horror of ceasing to be, of *nothingness* at death? Moreover, the knowledge that Jesus was in truth Lord would *not* be merely pleasant news gratifying some of our rare desires. It would mean overwhelmingly: (a) that Materialism was Error as well as ugliness; (b) that the several beastly futures predicted by the Marxists, the Freudians, and the Sociologist manipulators would not be real (even if they came about); (c) that one's growth towards wisdom—soul-building—was not to be lost; and (d), above all, that the good and the beautiful would survive. And so I wish it were true and would accept any humbling, I think, for it to be true. The bad part of wishing it were true is that any impulse I feel towards belief is regarded with suspicion as stemming from the wish; the good part is that the wish leads on. And I shall go on; I must go on, as far as I can go.

From C. S. Lewis (II)

The contradiction "we must have faith to believe and must believe to have faith" belongs to the same class as those by which the Eleatic philosophers proved that motion was impossible. And there are many others. You can't swim unless you can support yourself in water & you can't support yourself in water unless you can swim. Or again, in an act of volition (e.g. getting up in the morning) is the very beginning of the act itself voluntary or involuntary? If voluntary then you must have willed it, ∴ you were willing already, ∴ it was not really the beginning. If involuntary, then the continuation of the act (being determined by the first moment)

is involuntary too. But in spite of this we *do* swim, &
we *do* get out of bed.

I do not think there is a *demonstrative* proof (like
Euclid) of Christianity, nor of the existence of matter,
nor of the good will & honesty of my best & oldest
friends. I think all three are (except perhaps the second)
far more probable than the alternatives. The case for
Xtianity in general is well given by Chesterton; and I
tried to do something in my *Broadcast Talks*. As to *why*
God doesn't make it demonstratively clear: are we sure
that He is even interested in the kind of Theism which
wd. be a compelled logical assent to a conclusive argument? Are *we* interested in it in personal matters? I
demand from my friend a trust in my good faith which
is *certain* without demonstrative proof. It wouldn't be
confidence at all if he waited for rigorous proof. Hang
it all, the very fairy-tales embody the truth. Othello believed in Desdemona's innocence when it was proved:
but that was too late. Lear believed in Cordelia's love
when it was proved: but that was too late. "His praise is
lost who stays till all commend." The magnanimity, the
generosity wh. will trust on a reasonable probability, is
required of us. But supposing one believed and was
wrong after all? Why, then you wd. have paid the universe a compliment it doesn't deserve. Your error wd.
even so be more interesting & important than the reality.
And yet how cd. that be? How cd. an idiotic universe
have produced creatures whose mere dreams are so
much stronger, better, subtler than itself?

Note that life after death, which still seems to you
the essential thing, was itself a *late* revelation. God
trained the Hebrews for centuries to believe in Him
without promising them an after-life, and, blessings on
Him, he trained me in the same way for about a year.
It is like the disguised prince in the fairy tale who wins
the heroine's love *before* she knows he is anything more
than a woodcutter. What wd. be a bribe if it came first
had better come last.

It is quite clear from what you say that you have
conscious wishes on both sides. And now, another point
about *wishes*. A wish may lead to false beliefs, granted.
But what does the existence of the wish suggest? At
one time I was much impressed by Arnold's line "Nor

does the being hungry prove that we have bread." But
surely, tho' it doesn't prove that one particular man will
get food, it *does* prove that there is such a thing as food!
i.e. if we were a species that didn't normally eat, weren't
designed to eat, wd. we feel hungry? You say the materialist universe is "ugly." I wonder how you discovered
that! If you are really a product of a materialistic universe, how is it you don't feel at home there? Do fish
complain of the sea for being wet? Or if they did, would
that fact itself not strongly suggest that they had not
always been, or wd. not always be, purely aquatic creatures? Notice how we are perpetually *surprised* at Time.
("How time flies! Fancy John being grown-up & married! I can hardly believe it!") In heaven's name, why?
Unless, indeed, there is something in us which is *not*
temporal.

Total Humility is not in the Tao because the Tao (as
such) says nothing about the Object to which it wd.
be the right response: just as there is no law about rail-
ways in the acts of Q. Elizabeth. But from the degree
of respect wh. the Tao demands for ancestors, parents,
elders, & teachers, it is quite clear what the Tao *wd.*
prescribe towards an object such as God.

But I think you are already in the meshes of the net!
The Holy Spirit is after you. I doubt if you'll get away!

Yours,
C. S. Lewis

These letters gave us much to think on, then and later.
Seldom if ever have I encountered anybody who could
say so much in so little. And the letters frightened us, or
frightened me anyway—especially that shocking last paragraph. This was getting *serious*. Alarum bells sounded,
but I couldn't decide where to run.

Intellectually, our positions here on the brink were the
same. We had had that second look, and we had found—
what had we found? Much more than we expected to find,
certainly. Christianity now appeared intellectually stimulating and aesthetically exciting. The personality of Jesus
emerged from the Gospels with astonishing consistency.
Whenever they were written, they were written in the
shadow of a personality so tremendous that Christians

who may never have seen him knew him utterly: that strange mixture of unbearable sternness and heartbreaking tenderness. No longer did the Church appear only a disreputable congeries of quarrelling sects: now we saw the Church, splendid and terrible, sweeping down the centuries with anthems and shining crosses and steady-eyed saints. No longer was the Faith something for children: intelligent people held it strongly—and they walked to a secret singing that we could not hear. Or *did* we hear something: high and clear and unbearably sweet?

Christianity had come to seem to us *probable*. It all hinged on this Jesus. Was he, in fact, the Lord Messiah, the Holy One of Israel, the Christ? Was he, indeed, the incarnate God? Very God of very God? This was the heart of the matter. *Did* he rise from the dead? The Apostles, the Evangelists, Paul believed it with utter conviction. Could we believe on their belief? Believe in a miracle? The fact that we had never seen a miracle did not prove, or even imply, that there might not be miracles at the supreme occasion of history. There was absolutely no proof, no proof *possible*, that it didn't happen. No absolute proof that it did. It seemed to us probable. It had a sort of *feel* of truth. A ring of truth. But was that enough?

Emotionally, our positions were not the same. I was excited, enthralled even, by the intellectual challenge. I might not have admitted it, but I was coming to love the Jesus that emerged from the New Testament writings. I had impulses to fall on my knees and reach out to him. I suspected that all the yearnings for I knew not what that I had ever felt—when autumn leaves were burning in the twilight, when wild geese flew crying overhead, when I looked up at bare branches against the stars, when spring arrived on an April morning—were in truth yearnings for *him*. For God. I yearned towards him. But I didn't need him—not consciously.

But Davy's emotional position was not the same—there was need. What we talked about, mostly, were the intellectual things that can be put into words so much more easily than feelings, especially feelings that are not, perhaps, altogether known to oneself. But there were for Davy needs growing out of sin and pain. She had not forgotten of course that night when "all the world fell away"—the experience she painted in her "Sin Picture" with its prophetic shadow of the crucified Lord. Even then, intuitively, she had known what it all pointed to. That experience and the very different one of the evil man in the park—the frightful evil of the monstrous ego— had, I think, undermined her confidence in herself and even, perhaps, undermined her confidence in the beautiful "us-sufficiency" of our love. She didn't know it, nor did I, but the Shining Barrier was not *quite* invulnerable. Moreover, we were both a little worried about her health: nothing clearly wrong, but she didn't feel quite as chipper as she ought to have done. Finally, her mother was dying of cancer. Davy's sister, who was taking care of their mother, had practically commanded Davy to go on to England, partly because her not doing so would be a grief to her mother. But Davy was deeply aware of her mother's suffering. And then, two or three months after our arrival in England, her mother died. All of this I knew, sharing her feelings, but all at one remove. But for Davy, with a poignancy that could not be utterly shared, there was not only a shaken confidence but a vivid experiencing of sin, suffering, grief, and death.

Thus, though her mind, too, asked the intellectual questions—questions to which answers were flooding in through our books—Christianity was offering consolation and assurance and, even, absolution. It fell into her soul as the water of life. One evening, after a lively discussion of the faith with Lew and Mary Ann, I asked Davy if she felt that she was near to believing that Christ was God. She said, "Well, I think He might be." And I said that "thinking" he "might" be was not the same as believing. She put this exchange in the Journal; and then she wrote: "Underneath I kept wanting to say 'I do, I do believe in Jesus—Jesus the Son of God and divine.'" She added: "I owe this to C. S. Lewis who has impressed me deeply with the necessity of Jesus to any thinking about God."

She was on the brink, indeed—and then she leaped. Only two days later she wrote:

> Today, crossing from one side of the room to the other, I lumped together all I am, all I fear, hate, love, hope; and, well, DID it. I committed my ways to God in Christ.

She was alone when she took that walk across the room, and she told me when I came in an hour later. I was neither shocked nor astonished. It was as though I had known she would do it. I felt a sort of gladness for her, and told her. I also felt a bit forlorn, and perhaps there was an unformulated thought, which would not have borne the light of day, that she shouldn't have done it without me. I did not think about the implications for our future that day. Did I sense that I should follow her?

A few nights later, after a rather gentle talk about Christianity, she went to bed, leaving me lying upon the sofa in front of the fire reading Lewis's *Miracles*. A half hour passed. I let the book fall and switched off the lamp. Gazing into the glowing coals, I wondered with a strange mixture of hope and fear whether Christ might be in very truth my God. Suddenly I became aware that Davy was praying beside me—she had stolen into the room in her nightgown and knelt down by the sofa. I looked at the quiet figure for a few moments. I had never seen her pray. Then she spoke.

"When I was in bed," she said very softly, "it seemed to me that God was telling me to come to you. I have prayed to God to fulfil your soul."

She paused a moment, and then she whispered: "Oh, my dearest—please believe!"

Moved almost to tears, I whispered back—a broken whisper, she wrote in the Journal—I whispered, "Oh, I do believe." I was shaken by the affirmation that swept over me. She wrote that in the firelight I looked "gentle and sweet like some medieval saint." And she wrote, "We held one another tightly."

"Hold to this moment," she murmured. "Hold to it when doubts come. This is the true—I know it is."

But I did not hold on to it. I wish I had, if only for her sake. But, indeed, it was love for her that made me say it, not belief in God. Or so I told myself next morning. Or perhaps it was the assent of the heart and not the mind. Anyhow, the joy we might have shared that Advent, going together, hand in hand, was—except for that one holy night—denied. And yet I did not forget that sudden sincerity of believing, the affirmation welling up. Maybe it wasn't just love for her.

Still, I was back in the camp of the non-believers. And now I began to resent *her* conversion. I did not, I thought, resent her being a Christian; I resented her acting like one. Going to church without me—practically unfaithfulness. Going with all the other Christians, leaving me alone. I even resented her little special goodnesses, even goodness to me. I suspected she was doing it for God. I wanted the old Davy back. I didn't want her to be where I couldn't—or wouldn't—go. I didn't like my new isolation. The fun of *our* looking into Christianity was gone. I felt sulky.

The Shining Barrier came into my mind, mostly as an awareness of danger ahead if we remained a house divided. I did not think of the Appeal to Love, for it was not relevant to the situation. I hadn't rejected Christianity; I merely hadn't decided yet. There was a tacit understanding that this period was a hiatus until I did decide. It did not occur to me that if she were now committed to Christ, her commitment to our love must be lesser, as indeed mine must be if I followed her. At all events, I shied away from thinking about the Shining Barrier. Until later.

Here, on the brink, I hung for two months and more. I continued to read and think. I knew of course that Davy was praying for me. All our Christian friends were praying for me. Perhaps their friends. Perhaps whole churches. I regarded this activity with suspicion. I felt they were all waiting for something to happen. They gave me pleasantly questioning looks when we met on the street.

I was also suspicious of my own upsurges of feeling about this Jesus. I warned myself about emotion. It seemed to me sometimes that *Jesus* was giving me friendly but questioning looks, and at other times, intolerably severe ones. At the same time, I recognised that there was a place for emotion as well as reason, and wrote in the Journal:

> It would seem that Christianity requires both emotional and intellectual assent. If there is only emotion, the mind asks troubling questions that, if not answered, might lead to a falling away, for love cannot be sustained without understanding. On the other hand, there is a gap which must be bridged by emotion. If one is suspicious of the upsurge of feeling that may be incipient faith, how is one to cross the gap?

Christianity—in a word, the divinity of Jesus—seemed probable to me. But there is a gap between the probable and proved. How was I to cross it? If I were to stake my whole life on the Risen Christ, I wanted proof. I wanted certainty. I wanted to see Him eat a bit of fish. I wanted letters of fire across the sky. I got none of these. And I continued to hang about on the edge of the gap.

Davy and I, sometimes with friends, sometimes alone, were reading Dorothy Sayers's tremendous series of short plays on the life of Jesus. In one of them, I was forcibly struck by the reply of a man to Jesus's inquiry about his faith: "Lord, I believe; help thou mine unbelief." Wasn't that just my position? Believing and not believing? A paradox, like that other paradox: one must have faith to believe but must believe in order to have faith. A paradox to unlock a paradox? I felt that it was.

One day later there came the second intellectual breakthrough: it was the rather chilling realisation that *I could not go back*. In my old easy-going theism, I had regarded Christianity as a sort of fairy tale; and I had neither accepted nor rejected Jesus, since I had never, in fact, encountered Him. Now I had. The position was not, as I had been comfortably thinking all these months, merely a question of whether I was to accept the Messiah or not. It was a question of whether I was to accept Him—or *reject*. My God! There was a gap *behind* me, too. Perhaps the leap to acceptance was a horrifying gamble—but what of the leap to rejection? There might be no certainty that Christ was God—but, by God, there was no certainty that He was not. If I were to accept, I might and probably would face the thought through the years: "Perhaps, after all, it's a lie; I've been had!" But if I were to reject, I would certainly face the haunting, terrible thought: "Perhaps it's true—and I have *rejected my God!*"

This was not to be borne. I *could not* reject Jesus. There was only one thing to do, once I had seen the gap behind me. I turned away from it and flung myself over the gap *towards* Jesus.

Early on a damp English morning with spring in the air, I wrote in the Journal and to C. S. Lewis:

I *choose* to believe in the Father, Son, and Holy Ghost —in Christ, my lord and my God. Christianity has the ring, the *feel*, of unique truth. Of *essential* truth. By it, life is made full instead of empty, meaningful instead of meaningless. Cosmos becomes beautiful at the *Centre*, instead of chillingly ugly beneath the lovely pathos of spring. But the emptiness, the meaninglessness, and the ugliness can only be seen, I think, when one has glimpsed the fullness, the meaning, and the beauty. It is when heaven and hell have *both* been glimpsed that going back is impossible. But to go on seemed impossible, also. A glimpse is not a vision. A choice was necessary: and there is no certainty. One can only choose a side. So I—I now choose my side: I choose beauty; I choose what I love. But choosing to believe *is* believing. It's all I can do: choose. I confess my doubts and ask my Lord Christ to enter my life. I do not *know* God is, I do but say: Be it unto me according to Thy will. I do not affirm that I am without doubt, I do but ask for help, having chosen, to overcome it. I do but say: Lord, I believe—help Thou mine unbelief.

Davy sat beside me while I wrote, full of quiet joy. Of course I had told her first. Indeed, she had been in the

room when the series of thoughts about the gap behind
me had flashed through my mind. She had heard me
mutter, "My God!" And then, as she looked up, I'd said,
rather tensely, "Wait." A couple of minutes went by.
Then I said: "Davy? . . . dearling . . . I have chosen—
the Christ! I *choose* to believe." She looked at me with
joy. Then she came over to me and knelt. I knelt, too,
and committed my ways to my God. When we rose, we
held each other a long moment. It is perhaps significant
that we prayed first.

The sonnet I was to write about the choice was already
taking shape in my mind:

THE GAP

Did Jesus live? And did he really say
The burning words that banish mortal fear?
And are they true? Just this is central, here
The Church must stand or fall. It's *Christ* we weigh.

All else is off the point: the Flood, the Day
Of Eden, or the Virgin Birth—Have done!
The Question is, did God send us the Son
Incarnate crying Love! Love is the Way!

Between the probable and proved there yawns
A gap. Afraid to jump, we stand absurd,
Then see *behind* us sink the ground and, worse,
Our very standpoint crumbling. Desperate dawns
Our only hope: to leap into the Word
That opens up the shuttered universe.

Thou Art the King of Glory

We were now Christians. Davy perhaps had got used to it. But I—I a Christian! I, who had been wont to regard Christians with pitying dislike, must now confess myself to be one. I did so, with shrinking and pride. Indeed, I felt a curious mixture of emotions: a sort of embarrassment among my more worldly and presumably non-Christian friends, some of whom would have accepted by becoming a Buddhist or an atheist with less amazement, and a sort of pride as though I had done something laudable—or done God a favour. I was half inclined to conceal my faith, and yet it seemed to me that if I were to take a stand for Christ, my lord, I must wear his colours.

There was perhaps a want of humility. Even my saying at the moment of conversion "I *choose* to believe" instead of "I believe," although they may come to the same thing in the end, had something about it of a last-ditch stand. The banner of my independence dipped, lying in the dust and myself kneeling, but somehow proudly still. I did homage to Christ as one pledges his sword and his fealty to a king. In reality, I suspect, it was not like that at all: I did not choose; I was chosen. The loving prayers of Davy and the rest—the prayers of C. S. Lewis, not just his books and letters—these did the work of the King. And yet there is this to be said for the pledged sword, even though it be so only in one's own mind: if in some future year faith should weaken, one cannot in honour forswear the fealty tendered in "I choose to believe."

C. S. Lewis wrote, dropping the "Mr." before my name, though I continued to call him "Mr. Lewis" until he told me to stop:

> My prayers are answered. No: a glimpse is not a vision. But to a man on a mountain road by night, a glimpse of the next three feet of road may matter more than a vision of the horizon. And there must perhaps always be just enough lack of demonstrative certainty to make free choice possible: for what could we do but accept if the faith were like the multiplication table?
>
> There will be a counter attack on you, you know, so don't be too alarmed when it comes. The enemy will not see you vanish into God's company without an effort to reclaim you. Be busy learning to pray and (if you have made up yr. mind on the denominational question) get confirmed. Blessings on you and a hundred thousand welcomes. Make use of me in any way you please: and let us pray for each other always.

Davy and I were already Anglicans. All our Christian friends, and Davy lately, had been going to the ancient Norman church of St. Ebbe's, evangelical and Church of England, so of course I went there, too. It was a church full of faith, and it had a splendid Rector, M. A. P. Wood (since become the Lord Bishop of Norwich). He was a great preacher and a wise counsellor on the Christian way. Davy and I had a series of conversations with him at the Rectory in Paradise Square, and sometimes we stayed for a meal. I was impressed by the Rector's discerning view of the relationship between mind and heart in conversion. In the church our first Christian communion together was moving. Later Davy and I were to go about a little to sample the riches of the many Oxford churches—the University Church of St. Mary the Virgin and the high-church Anglo-Catholic beauty of St. Mary Magdalen among others. But wherever we went, our young Christian life was shaped by the Church of England; and we always came "home" to St. Ebbe's. There was the lively life in Christ. St. Ebbe's sang the *Te Deum* to a setting that made a triumphant proclamation of the line: "Thou Art

the King of Glory, O-O-O-O-O Christ!"—the O's ascending to the mighty "Christ!" That setting came to mean
St. Ebbe's and its strong faith to all of us.

One night late several of us went round to the place
where Peter and Bee lived in an upper-storey flat and
found the staircase door locked. So there in the silent
street we launched into "Thou Art the King of Glory."
As we hit the word "Christ!" the windows were flung
open and the astonished heads of Peter and Bee looked
down.

At first I had, as Davy had had, an astonishing assurance and certainty about my choice, despite the doubts
that had harried me so long. I believe that a new Christian
is given a special grace—joy and assurance—in the beginning, however feeble the choosing. Until the new-born
Christian has learned to stand and walk a little. I wrote
in our Journal:

> Forty days after: The decision made, one begins to act
> on it. One prays, goes to church, makes an incredibly
> meaningful first Christian communion. One tries to
> rethink everything one has ever thought in this new
> Light. One tries to subordinate self—to make the Sign
> of the Cross, crossing out the "I"—and to follow Christ,
> with something less than brilliant success. C. S. Lewis
> prophesies the enemy's counterattack, and is right as
> usual. Feelings surge in that it's lies, all lies, that yonder
> red bus, the hard pavement under one's heels, the glory
> of the may tree are the *only* realities. But one remem-
> bers that the Choice was based on reason, the weight of
> the evidence, and is strengthened. But that's not quite
> all. Not only can the doubts be coped with, not only do
> prayers go better, but the doubts come less often—and
> when they do are often met with a surge of inexplicable
> confidence that the Choice was right. *We* are winning.

Discussing every line with Davy, I completed my poem
on the choice, "The Gap." Even as I worked on that one,
I was diverted to another one in which the soul's act of
choosing—though choose she must—is subordinated to the
action of grace. These poems, when completed, I sent to
C. S. Lewis. Here is the second of the two:

THE SANDS

The Soul for comfort holds herself to be
Inviolate; but like the blowing sands
That sift in shuttered houses, Christ's demands
Intrude and sting, deny her to be free.

She twists and turns but finds it vain to flee,
The living Word is in the very air,
She can't escape a wound that's everywhere,
She can but stand or yield—to ecstasy.

Her Lord is seeking entrance; she must choose.
A thickening callus can withstand the pain
Of this rough irritant, the sands that swirl
Against her thus defied. But if she lose
Her self, Christ enters in—the sharp-edged grain
Of sand embedded grows a shining pearl.

C. S. Lewis replied:

Thank you for a letter I prize very much. The sonnets, though in a manner which will win few hearers at the moment (drat all fashions) are really very remarkable. The test is that I found myself at once forgetting all the personal biographical interest and reading them as poetry. The image of sand is *real* imagination. I thought this was the better of the two at first: but now I don't know. The second quatrain of *The Gap* is tiptop argument—and then the ground sinking be*hind*. Excellent.

As a new Christian, fascinated by Christianity, I might well at this point have considered switching my area of research in that direction. I didn't, because I had already considered it—*before* I was a Christian. Subsequently, I was amazed that as a non-believer I could have contemplated, not only a theological subject but even the priesthood. Davy, by then a Christian, was curiously unenthusiastic, not about historical research in the area—after all, history was my field—but about the priesthood.

The strange thing was that I, interested in Christianity, saw nothing wrong with the idea of being a priest of a faith I did not accept—a sort of walking lie. Perhaps I felt a need for faith and thought I would find it so. Anyhow, I was interested, as a man might be interested in war and so become a soldier. Nothing so clearly illustrates the radical difference between the believing Christian and the non-Christian as the concept of what a priest should be: a man of faith or a man who can choose it for a career, like law. A priest or bishop without belief is as false as, quite precisely, hell to the one and a nearly innocent careerist to the other. The element of need that may persuade the non-believer to go into the church might offer a clue to the not-altogether-dissimilar phenomenon of unbalanced people, even nuts, becoming psychologists. At all events, men's need for faith as well as the view of the church as a career like any other presumably explain the unbelieving priests and bishops—shepherds of the flock!—who do the church so much harm yet feel no need to resign, and appear to be almost blind to their own dishonesty.

In the grip of this deplorable idea I wrote C. S. Lewis about it, arguing further after his first reply. The two letters from him were in January, three days apart, and two months before conversion. The "tent-making" letters follow:

> We must ask three questions about the probable effect of changing your research subject to something more Theological.
> (1.) Wd. it be better for your immediate enjoyment? Answer, probably but not certainly, Yes.
> (2.) Wd. it be better for your academic career? Answer, probably No. You wd. have to make up in haste a lot of knowledge which wd. not be v. easily digested in the time.
> (3.) Wd. it be better for your soul? I don't know. I think there is a great deal to be said for háving one's deepest spiritual interest distinct from one's ordinary duty as a student or professional man. St. Paul's *job* was tent-making. When the two coincide I shd. have thought there was a danger lest the natural interest in one's job and the pleasures of gratified ambition might be mistaken for spiritual progress and spiritual consolation; and I think clergymen sometimes fall into this

trap. Contrariwise, there is the danger that what is boring and repellent in the job may alienate one from the spiritual life. And finally, someone has said "None are so unholy as those whose hands are cauterised with holy things"; sacred things may become profane by becoming matters of the job. You *now* want spiritual truth for her own sake; how will it be when the same truth is also needed for an effective footnote in your thesis? In fact, the change might do good or harm. I've always been glad myself that Theology is not the thing I earn my living by. On the whole, I'd advise you to get on with your tent-making. The performance of a *duty* will probably teach you quite as much about God as academic Theology wd. do. Mind, I'm not certain: but that is the view I incline to.

[Second letter] Look: the question is not whether we should bring God into our work or not. We certainly should and must: as MacDonald says "All that is not God is death." The question is whether we should simply (a.) Bring Him in in the dedication of our work to Him, in the integrity, diligence, and humility with which we do it or also (b.) Make His professed and explicit service our job. The A vocation rests on all men whether they know it or not; the B vocation only on those who are specially called to it. Each vocation has its peculiar dangers and peculiar rewards. Naturally, I can't say which is yours. When I spoke of danger to your academic career in a change of subject I was thinking chiefly of *time*. If you can get an extra year, it would be another matter. I was not at all meaning that "intellectual history" involving Theology wd. *in itself* be academically a bad field of research.

I shall at any time be glad to see, and hear from, you.

After these letters, so admirably sane and logical, I got on with my tent-making, both then and after conversion. But of course Davy and I continued to read theology—for instance, Austin Farrer—on the side. We were both deeply impressed by *The Descent of the Dove* and *He Came Down from Heaven* by Charles Williams.

Then we encountered the Germans—the "demythologisers"—and were dismayed. The Resurrection was a myth, the Ascension was a myth, all miracles and prophecy were myths, perhaps Christ's very existence was a myth—and by "myth" they meant lies or devout fictions. If Jesus wasn't a myth, he—the real historical Jesus—was quite unknowable. What, then, were we doing, being Christians? What, for the matter of that, were these demythologisers doing, calling themselves Christians still and even being ministers? That perhaps would be taken up with them later. And we, after our first dismay, rallied and began to think. First of all, it appeared plain to us that these fellows were in the position of the man who couldn't see the wood for the trees, for one thing was absolutely certain: the personality of Jesus that emerged with perfect consistency from all four gospels and from St. Paul was so powerful, so individual, and so remarkable that it was obvious that the New Testament writers knew him, perhaps through others, as we know Winston Churchill or Abraham Lincoln. They lived in the shadow of a Man so immense that his spirit and words burned in Christian minds. But our real "salvation" from these wreckers came through our recognition of the quite unverifiable fundamental assumptions, in no way derived from the New Testament text, that they brought *to* it. If Oxford consistently teaches any one thing, it is that fundamental assumptions *must* be verified. But not the demythologisers: When they say that prophecy must have been inserted after the event, their unverified assumption is that true prophecy cannot occur. They assume—*merely assume*—that miracles cannot happen: no proof and, by the nature of the case, no proof possible. Apart from being miraculous, the Ascension could not have happened because it contradicts modern cosmology—heaven cannot be "up" or "out"; the assumption is that God could not have had purposes obscure to critics. They argue that something could not have been said or written when it was supposed to have been because its theology or ecclesiology is too advanced, assuming that no man could have been ahead of his times. If a New Testament event is akin to an earlier myth, it cannot have happened, on the assumption that God couldn't have intended to turn anticipatory myth into fact. Moreover, Christ's words were misunderstood by His followers and the early church though quite clear to critics. Assumption: the mind of the infinite God is not unlike that of a German critic. We had no quarrel with legitimate Biblical criticism and scholarship, only with those, like the demythologisers, who bring their unverified assumptions and philosophies to the text. As for them, we retitled Hilaire Belloc's little thing on a puritan to "On a Demythologiser": "He served his god so faithfully and well/That now he sees him face to face in hell." The emperors of demythologising had no clothes on; and they themselves required "demythologising."

I wrote another of my "Oxford sonnets" on the Veronica legend about the woman who wiped the sweating face of Jesus on his way to the crucifixion, and dedicated it both to Davy and to swift, impetuous Bee Campion. I could see either of them doing just that.

THE SWORD

Yes, Mark was posted to the Tenth that year.
The day we got there priests contrived to bring
This "god" to death, and mobs that made me cling
To Mark surged round us, all one mocking jeer.

No omen warned me when Mark led me near
The yelling street that I should be implored
By God to wear my girlhood like a sword
So edged with mercy men would freeze in fear.

Mark's armour made the crowd draw back a space.
Just there beneath his cross the god limped by.
I saw his eyes and rushed into the street
Through sudden stillness and I wiped his face.
"My child," he said and staggered on to die.
—My girlhood lay in fragments at my feet.

It was only a short time after I announced my choosing to believe to C. S. Lewis and got his "hundred thousand welcomes" that I got a card from him inviting me to dine with him at Magdalen College. I had never so much as seen a photograph of him, and in reading his books and letters I had vaguely pictured him as slender, perhaps somewhat emaciated, and slightly stooped with a lean, near-sighted face. What I met, when I turned up at his rooms, was John Bull himself. Portly, jolly, a wonderful grin, a big voice, a quizzical gaze—and no nonsense. He was as simple and unaffected as a man could be, yet never was there a man who could so swiftly cut through anything that even approached fuzzy thinking. Withal, the most friendly, the most genial of companions. Knowing that I would be burning with my new-found Christianity, he suggested that it would be best not to talk of Christian matters in hall or common room. That was my first intimation that some of the other Fellows at Magdalen, as well as other dons in the university, were not altogether cheerful about his Christian vocation. They would no doubt have tolerated his being, quietly, a Christian; but his acting like a Christian, writing widely read books about Christianity, was another thing. Much later, when Lewis was nominated for the Professorship of Poetry, Thad, who was walking along the High Street behind two dons, heard one of them remark: "Shall we go and cast our votes against C. S. Lewis?" Not, that is, *for* the other chap. At all events, I refrained that night from talk of Christianity, at least until we returned to his rooms, and I therefore saw and heard, both at table and at the semi-circle by the fire in the common room as the port went round, the Lewis who, in brilliance, in wit, and in incisiveness, could hold his own with any man that ever lived.

That evening began my friendship with Lewis. It was a very deep friendship on my part: no man ever did so much to shape my mind, quite aside from Christianity, which of course shaped my whole life. I have never loved a man more. And I must believe, from things he said and wrote to me, that he felt both friendship and affection for me. Later, he became very fond of Davy—or Jean, as he called her—too. After his death, his brother, Warren, remarked to a friend: "Oh, Jack adored Van and Jean." I dined with Lewis—or Jack (not that I called him that for years)—a number of times at Magdalen, and there were happy hours of genial conversation in his rooms in college, rather bare rooms with a splendid view. Sometimes I walked with him round Addison's Walk. The first time he proposed it, I prepared to modify my stride to suit an older man—and he nearly walked me off my legs. He was the Legions on the march. I was not wholly sorry when we came round again to the entrance; and Lewis said, "Around again, eh?" And away we went. I also on occasion saw and heard him about the university, both lectures at the Schools and at the Socratic Club where Lewis was in his element. But our most usual meeting place was the Eastgate Hotel for lunch, where Lewis would immediately boom out: "Any pies today?" A hearty helping of steak-and-kidney pie and a pint of bitter was standard fare.

Once he forgot a lunch at the Eastgate that he had suggested, and next day he sent round to Jesus the following card:

Porcus sum, I am a pig, *porcissimus,* the piggest of pigs. I looked at my diary at about 3 o'clock on Sat. afternoon and found to my horror that I had failed a tryst with you at 12. Please forgive a nit-wit. Will you prove your charity by meeting me at the Eastgate 12 o'clock next Saturday? Even I seldom make exactly the same howler twice! I really am very sorry; I had been much looking forward to it. C.S.L.

We talked, Lewis and I, about everything under the sun, and beyond the sun, too. There were several good discussions of science-fiction, which we had both read a lot of. And of course we talked of Christianity and of Christian morality. I remember one afternoon in his rooms I asked him whether I should have said a certain harsh thing to someone who quite deserved it; and Lewis went instantly to the heart of the matter with the question: "What was your motive?" In the course of a discussion about the efficacy of prayer, he made the point that it was altogether healthier to find yourself being used as the answer to someone else's prayer. And he told the story of his nagging impulse to go and get an unneeded haircut, finding when he gave in to it that his barber had been steadily praying that Lewis would come by. Several of his stories, like that one, later found their way into his writing. One night at Magdalen, we talked of "the Island in the West" in *Pilgrim's Regress*—that something we long for, whether it be an island in the west or the other side of a mountain or perhaps a schooner yacht, long for it in the belief that it will mean joy, which it never fully does: because what we are really longing for is God. There was no idea of Lewis's that I more deeply understood, and our conversation about it was deep and enthralling. Finally we made tea and drank it, and then I walked home through the misty silent streets of Oxford, still in the spell of the talk, to tell an eagerly waiting Davy all about it. On other occasions Lewis and I talked —so my little blue Oxford diary informs me—of definitions of the novel and of what the novel should be (a good story), of poetry, of the "bent world" in both his science-fiction and in G. M. Hopkins' "God's Grandeur." Lewis believed that he had thought of it independently, since it was so natural and right in his story. But in his poem "Pilgrim's Problem" where, at the end, "earnest stars blaze out in the established sky/Rigid with justice," he thought he must have unconsciously borrowed the "earnest stars" from Keats. We talked at other times of human frailty, of beer, of prayer, of literary sources, and of favourite books. Rereading books, we said with immense agreement, was the mark of the real lover of books.

Davy and I had been moving about a bit among the Oxford churches, and we came to accept, essentially, the high-church position that the Anglican church was part of the Church Catholic. And we found the Anglo-Catholic mass very beautiful. As a result of the high-church veneration of Mary, the Blessed Virgin, I wrote a sonnet on her:

THE HEART OF MARY

Dear sister, I was human not divine,
The angel left me woman as before,
And when, like flame beneath my heart, I bore
The Son, I was the vestal *and* the shrine.

My arms held Heaven at my breast—not wine
But milk made blood, in which no mothering doubt
Prefigured patterns of the pouring out,
O Lamb! to stain the world incarnadine.

The Magi saw a crown that lay ahead,
But not the bitter glory of the reign;
They called him King and knelt among the kine.
I pondered in my heart what they had said,
Yet could not see the bloody cup of pain.
I was but woman—though my God was mine.

In June, at the end of Summer Term, Davy and I
inherited from a friend going down, a tiny mews flat, the
Studio, in the centre of Oxford. We were saddened at
the loss of the piano, but, all the same, we gladly moved.
It was located on cobbled, gas-lit Pusey Lane. A red door
opened into an alleyway where another door announced
"The Studio." There was a closet-sized kitchen on the
ground floor, a staircase so narrow that two skeletons
could not have passed on it, and one long upstairs room.
That was all—the bathroom was across the garden in the
main house. Our one long room had two windows over-
looking the garden, and a large skylight was set in the
gently sagging roof. At one end of the room was a fireplace, which would immediately fill the room with dense
coal smoke if the wind veered into the wrong quarter.
Wherever the wind was, we could hear all the bells of
Oxford, including the deep boom of Great Tom at Christ
Church. This was the Studio—or St. Udio's—inconven-
ient, damp, smoky, and very dear to us and to many.

Because the Studio was central and, incidentally, on
the way from North Oxford to St. Ebbe's, and because,
perhaps, of its extraordinary atmosphere, compounded of
the gas-lit cobbled lane outside and the warm upper
room, with its skylight black with rain and its cheerful
fire (except when the wind was wrong, of course), it
became the centre of a lively life in Christ for a great
many people. We soon accepted that if we hoped to get
any work done we must do it in the Bodleian Library;
and even then we often came home to find that friends
had arrived and were already deep into some absorbing

discussion. The diary indicates that in one week, taken at random, twenty-four people came, six of them twice, so there were thirty times that the brass knocker sounded and one of us leaped down the narrow stairway. For nearly two years, except when we went up to London to see plays or went visiting or travelling, there was hardly a day or night that people did not come, both Christians and non-Christians (those who said they weren't); and there were literally hundreds of absorbing conversations. Oxford.

As a result of our embracing the faith, the circle of our Christian friends of course enlarged, nearly all being university people. We continued to see a great deal of the original five, Lew and Mary Ann, Peter and Bee, and Thad—and I have mentioned the bushy-headed Welshman, Geraint Gruffydd, who could read poetry in his vibrant voice so magnificently that it would send chills down the back of a statue. He was himself a poet, though we only saw his poems in his own translations from the Welsh. Once at his house in Wales, as the result of an argument about the relative merits of burgundy and claret, we scoured the wine merchants for vintages and had a grand series of wine-tasting sessions, rather in the "Brideshead" manner. Claret was rather ahead, until, back in Oxford, I opened a treasured bottle of a velvety Chambertin of a great year in Burgundy. Another poet—an extraordinary poet—and a deep Christian friend through the years was Julian—Dom Julian of St. Benet's Hall. Although born in England, he had partly grown up in Maryland; and his Benedictine priory in New England had sent him first to Rome and then to Oxford, where, in due course, we attended his priesting. Also reading theology for the priesthood were David Griffiths of Kent and Worcester College and Tom Harpur of Toronto and Oriel College, only, for them, it was the Anglican priesthood. But it was with David that we shared the exciting discovery of the Catholic Faith within the Church of England, and many a night we talked long about it. Tall, blue-eyed Tom, despite the tradition of Newman and the Oxford Movement in his college, was more Evangelical. But that was the Studio: Catholics and Evangelicals and Atheists and all shades of Betwixts and Betweens, all talking happily and spiritedly on equal terms. Sometimes, when Tom stayed late, I would walk back to Oriel with him to make a back for him so that he could reach up and remove a bar from one of the barred windows that all colleges have and climb in. Once he dropped the bar with a clang that echoed across the silent night, and seconds later a proctorial party turned into the lane. We —Tom still holding the bar—ran rapidly away among the shadows, later returning for another go. Davy, in heavenly compensation for the lost piano, was sometimes asked to play the organ at St. Ebbe's. In the choir, looking very much like a small dark angel, was a young girl named Jane, whom Davy brought back to the Studio. After that, Jane and sometimes her friend, Mia, both studying for university entrance, came often. Jane was very silent, but she, too, was a lover of poetry, and a poet. We read a lot of poetry aloud at the Studio, and when I would read, especially T. S. Eliot's *Four Quartets*, I could almost feel the intensity of Jane's listening.

Poetry was no small part of the magic of the Studio, not only the great poems but our own—the poems we wrote and read to each other and discussed, poems in which the Incarnate God was very much present. Geraint in a poem to Luned, the Welsh girl he was to marry, spoke of their "holy hours/When our spirits flowed quietly at one/In the streams of our Christ's love." And Julian's poetry was pure prayer, deep and holy. He spoke of himself: "Walking in the garden . . ./Pawing with the foot of my philosophy the dust of the path/[seeking] uncaring unknowingness and unreasoned trust." At his Oxford ordination, he offered Christ: "Tormented thought and worn-out shoes/Take all and dwell therein." One of his poems was about going away from the Studio at night:

> Cry to the night
> To the gaslight
> After the rain
> What shall I cry?
> Farewell, goodbye

I leave you with your pain
The Lord be with you
And in your hour, again
Tread in this cobble lane
And rain His faith within you.
Amen.

One night Julian and Davy and I had a deep and gentle talk about poetry and Mary Virgin—what she means to man and her rôle in the Kingdom. Out of that long night's talk there came another of my Oxford sonnets, dedicated lovingly to Julian:

OUR LADY OF THE NIGHT

When this world hides the constant heart of light
We sink to chill despair through stars that wheel
In deathless unconcern, our senses reel
At nothingness, and darkness steals our sight.

Appearing wrapped in deep blue heaven, bright
With secret sun, the moon for tenderness
Looks down to earth where, reassured, we bless
The sun in her, our lady of the night.

O lady, eyes can neither bear the pain
Of utter light, nor see without it how
To walk, so blindly stumbling we are drawn
To seek that light in you who see it plain.
Be with us, lady, through the darkness, now
And at the awful hour of the dawn.

Although our Christian friends came often to the Studio, our non-Christian friends were, of course, equally welcome. Indeed, in some of the best discussions on Christian subjects, there would usually be a couple of non-Christians there, too, joining in with healthy scepticism. Our experience of Oxford was that everybody talked about everything. And for that very reason, we usually knew who was Christian or non-Christian or semi-Christian or Hindu or whatever because it came out in conversation.

One afternoon Davy and I walked in the University Parks and Mesopotamia, talking of some day writing a novel, catching something of the extraordinary variety of Oxford life, including the Studio, a novel that we would put ourselves in as characters. Then, saying "Some day, maybe," we went to the Copper Kettle on the High for tea. That night, as usual, a couple of friends came by. One was Julian and the other was a non-Christian friend from Corpus Christi College named Richard, and it was Richard who wanted to talk about Christianity. After considerable talk, he said: "The thing that stumps me is the Trinity: The Trinity and, above all, the Incarnation. You all seem to believe that Jesus was, at the same time, completely a man—and completely God. In the name of common sense, how *could* he be? You Christians always take refuge in mysteries."

"Not at all," I said. "We aren't hiding behind a mystery in this, at least."

"Well," said Richard. "Explain it in some way that makes sense."

Julian began to say something about the Persons of God, and I could see that Richard wasn't finding it very helpful. Then I thought of the novel Davy and I had been talking about and murmured to Davy, "I've got it!"

"It's still no good," said Richard when Julian had done.

"Look, Richard," I said. "This afternoon Davy and I were talking about writing a novel of Oxford with the Studio in it, and us, and everybody. Now, assuming we could do it—"

"Assuming you could do it," said Richard, "I'd buy a copy. Not more than five shillings, though."

"Listen," I said. "We're talking about the Incarnation. Okay, suppose *I* write it—it's too complicated with two authors—and I put myself in it. There I am, walking down the High, wearing a Jesus tie—in the book. And let's say I make up a lot of characters, not using real people for fear of hurting their feelings. But I am in it, and I, the character, say whatever I would say in the various situations that occur in my plot."

"What about the Incarnation?" said Richard.

"That's what I'm *telling* you, stupid fellow," I said with a grin. "Don't you see? I am incarnate in my book. I am out here writing it, so I'm like God the Father. But it's really me in the book, too, isn't it? So that's Jesus, the Son, right? The me in the book speaks my words—and yet they are speeches that I've probably never made in real life, not being in those situations. And yet can't you see that it's really me?"

"Um," said Richard. "Yes, right. I see. Go on."

"Well," I said. "All right. I'm out here, being 'the Author of all things' *and* I'm in the book, taking part in scenes of 'drammer' Incarnate in my book. Now, the me in the book: he's *all* me, isn't he? *And* he's *all character*, too, isn't he? Like the doctrine: All God and All man. It makes sense, doesn't it? And one more thing: suppose the characters run away with the story—authors are always saying that that happens. It might be necessary, whatever I had originally intended, for me to get killed—um, crucified . . . Anyhow—you see?"

"You win," said Richard. "It does make sense that way. I'll have to think about it."

"There's something else, though," said Davy. "The other characters—made-up ones. Invented ones. If Van invents characters, they'll *all*, even the bad ones, have something of Van in them, won't they? So, you see? We all have something of God in us—God's spirit—but only the One, Jesus, is God Incarnate. But God's Spirit in us . . . Well, that makes the Trinity, doesn't it? God the Father, God the Son, and God the Holy Spirit. Actually, I've never seen it so clearly myself. More tea?"

At intervals during the Oxford years, in the vacs, we went off on visits to friends or on longer exploring journeys. There were many one-day or two-day trips to London. There was a jolly Christmas in Yorkshire, full of family games and carolling in the misty streets, at the home of a college friend, Trevor. And a fortnight in Wild Wales with Bee and Peter, and Geraint part of the time, mainly climbing Cader Idris when it was fine, and reading John Buchan in the farmhouse when it was wet. We and

Thad borrowed a car and wandered for days about the lovely Cotswolds country, exploring ruined abbeys and stopping to see friends. Another friend, an Irishman, Paddy O'Leary, whom I'd met whilst drinking bad sherry at our Moral Tutor's in college, and his sweet English wife, Margaret, invited us to her house, where we stood as godparents to their son. With Edmund, my dining companion, and a girl named Lore, we travelled in France for a fortnight, exploring cathedrals and Roman ruins and the Caves of Lascaux, as well as dining at some great restaurants, as indicated by the Guide Michelin. We also drank a great deal of the wine-of-the-country wherever we were; and we ended up with a joyous drive into Paris, top down, on the first balmy day of spring. The sky was blue, the parks full of lovers, the river sparkling, and Notre-Dame on the Ile de la Cité looking awfully noble. One of the happiest visits was to the Hampshire home of a very dear friend in the college, a frequent caller at the Studio, Peter Crane. His huge and rambling house, Fritham, was in the New Forest; and we were to remember the house itself and the kitchen garden full of lavender, the warmly hospitable Major and Mrs. Crane, the pleasant drawing-room, and the mysterious window on an upper storey that opened into no room—unless it were a small, walled-up one. One soft, dark night without a star, Davy and Peter and I walked a long way on the small roads running through the ancient forest. After awhile we saw firelight ahead and heard a girl's voice singing. We crept closer. Then we saw, in a firelit glade with the great trees all around, a number of gypsy caravans drawn up. The men were sprawled about in the grass, and the girl, dark and lovely in the firelight, was stirring a pot on the fire and singing, almost as though she sang to herself, some lonesome-sounding song in Romany.

Although there were these journeys full of vivid memories, and although there were also, of course, hundreds of hours in the depths of the great Bodleian Library, the centre of our Oxford experience, one which Davy and I wholly shared, was the Studio. Even at some cost to our time alone together, we had decided from the first to reach out to or draw in all we could of the extraordinary richness of the great university round us. In a way all of us at Oxford knew, knew as an undercurrent in our minds, that it wouldn't last for ever. Lew and Mary Ann expressed it one night by saying: "This, you know, is a time of taking in—taking in friendship, conversation, gaiety, wisdom, knowledge, beauty, holiness—and later, well, there'll be a time of giving out." Later, when we were scattered about the world. Now we must store up the strength, the riches, all that Oxford had given us, to sustain us after. She stood there, Oxford, like a mother to us all with her hands heaped with riches. We could take what we would. We, Davy and I, would, for one thing, take all who came to the Studio. Whoever came, whatever the hour, was always welcome.

No account of our Oxford Christian life could be complete without some reference to the pervasive influence of C. S. Lewis upon our whole group of friends. In addition to our constantly hauling down some Lewis book to read a passage, dozens of things from the "canon" were woven into our conversations and jokes. "By Jove! I'm being humble," one of us would say with slight self-mockery. We referred constantly to "red buses," meaning the red bus that Screwtape used, along with thoughts of lunch, to divert the chap in the British Museum from dangerous thoughts of God. We meant by "red busses" the screen that the "real world" interposes between us and true Reality. We jokingly spoke of "Our Father Below," usually accompanying the words with an upward glance and a murmured "Pardon, Sire!" There were many references to the people in Lewis's *Great Divorce*, particularly the unctuous bishop who refused to believe. Often one of us would say, "Oh, I forgive you as a Christian, of course; but there are some things one can *never* forget!" Sometimes we said it in self-mockery. Sometimes we said it seriously and questioningly if we thought one of us might not be wholly forgiving. And sometimes we said it with utter, joyous forgiveness as a kind of luminous "heavenly irony."

All our friends and acquaintances, Christian or otherwise, came by, sometimes bringing others—sometimes only for a few minutes, sometimes for hours. There were conversations upon almost every imaginable subject, yet sooner or later, it seemed, the talk would drift round to ultimate things and Christianity. Never was there such talk as there was at St. Udio's, as we sometimes called it, talk gay and serious by turns, or both at once. No one who was a part of that scene has ever quite forgotten it. And as a background, accepted, hardly noticed, yet a part of the texture of the hours, there were the bells of Oxford, ringing across the night. Hardly less part of it was the rain on the skylight. And, as in Julian's poem, the goodbyes: going down the narrow staircase and out into Pusey Lane to speed the departing friend with "Goodbye, goodnight. Go under the Mercy." The phrase comes from Charles Williams, and we all used it—indeed, still use it, some of us, after the years. There would be a halo round the gas lamp in the lane, and the slight English rain like a mist, and the cobblestones of the lane would be glistening. "Goodnight. Go under the Mercy." And the friend would say perhaps: "Sleep under the Protection. Goodnight." And then the sound of heels marching away into the Oxford night and perhaps bells marking the midnight.

We went to see other people, too, of course—parties in college rooms with mulled wine by the fire or flats in North Oxford. But the Studio was central, more or less on the way to anywhere, so the knocker sounded day and night. People were always welcome.

Except once. We had got up late and were, consequently, grumpy. The place was a ruin of dirty cups and glasses and books spread out on the floor. Grey light fell upon the room from the skylight. The fire of course was cold and dead. Finally I got it together enough to go down and get some coal and make a fire. It had just got going well when, simultaneously, two things happened; Davy plugged in the vacuum cleaner which blew all the fuses, and the wind veered round and smoke poured into the room. We staggered about in the gloom, treading on coffee cups, carrying pots of water to put out the fire. At that moment came a cheery tattoo on the door knocker. Davy and I looked at each other in the smoke with mad red eyes and, in unspoken agreement, did not move. The knock came again. We did not stir. Whoever it was—we never found out—gave up. Heels went away. Probably it was Jesus.

Later in the day we went out and had lunch at the Trout and then crossed over the river and, after pausing to contemplate the ancient walls of Godstow nunnery, now used by a farmer to keep hay in, walked far on to the west. Although so many people came to the Studio, we were mindful of the need to keep close and mindful, too, of our old injunction about having time "Outdoors alone" together. So we walked a lot in all weather, talking as we walked; or took a punt out on the river. In spring and summer, we would take a book of poetry—or *The Wind in the Willows*—and go out to some pleasant grassy nook along the Cherwell to read and talk. Although we were Christians now, we were Christians together, perfectly agreed about what we were doing. All the principles of the Shining Barrier, now that we had got by that brief time when she was a Christian and I was not, seemed to us to be operating as of old. In the Studio, however many people were about, we were constantly aware of each other and in wordless communication, quick to sense anything that might bother one of us and do something about it.

One night to the Studio for dinner came C. S. Lewis. It was in Summer Term or the Long Vacation, so there was no fear of the fire smoking; it almost never did at night, anyhow. Lewis arrived and wedged himself up that narrow stair like a good one, and his great genial voice practically made the walls bulge. After sherry, we had mutton and new potatoes. It was a grand evening. We talked gaily about word origins, and about differences of usage between Great Britain and the United States, such as the use still in American of "gotten," now archaic in England. Davy talked of the old words and the faintly cockney accents of the Chesapeake islanders when we were cruising there in *Grey Goose*. Lewis seemed interested in our sailing adventures, so we talked a little about boats. He stayed quite late, and eventually the conversation turned to a more serious vein as we talked about prayer. At one point Davy asked him about prayers to enlist the help of the Blessed Virgin. Lewis would never commit himself on anything having to do with differences between high church and low. He did say, though, that if one's time for prayer was limited, the time one took for asking Mary's help was time one might be using for going directly to the Most High. We talked, too, of praying that someone might become a Christian—whether such prayer was useful, since (1) God must presumably want it to happen anyway, and (2) the person prayed for presumably has the free will to reject. All the same, Lewis was firm that we should and must pray for it. Pray for it as, he might have added, he and Davy had prayed for me to become a Christian. When he finally took his leave, we both went down with him to the lane; and then we both walked part of the way back to Magdalen with him, parting near the Martyrs' Memorial.

That year Summer Term was extraordinarily lovely. On May Morning, not long after the light appeared in the east, we had sat in a punt under Magdalen Tower with friends, hearing first a belated nightingale and then, from the top of the tall tower, the pure voices of little boys singing their Latin madrigal. When they had done, the tower bells rang out to welcome the Maytime in, and we, with the great bells still ringing astern, went off down the river to eat the breakfast we had brought.

And one Sunday with the may trees all in bloom we and Peter and Bee walked across the meadows to the tiny village of Binsey and on down the lane of beeches to go to Mattins at St. Margaret's, as we had long planned to do. But we had got the time wrong; nobody showed up. We decided, therefore, to have our own little twopenny-halfpenny (tup'ny-ha'p'ny) Mattins. Davy played the little organ. Peter read the first lesson, and I read the second. Then we all knelt and said the General Confession, though of course no Absolution, except, we trusted,

from on high. We sang at least one hymn, and Bee gave
us a sermon of exceptional merit, lasting about one minute, on the theme of loving one another. But what I
remember most vividly is our singing the *Te Deum
Laudamus*: our voices filled the little church when we
swept into "Thou Art the King of Glory." After it was
over and we emerged into the bright country morning,
we all felt as churched and holy as we would have done if
the vicar had come.

Looking back to that first Advent when Davy had
become a Christian—and I, one holy night, almost had,
I wrote the last of my Oxford sonnets, with Davy's help,
as always:

ADVENT

Two thousand years go by while on the Cross
Our Lord is suffering still—there is no end
Of pain: the spear pierces, nails rend—
And we below with Mary weep our loss.
The chilling edge of night crawls round the earth;
At every second of the centuries
The dark comes somewhere down, with dreadful ease
Slaying the sun, denying light's rebirth.
But if the agony and death go on,
Our Lady's tears, Our Lord's most mortal cry,
So, too, the timeless lovely birth again—
And the forsaken tomb. Today: the dawn
That never ended and can never die
In breaking glory ushers in the slain.

I sent round the whole six sonnets, though he had seen
two of them, to C. S. Lewis, and he replied, in part: "I
think all the sonnets really good. *The Sands* is v. good,
indeed. So is *Advent*, perhaps it is best. (L. 5 is a corker)."

After Summer Term, several of our friends were going
down, including a sad Julian, for whatever part of the
world claimed them. For us the Long Vacation and the
early autumn was a time of immense work, academically,
although we had time for such friends as still remained or
who, like Jane, came for a gay visit and a poem or two.

In the autumn the end of our own Oxford day was drawing near. We should be going down in the dead of winter. Julian, now back in his monastery, wrote of wishing to be in Oxford again and spoke of "eager" Davy, that quality that seemed the very essence of her being. And he sent us a poem:

EVENING

Sometimes I light my pipe and the fall evenings are long
And getting cool, gone the summer song,
Somehow my mind returns
My mind and heart long to return
To the Studio fireside, to Van and Jean.
We will talk of prayer.
And the gaslight and perhaps the evening rain
Will rise in mist from the lane,
As our wills to God to mortal eyes unseen.

We went often that autumn to our local pub, the Lamb and Flag. There amidst the dart throwers we would sit in the corner and drink brown ale and talk. There was a sort of realisation in us that it was we two again. All this grey magic of Oxford would fade away, but we—we should go on, we should be together, back-to-back if need be. We knew what it was to be Christians at Oxford, and we knew what it was to be gay pagans elsewhere. But now we were about to head for elsewhere as Christians—Virginia, to be precise—and that would be a new thing. But the dear God would be with us, and we should cope.

We talked about our Oxford years from the point of view of "us." How much, despite all the people, how very much of comradeship and love there had been. We thought of all the gay moments together, walking in the Parks, going somewhere on the train, lying in the grass along the Cherwell, wandering out to the Perch or the Trout. But we both felt, and said to one another, that the whole experience of both Oxford and Christ was not less than overwhelming. We both felt that we needed a long time alone, on some isle, desert but for us, to talk and talk in order to harmonise Oxford and Christ, *Grey Goose* and Shining Barrier. The pagan philosophy and the Christian truth in our own "Summa." We planned, then, that in a year or two, somehow, we would take off a year or half year and find some country place where we could "hole up" and do just that. We thought with longing of vanished Glenmerle. The place we would find, though—perhaps in England, perhaps Virginia—we named "Ladywood." At Ladywood we would talk, find ourselves and each other, and set our course for the future. We still thought in terms of *Grey Goose*, but we were not certain —not with Christianity. At all events, we needed to recoup our fortunes a bit. In us in all thsee talks there at the Lamb and Flag was the sense that the time was ending, the Oxford time, and was ending, we felt, at the right moment. Because we had not, during these Oxford years, talked much of the future—the present being such a glorious whirlwind—we felt almost as though we were finding each other again. And we had a curious sense, there at the pub, of being poised in a timeless way between two worlds.

Suddenly it was our last full day in Oxford. Tomorrow morning Edmund Dews would give us breakfast—he was already exercising his mind to select the perfect light wine for a farewell breakfast. And then he would take us to the train up to London. There we should just have time to lunch at my club in Pall Mall, the Oxford and Cambridge, and then the train called the Red Rose to Liverpool. And by nightfall our ship would be standing out into the wide and wintry North Atlantic.

But now it was the last day in Oxford, a sunny winter day. In the afternoon we should say goodbye to friends and in the night wander about Oxford. This morning we walked by way of New College and Queen's Lane to Magdalen Bridge where we turned round to walk up the High Street. The High, gently curving, ancient colleges on either side, may well be the most beautiful street in the world, not least because of the soaring beauty of St. Mary's spire. Just as we came up to it, the bell-ringers within, as if they had seen us coming, pulled their ropes, and the bells rang out. We stood there a few minutes submerged in the cheerful clamour of the change-ringing bells.

On that last day I met C. S. Lewis at the Eastgate for lunch. We talked, I recall, about death or, rather, awakening after death. Whatever it would be like, we thought, our response to it would be "Why, of course! Of *course* it's like this. How else could it have possibly been." We both chuckled at that. I said it would be a sort of coming home, and he agreed. Lewis said that he hoped Davy and I would be coming back to England soon, for we mustn't get out of touch. "At all events," he said with a cheerful grin, "we'll certainly meet again, here—or *there.*" Then it was time to go, and we drained our mugs. When we emerged on to the busy High with the traffic streaming past, we shook hands, and he said: "I shan't say goodbye. We'll meet again." Then he plunged into the traffic. I stood there watching him. When he reached the pavement on the other side, he turned round as though he knew somehow that I would still be standing there in front of the Eastgate. Then he raised his voice in a great roar that easily overcame the noise of the cars and buses. Heads turned and at least one car swerved. "Besides," he bellowed with a great grin, "Christians NEVER say goodbye!"

──❖{ VI }❖──

The Barrier Breached

In the dead of winter we came to Lynchburg in Virginia. As the new year began we were established, along with our blithe collie bitch, Flurry, in a drab bungalow, which after one look we named L'il Dreary, on a street of drab houses. We had no car, but it was only half-a-mile to walk to Lynchburg College where I taught, and less than that to shops and to our parish church. We had come home. Or was it the other way round? Was it, indeed, that we had left home, England and Oxford, the city of our souls, for foreign parts? It felt more like that.

We were, in fact, suffering from what was to be called "culture-shock," the more devastating for being unexpected. There had been no corresponding shock in going to England. We had then been prepared for cultural differences, most of which we had taken to anyway. But now we were shocked and dismayed. The local newspaper after *The Times* was incredible. American lager beer was too cold and bubbly. Houses were too hot. The grass was not a proper green. The houses looked flimsy. The students at the college were not only not students but were semi-illiterate.

Shortly after our return I spoke to the college women's club, but all the polite welcoming smiles faded, except Davy's which got broader, as I began to lash at American barbarisms: car horns blasting to summon friends, drinking attitudes as well as anti-drinking attitudes, and McCarthyism. I contrasted the anti-communist hysteria with an early experience in Oxford: walking along the Broad one night, we had come to a little knot of people listening, mostly with amusement, to a "Commie" ranting on a soapbox, while a fascist-type heckled him, and a bobby stood watching. When it began to look as though the fascist was going to start a fight, the bobby shouldered his way through the crowd, a large hand descended on the angry fascist's shoulder, and the bobby said soothingly: "Now, now, lad. Let 'im 'ave 'is say."

We had sunk so deeply into England and the high civility of Oxford, unaware that we were doing so, that the cultural shock was quite genuine. And it was compounded by discomfort. Every interior was suffocatingly too hot—trains, buses, houses—too bloody hot! And our tweeds and flannels, all we had, were too heavy. I would fling the classroom window wide, and the students would shiver like leaves and complain. At home, at least, we pushed the thermostat back to the peg and kept a friendly coal fire on the hearth. We drank "proper tea" morning, noon, and night and even, for awhile, tried to continue eating tea as a meal. We read Theodore Maynard's poem "Exile" with empathy and murmured with him: "And English air that was my breath/Remained my mortal life till death . . ." We wrote homesick letters to friends still in Oxford, and received homesick letters from friends who, like us, had gone down and weren't happy about being in Kansas or Kenya Colony. Later, when summer came, we were startled by the creepers and lush undergrowth and frightful heat: Virginia, though we had never noticed it in past years, seemed tropical, even jungly. Davy and I were drawn closer in a back-to-back sort of way by our shared dislike, partly temporary, of so much around us and by our longing for England.

Compounding the cultural shock was a religious one. At Oxford we had remembered Lynchburg as a city of churches, not such venerable and beautiful churches as the English ones perhaps but full, no doubt, of the Holy Spirit, full of constant lively searching into the meaning of the Christ-centred life. To be sure, we had not noticed

this vivid Christian life, doubtless surging all about us—
but, then, we had not been Christians. Now it appeared
to us that there was very little interest in living a life
centred in the Incarnate Lord. People went to church of
course, but their conversation was about the convivial
Couples Club or the radical racial ideas of the bishop. No
doubt Christ was in the churches, somewhere, but He
was not easy to find.

Even more dismaying, in other circles, was the watering-
down of the Faith to little more than a few of Christ's
moral precepts. "Yes," said these unbelievers who called
themselves Christians, "yes, indeed, Jesus was the divine
Son of God; so are we *all*, divine Sons of God. Of course
there was an incarnation: *each* of us is the incarnation
of God. If St. John suggests anything else, or St. Paul
does, they are not to be depended on. Miracles—well, no,
we happen to know God doesn't work that way. No, of
course our knowledge of how God works doesn't come
from the Bible, but we know all the same. There was no
resurrection, except in some very, very spiritual sense,
whatever those naïve Apostles thought they saw. Of
course we're Christians—how could you doubt it?—though,
naturally, Buddhism and Islam and all religions except
the Catholic Church are equally Ways. Truth? What is
truth? What has truth got to do with it?"

All this, to us who had accepted the ancient Christian
faith, was depressing. It was about as far from the strong
red wine of the Faith as grape juice. The Faith was too
strong: the wine must be turned to water in an anti-
miracle. In other ages people who could not believe in
Christianity (and, admittedly, it takes some believing)
had called themselves Deists or Unitarians, but these
people, for reasons we did not understand, were intent to
shelter under the *name* of Christianity and at the same
time to reduce the *Faith* to a hollow thing that required
no believing beyond a mild theism.

We resolved to stand firm for the Faith once-given,
and we began to be glad for the unswerving faith of
Rome. The place of last resort.

Oxford had really represented to us two things so inter-twined that we did not clearly distinguish them. One was the apostolic faith in its fullness, as represented by C. S. Lewis and Charles Williams. The other was high civilisation, sweet reason, and the life of the mind, which was no less represented by Lewis and Williams as well as many others. Religiously, we longed for the lively life in Christ, but we did not fully see that we were equally longing for the lively life of the mind—the delights of conversation at once serious and gay, which is, whatever its subject, Christ or poetry or history, the ultimately civilised thing. When we spoke of the lively life in Christ, we meant keenness, to be sure, but we also meant the subtle discourse on the meanings of Christ's way that is, in fact, only possible among highly articulate and civilised Christians. There was perhaps more faith in the Virginian churches than we perceived, faith that was real but in-articulate and not thought about. But we, seeing what looked like apathy in one direction and, in the other direction, watered-down Christianity, began to wonder whether in Protestantism the apostolic faith were not dying. We were comforted by thoughts of Julian, radiant with his deep faith, and other friends scattered about the world, holding the faith.

We lived in the parish of Grace Church, a small and beautiful church built of a local green stone as soft in colour as Cotswold stone. Rector Jeffrey and his wife were English—Cornish, actually—which of course pleased us. And we soon came to know a neighbour, in the church, Miss Preston Ambler, who was not only a lady but a firm and articulate Christian. And another Anglican, Shirley Rosser, in physics at the college, was no less firm in the faith. The fact that he, like Peter and Lew at Oxford, was a physicist and a Christian led me to formulate a theory as to why so many physicists—I knew of still others—were committed Christians. The theory went like this: The non-scientists say, well, we don't know the answers, but the scientists do; and the scientists who are not physicists say, well, we don't know the answers either, but the physicists do; and the physicists know that they do not, in fact, have the ultimate answers and, accordingly, turn to Christ who does.

We also became part of a rather more worldly group of friends in the college, who, if not ardently interested in Christianity, were lively and intelligent people, interested in books and the artistic life of the community. One of them in particular, Belle Hill, a woman who had lost her husband a year or two earlier and was now cheerfully and bravely making a new life in college teaching, became a close and trusted friend.

Gradually we settled-in to the patterns of our new life, still not liking it much. I taught a fairly heavy schedule at the college, and Davy, in March, got a job in the book-keeping department of our bank. She also took on a high-school-level class on Sunday at Grace Church, working hard on her preparation for it. We faithfully went to church and sometimes went with the Rector to another church where he had Evensong. At home, morning and night, we had family prayers from the Prayerbook, the two of us kneeling at a wooden cross, reading and praying the well-loved prayers and holding hands.

One day in early March in a class in world civilisations I pointed out that no textbook writer was ever purely objective and that his particular bias could often be discovered through his choice of adjectives. Among my examples was that of an "enlightened emperor" of China who, doubting his own religion, invited missionaries of other religions into China to present their beliefs. The class was puzzled. The emperor, I said, might be called "open-minded" but to call him "enlightened"—having the light of spiritual truth—when he did not, in fact, believe anything, must mean that the author, if not simply careless, must hold that to believe in nothing was to have the light of truth. This at once threw the class into furious argument for the rest of the hour. One girl, a very good student, continued to argue that he *was*, somehow, enlightened after class, and finally asked if she might come round to my house that night and talk further.

She came and Davy and I discussed the thing with her. Inevitably we moved into talk of the sort of enlightenment—the ancient and apostolic Christian faith—that had fallen upon us at Oxford. The girl was a more-or-less nominal Christian of the "liberal" or watered-down variety; and she was fascinated by the suggestion of a Christianity that was at once civilised and magnificent and maybe—just maybe—supremely true. Could she come again, please? And bring a friend? Of course.

Thus, completely unplanned, our Christian group was born. The girl and her friend became a dozen students. Week after week they came and were welcomed. Some dropped away and others took their places. We had not started it. It had just happened, and it went on of its own accord. We simply accepted, though, as I wrote in the Journal, we were "awed and joyful"—awed at the work of the Spirit, joyful that God was using us. It was all, in the C. S. Lewis words we loved, the Great Dance. Many of these students became real Christians, a great many indeed over the years. We read things from C. S. Lewis and Charles Williams and Dorothy Sayers. We discussed the Apostolic faith and answered the hundreds of questions. At the same time we scoffed at solemnity and the mushy sentimentality of some Protestant circles, as well as the incredible view that "alcohol" was sin. The Christianity we represented was sunny and joyous, with all the room in the world for humour and gaiety, and yet at the same time rigorous and glorious. So we laughed and joked and poured out the wine but challenged their minds and souls. And the students smiled and abandoned the solemn voices they had been taught to use in speaking about such things, gaily drinking the wine and discovering a Christ who was a blazing reality.

Davy and I, with our closeness of understanding and love, made an almost perfect team. No doubt it was I who insisted upon the intellectual rigour and logic that C. S. Lewis had taught me. And Davy, "so eager and loving" as I wrote then, was the one who made the love of God a flame in the room. Both of us felt that this group in this moment of time was our vocation. When we and the students knelt at the end of an evening in silent prayer—the only spoken words being my "In the name of the Father, the Son, and the Holy Ghost" at the beginning and the whispered amens as each one finished his prayer—the room, lighted then only by glowing fire, seemed charged with holiness.

Even Flurry seemed to pray. She, too, daughter of Gypsy, and former seadog on *Grey Goose,* was a part of our team. She made the students laugh, and she amazed them with her obedience and intelligence. She even taught them something, for she refused to obey the command "Lay down!"—only "Lie!"

One night, with Flurry lying in the centre of the room, I told the group a true story of Flurry and Gypsy to illuminate the difficult doctrine of the Fall and Original Sin, which next day I wrote down. As I told the tale, Flurry pricked up her ears at every mention of her name. Here is the story I told that night:

THE FALL

Gypsy, a furry, wheat-coloured collie, found herself in possession of several hundred acres of hills and woods, full of good things like rabbit trails and streams and intriguing burrows, and she delighted in it all. She was given a comfortable bed and good meals. Perhaps she rather took it all for granted. Of obligations there were few, and they not heavy. She was, to be sure, supposed to worship her Master and be right joyous to be with him. She knew she must not chase the chickens. While she must obey certain commands—to follow, to come, to lie down—there were no unreasonable ones, and no tricks. After all, to obey and to worship were natural to her dog nature.

There came a day when, as Gypsy was prowling on the far hill past the springhouse and pasture, two things happened at once: the Master called her and a rabbit fled across the hill. Gypsy wheeled and raced towards the Master, as she had always done. Then she stopped. It entered her mind that she didn't have to obey. Perhaps the Master didn't understand about that rabbit.

Anyhow, these were *her* hills. The rabbit was hers, too. Very likely it was all lies—that story of everything, including herself, belonging to the Master. How did she know that the food in her dish came from him?—Probably there was some natural explanation. She was a free dog and that was the end of it. These thoughts went through her mind swiftly while she stood irresolute. Again came the Master's command; the rabbit crossed the hilltop. Gypsy whirled and raced after the rabbit. She had made a choice. She was free to choose.

Hours later she came home. She saw the Master waiting for her, but she did not rush gladly to him, leaping and frisking, as she had always done. Something new came into her demeanour: guilt. She crept up to him like a snake on her belly. Undoubtedly she was penitent at the moment. But she had a new knowledge—the knowledge of the possibility of sin—and it was a thrill in her heart and a salt taste in her mouth. Nevertheless she was very obedient next day and the day after. Eventually, though, there was another rabbit—and she did not even hesitate. Soon it was the mere possibility of a rabbit. And then she dropped the rabbit thing altogether and went her way.

The Master loved her still but trusted her no longer. In time she lived in a pen and went for walks with a rope round her neck. All her real freedom was gone. But the Master gave her, from time to time, new chances to obey of her own free will. Had she chosen to obey she would once again have had perfect freedom to wander her hundreds of acres. But she did not return to the obedience. She always chose, if she were out of reach, to run away. The Master, knowing hunger would bring her back to her pen, let her run. He could have stopped her: the rifle that would have ended her rebellion with the crack of doom stood in the corner. But while she lived she might still return to the obedience, might still choose the obedience that was freedom.

One day, during a journey by car, Gypsy and her good little daughter, Flurry, were taken into the edge of a wood. Always Gypsy had limited her disobedience to her own hills. But now, coming back to the car, she suddenly felt the old thrill. She turned and fled. The Master called with a note of sharp urgency. Flurry, with the courtesy that always ruled her, came at once. Gypsy, her ears dulled to the meanings of the Master, continued her rush into the dark forest. After hours of search and calling, the Master sadly abandoned the lost one and, with Flurry beside him, went home.

There Flurry continued to live in freedom under the obedience. She was right joyous to be with the Master and gay when she did a thing that pleased him. She knew that in his service was perfect freedom. She obeyed gladly of her own free choice.

But lost Gypsy, if she still lived, wandered the woods and roads an outcast. She became dirty and matted with burs. No doubt stones were thrown at her and she was often hungry, but she had lost the way home. If she had puppies, they, too, and their children had lost the way home, for Gypsy's perilous and bent will to disobey must infect them; and the comforting hand of the Master would be unknown to them, except as a tale. This is the way Gypsy chose on the Day of the Rabbit and continued to choose until, suddenly, there was no more choosing.

When I had done telling this tale of Horsebite Hall, all the students wanted to pat Flurry, a tribute that she was only too pleased to accept. And the parable evidently made sense to them; years later, some of them would say that they still thought of Gypsy whenever there was a reference to the Fall.

About the time the Christian group began I wrote to C. S. Lewis, telling him that he had virtually created us anew through the books and letters leading to our conversion. I expressed my disgust at certain clergymen—men called, supposedly, to represent Christ—who neither believed nor had the honesty to resign. I also expressed my astonishment, at moments, at the thought of myself being a Christian. Lewis replied, as follows:

It was very nice to hear from you. I hope my interest in you both is something less blasphemous than that of a Creator in a creature (it wd. anyway be *begetting* not *creating*, see *Philemon* 10). My feeling about people in whose conversion I have been allowed to play a part is always mixed with awe and even fear: such as a boy might feel on first being allowed to fire a rifle. The disproportion between his puny finger on the trigger and the thunder & lightning wh. follow is alarming. And the seriousness with which the other party takes my words always raises the doubt whether I have taken them seriously enough myself. By writing the things I write, you see, one especially qualifies for being here-after "condemned out of one's own mouth." Think of me as a fellow-patient in the same hospital who, having been admitted a little earlier, cd. give some advice.

The semi-Christians (in dog-collars) that you speak of are a great trial. Our College chaplain is rather of that kind. I'm glad you have something better in your own church.

I feel an amused recognition when you describe those moments at wh. one feels "How cd. I—I, of all people—ever have come to believe this cock & bull story." I think they will do us no harm. Aren't they just the reverse side of one's just recognition that the truth is amazing? Our fathers were more familiar with the opposite danger of taking it all for granted: which is probably just as bad.

God bless you both: you are always in my prayers. I hope we may meet again one day.

The moments of astonished incredulity at one's own belief were, as Lewis said, rather amusing. I smiled at them myself. I knew of course that they were much more likely to occur here in Virginia, where my past experience was pagan, than in Oxford, which, to Davy and me, was almost entirely associated with Christianity. I tended, indeed, to feel, here in Virginia, that God Him-self dwelt in Oxford, His holy city, where He could hear the bells. My moments of astonishment did not of course mean that my faith was endangered. At the same time, my pagan impulses were somewhat troubling.

I became more troubled as the year moved on, which, in turn, troubled Davy. While still in Oxford, we had talked at the Lamb and Flag of the need to be alone, with leisure, in order to reconcile and bring into harmony our pagan dream of love and beauty and this overwhelming Christianity. And we had given the name of Ladywood to the place where we should, when we could, do it. How did the Shining Barrier stand under the Light? But Li'l Dreary was not Ladywood. There was little of leisure or being alone together. And I was remembering—being stabbed by remembrance—the images from the old pagan days: the gay companionship, the love of life and beauty, the dedication to our love, the schooner outward bound to far islands.

But we were Christians now. Davy, with the eagerness that was part of her very being, was flinging herself into the service of the Incarnate God. I, too, was serving Him: the morning and evening prayers with Davy, the church, the student group, the challenges that I tried to make implicit in my teaching. Indeed, it was I who at Oxford had seen and written in our Journal: "It is not possible to be 'incidentally a Christian.' The fact of Christianity must be overwhelmingly *first* or nothing." And I would no doubt have affirmed that statement still, with my mind. Davy was affirming it with her whole being. And Christianity *was* first in my concerns. Intellectually I was wholly committed to its truth. And yet I was holding something back. But for Davy it really was "overwhelmingly first"—nothing held back. She was literally pouring out her life in Christ's service.

I wanted—what did I want? I wanted the fine keen bow of a schooner cutting the waves with Davy and me—just Davy and me and Flurry—happy and loving and comradely on her decks. Well, there was nothing unChristian about that, as long as God was there, too, and as long as we were neglecting no service of love. But, though I wouldn't have admitted it, even to myself, I didn't want God aboard. He was too heavy. I wanted Him approving from a considerable distance. I didn't want to be thinking of Him. I wanted to be free—like Gypsy. I wanted life itself, the colour and fire and loveliness of life. And Christ now and then, like a loved poem I could read when I wanted to. I didn't want us to be swallowed up in God. I wanted holidays from the school of Christ. We should, somehow, be able to have the Shining Barrier intact *and* follow the King of Glory. I didn't want to be a saint. Almost none of this did I consciously know—just longings.

But for Davy, to live was Christ. She didn't want to be a saint, either; she was too humble even to think of such a thing. She simply wanted God—almost totally. His service *was* her freedom, her joy. She loved me, she loved our sharing; but, ultimately, all there was to share was Christ and His service. I knew it was so with her.

She served God and she served our neighbour, gladly. She worked hard and long—to my mind too hard and long—preparing for her Sunday school class. If I had done it, I'd probably have done it without preparation. But the very idea of a Sunday school bored me. Davy wanted some of her more obdurate boys to talk to me. It never came about because I did nothing to bring it about. I knew she would be delighted if I were to offer to be a co-teacher of that class; perhaps God would have been delighted, too, and the work of the Kingdom furthered; certainly it would have been sharing. But I did not do it. I felt that, with the church and the group and our prayers, I was doing enough. I did not, needless to say, ask myself what I meant by "enough." Enough for what?

When Davy wasn't reading the Bible to prepare for her class, she was reading it for her soul's sake. She was always reading it, or reading Brother Lawrence and other devotional works. I wanted to protest that it was too much; but how could I do that? It's not possible for one Christian to say to another: You love God too much. Nor to say: You are holier than necessary. I couldn't even *think* such thoughts. They would have been dangerous. I might have seen things. I merely *felt* a sort of helpless protest. I didn't quite like to see her poring over Isaiah or St. John. I think I'd have smiled to see her curled up with an Agatha Christie. I knew that everything had to be different now we were Christians—but *this* different? I may even have read the Bible less as she read it more, as a kind of dumb protest. Some witty tongue defined a martyr as a person who lives with a saint. I might have given that a wry smile. The martyrdom consisted of being unable to say anything and of not knowing what to say, anyhow.

Davy of course knew that all was not well, despite my silence. I expect she prayed about it, but she, too, must have found it hard to speak of anything so vague, something she merely sensed. Once, before Oxford, if one of us had felt that something was not right, or that something was dividing us and was, therefore, a threat to our love, a Navigators' Council would have been called for. The whole thing would have been discussed, and, if need be, the Appeal to Love, bright and irresistible, would have been brought forth: what is best for our love? Always, the Appeal to Love had been the one, the sufficient, basis for action. But now—I knew it and she must have known it—the Appeal was broken. The simple, perfect Appeal, without a word said, was blunted. Now, the only appeal was to God. It would not be best for our love for Davy to be crucified—but how if it were best for God? It might be what God required of her. And I certainly could not suppose or maintain that I knew better than Davy what was best for the Kingdom. Indeed, I had an uneasy suspicion that she knew a great deal more about it than I did. And yet I could not—or, at all events, did not—go all the way with her.

We still prayed together hand in hand. We went to church and discussed what we should do in the student group. We were still a team and we loved each other dearly. But we did not talk of what I was feeling. And yet the knowledge that the Appeal was broken sank deep into me. I did not consciously think—let alone say—that I ought to be able to invoke the old Appeal; but I *felt* it. It was like having something I had always trusted, my right arm perhaps, suddenly useless. I was deeply confused. I spoke on an earlier page of our love as like a fine watch that could be thrown off by a grain of dust. But this was not a grain of dust or even a mustard seed: it was the eternal God. After all, as C. S. Lewis had said, I was not finding the existence of a Master and a Judge "*simply* pleasant." My intellectual commitment to that Master was perfectly clear, as was Davy's. And at Oxford it had all been challenging and beautiful and exciting. But now it seemed different. Duller. Davy was simply living up to her commitment, wherever it led. For me, that was the trouble: where it led. I was ready to play in a match, Christians *v.* Atheists. I was ready to level my lance and charge under the Cross of Gold. I was ready to follow the King into battle. But—Sunday school? Where was the glory? Poring over the Bible—when we could be reading poetry? Where was the army of the King with banners? Where was the cathedral, beautiful and holy?

So Davy went on reading the Bible, and I went on not reading it much. I read other things, novels and mysteries, which she didn't have time to read. No longer in loyalty to our love were we reading the same books. How could I say: Stop reading Isaiah and read Margery Allingham? Besides, if she did, I'd have to read Isaiah. And the old sharing was going in another way. She was becoming *wifely*. She was accepting St. Paul on women and wives. She seemed to want to be domestic and make things in the kitchen. I was afraid she might actually obey me if I issued a command. There was something very humble and good in her attitude towards me as well as towards Christ. A humble vocation. But it wasn't like her. I almost wanted a fight.

As spring came on with its blossoms, its stir, its soft and cajoling breezes, its lilacs, I felt that stir in me as I walked to college. Images of blue water and a yacht heeling under a fresh breeze came into my mind. Images of far islands. The "divine discontent" that spring is supposed to foster was, in me, not a bit divine. But it *was* discontent. I talked about yachts that spring, when we sat after dinner on our small back porch, and Davy herself spoke of them with love and nostalgia. We spoke, with a faintly tentative air, of when we should have a *Grey Goose* again. The sense of being outward bound that had marked our whole life was with us again, a little. But we did not come to grips with the big question: how can the old pagan joy, the Shining-Barrier love, symbolised by a schooner named *Grey Goose* heeling under the wind, be reconciled with Christian joy?

What I wanted, emotionally if not intellectually, was the old Davy back along with the old love of life and beauty and poetry for their own sakes. It was a longing of the heart that seemingly could not be reconciled with my intellectual commitment to Christ. Even less could it be reconciled with Davy's wholeness, both mind and heart, of devotion. Perhaps if we had been given time—unpressured time alone together—we could have reconciled all and found our way. But we were not given time.

The college term ended, but this once, for the sake of the exchequer, I taught summer school. And Davy was working in the bank.

The heat that summer was frightful. The heat and the jungle. And we were used to England. No air-conditioning. We should hardly have had the energy to talk if we had had time. In July I became worried about Davy's tiredness—tiredness coupled with a slight swelling of her ankles—and insisted that she see our doctor. He said she was overdoing and must work part-time only. So now I did issue a command: she must stop working altogether. Accordingly, she gave in her notice.

Davy did not say so then, but she secretly thought—perhaps only briefly—that she was going to die. She prayed that she be allowed to live one more year for the sake of the Christian group. But I did not know.

In August came Jane from England. For three weeks. Davy had brought her from the choir at St. Ebbe's to the Studio, and then she had come often. Just before we left England, she had come back to Oxford for a brief gay visit. Now, her parents being in New York on business for awhile, she had come over. Jane was country-bred and loved country things, as did we. She also loved poetry. So those were bonds. On the other hand, she was very young and, sometimes, moody and silent. Our early feelings about her in Oxford had varied between thinking her "a nice child" and being annoyed with her moodiness, but the nice child had won out. Then I began to notice her perceptiveness and intensity of listening when I read poetry. She also loved Charles Williams. When she came back on that last visit to Oxford, we felt a real bond with her.

We looked forward to her visit. She would be a breath of England. And Oxford which we all loved. Unfortunately Davy had just given in her notice, so she would still be working during most of Jane's stay. It would be up to me to cope in the daytime.

So the "nice child," rather distinctly less the child now that she was in the university, came, and I coped. Every morning she walked into college with me and came to my class in English literature. She even took the tests with Alpha double plusses. After class we sometimes walked about the town, looking at houses and talking of England. Eventually we would go home and talk some more. And read poetry. All manner of poem. But, especially, I would read T. S. Eliot's *Four Quartets*, which was already a bond between us. And she would read Emily Brontë's poems, poems that she had always loved, which became a bond between us. We talked a lot of Emily Brontë: of the strange love that linked Heathcliffe and Cathy, and of the sisters, Emily and Charlotte, growing up in that lonely Yorkshire house, running in ragged frocks across the moors. We also talked endlessly about Oxford, very dear to us both. So the hours happily sped.

Jane was a Christian. She had not grown up as one but had been converted not long before we knew her, converted almost at the same time as I had been. So we jokingly said that she was my "godsister." If godparents, why not a godsister? Although low-church St. Ebbe's had brought about our meeting, she had become higher. What moved her was Anglo-Catholic worship with its emphasis on the altar and the sacraments, as well as its deep aesthetic appeal. I, too, was inclined that way, rather more than Davy was. It had not been an issue between us, partly because we were united in our dislike of the

watered-down "broad church" and partly because there
was no high church in Lynchburg anyhow. But now
Jane and I were finding a bond in the Anglo-Catholic
approach to the faith: the beauty, the mystery, the holiness. The beauty of holiness. A less workaday sort of
Christianity. No Sunday schools, perhaps. It may be that
Jane and I were drawn more by the beauty than the
holiness. We remembered St. Mary Magdalen in Oxford
—an aesthetic and, indeed, romantic appeal. And of course
we were finding an aesthetic bond in the poetry—poetry
that we were loving for its own sake. I had always served
beauty. Davy and I together had loved beauty. Now,
maybe, I was worshipping beauty in the Christian God
while Davy was worshipping God. There may be danger
in the love of beauty, though it seems treason to say it.
Perhaps it can be a snare. If so Jane and I were snared.
And Davy went tiredly off to work, thinking she might be
going to die, and faithfully taught her Sunday school class.
And Jane and I entertained each other.

Jane's weeks with us sped tranquilly by, marked by
small events. The Rector and his wife came to tea. Other
people called. My colleague, Belle, took us all for a
Sunday drive in the country, and we were caught in a
frightful storm that rocked the car while trees and barns
blew down around us. We made our communion at the
beautiful white altar of Grace Church. And imperceptibly
Jane and I grew closer and laughed at little jokes that
grew out of our hours together. Early in her stay with us,
a strange gloom and silence fell upon Jane; and I went im-
patiently off and left it to Davy to do something. Later
in the visit it occurred again, and this time it was I that
stroked her hair and soothed her. The gloom was caused
by the approaching end of her stay with us.

Since Oxford Davy and I had longed for one of the
beautifully designed TC or TD MG two-seaters. Now,
a few days before Jane was to leave, I spotted a black TD
with a For Sale sign on it and entered into discussion
with its owner. I took Davy, now at last not working, for
a spin. Then we bought it. Jane, imitating a cockney
child, said, "Coo, Miss!" when she saw it.

The next three nights—Jane's last—the three of us drove
under a full moon, Davy and I rediscovering the real
Virginia, the country, that we loved. We went up into
the high Blueridge, mysterious and beautiful under the
moon. Once while we lay in the grass on the mountain
a huge white owl drifted over us. Once we stopped at
the little country church, St. Stephen's, that we had used
to go to occasionally. We sat there beneath the great oaks
of the churchyard and talked. Then, after our drive, overwhelmed by the cool beauty of the night, we would come
home. Davy, no longer working but still tired out, would
go to bed; and Jane and I would sit up awhile, talking and
reading some poems. We were very conscious that her
stay was ending and were sad, Jane perhaps especially.

The third night's drive was the most lovely of all—
unearthly in its moon-blanched beauty. And it was the
last, for Jane was to go in the morning. When we came
home, perhaps about one, Davy went to bed and Jane
and I, again, sat up. We read "Little Gidding" from the
Four Quartets and talked a little. There was a sort of
anguish in me that she was going away. I wished we
were all sailing for England. I wished she were my sister
in truth. I said something and she did not reply. I looked
at her: there were tears in her eyes. I reached out and
took her hand. Perhaps I murmured, "Oh Jane!" No one
said anything further. I may have started to withdraw
my hand, but her clasp tightened. I did not withdraw it.
Minutes passed. Then hours. Silence. I do not know
what I thought. I do not know whether I thought. I felt,
mostly. Grief at her going, certainly. A feeling that she
and England were one. Images of the Yorkshire moors
and children running over them. The hours passed unaware. The grey light of dawn seeped in the windows.
A few hours later Jane was on her way to England.

Naturally I told Davy about the silent night—what
there was to tell. About holding hands and about wishing
Jane were my sister. I had told her all along what Jane
and I had said and done. Davy and I always told each
other things.

But what was there to tell? Something had happened,

but what was it? Was I in love with Jane? The thought
had never crossed my mind. It didn't cross it now. No,
but was I? Was Jane in love with me? I hadn't thought
of that either; but now Davy and I thought that perhaps
she was. I was not pleased at the thought. I was enamoured with Jane as sister, a sister in England. One may
have a strong bond with a sister. But enamoured by it I
was. I was caught up in it and remained so for weeks,
exchanging many letters with Jane, all of which Davy
saw of course and we talked over. Nothing hidden.

In an earlier chapter, writing about the Shining Barrier,
I said that with the closeness we were bringing into being
it would be unthinkable for either of us ever to love another. Unthinkable. Literally unthinkable. And I literally
had not thought of being in love with Jane, nor did I
think of it in the next weeks. The Shining Barrier, even
breached by Christ, was still immensely strong. And, indeed, whatever might be the truth of my feelings for
Jane, Davy was my life. Davy was the air I breathed. I
knew that steadily.

But I *was* in love with Jane. And she with me. I do
not doubt it now. We never so much as kissed each other,
but that's what it was. She did not know it for what it
was then either. She and I were caught up in a dream
of beauty. Poetry was at the heart of it. There were
elements of high-church mystery and elements that were
virtually pagan, like the Yorkshire moors and the wild
powerful love of Heathcliffe and Cathy, a love of the
spirit that was almost sexless. Often when people are
falling in love, physical desire is in abeyance: had it not
been so with Jane and me, alarums would have rung.
But it was a thing of the spirit, its true nature precisely
unthinkable by me—or, in a different way, by her. And
I said to myself, as I wrote letters to Jane or walked in
the night, that my dream of Jane as sister was made up of
elements—poetry and pagan beauty—that Davy, in her
deep Christian commitment, didn't have time for any
more. A strange and subtle betrayal, almost innocent. But
not quite: corruption is never compulsory.

The most important thing about what happened with Jane is that it was a consequence. It was the consequence of God's breaching the Shinning Barrier, of the failure of the Appeal. This I believe to be certainly true. It *could not* have happened, even in that nearly innocent form, in the years when the Shining Barrier was intact. Of course, if I had been as wholly committed to Christ as Davy was, it wouldn't have happened either. It happened because in my heart I wasn't that committed and because I wanted the old pagan joy—and couldn't appeal to Davy on the grounds of our love. It was the "old Davy" I had been wanting, and a schooner under the wind. If Davy—Davy my comrade and my love—had wanted what I wanted, the Shining Barrier would have stood. But I had begun to despair of having the old pagan joy with her, ever again. And Davy, meanwhile, was longing, a little pitifully, for me to find the joy she was finding in the Obedience: the joy that is perhaps the only perfect joy.

The hot weather broke that year in early September; and Davy, through rest and coolness, began to feel good again. The autumn term would be beginning soon. In the meantime we drove out morning, noon, and night in the MG, very frisky and Oxonian, with Flurry riding gaily in Flurry's 'Ole behind the seat. Once, when Flurry was attractively in heat, we were pursued by a wolf pack of half a dozen of her more spirited suitors, the neighbours looking on in astonishment and we laughing until we had tears in our eyes. In the MG, named now the Trout, we explored all the country round including the Blue Mountains. We often stopped at night at St. Stephen's and prayed together, kneeling by an old stone cross in the graveyard. This led us to come, sometimes, to church there. We could not desert Grace Church because of our love for the Rector and Preston Ambler, but we found the little country church, very old for this part of Virginia and set amongst great oaks, so appealing that we declared we were "half members." Not far from St. Stephen's, out there in Bedford County, we found an old and deserted house, rather small but with great dignity and with fine trees all about. We decided that it would be a perfect "Ladywood"—the house we had planned to find, back in the Lamb and Flag, where we could be alone together and talk. Next year, we said, we might be able to buy it.

But even as we were renewing our comradeship through that blessed little MG, I was writing to Jane and still caught up in that particular web of beauty, still with the restless longing of the heart for some "island in the west." Davy was sympathetic and loving when I talked about Jane; and when I wrote a couple of poems to "my sister," I think Davy loved them more, albeit somewhat wistfully, than the sister did.

Then Davy, who did not write poems, wrote one about Dom Julian, far away in his monastery. We exchanged letters with him and loved him always, reading often his splendid Christian poems. This is Davy's poem to Julian:

> Dear dying Julian
> Gracious and just
> Dying to self
> And hid deep in Christ
>
> Still thou dost live
> In pain and thirst
> And bit by bit
> Consume to dust
>
> Thy soul's dark night
> Works life in us
> To our dim vision
> There shines forth Christ
>
> Ah, but how fair
> Thy bare faith is
> Refuge for us
> Who still do not trust

Davy, whom I saw as far ahead of me on the Way as she saw Julian to be ahead of her, fell far short, in her own eyes, of the glory of God, as of course Julian, in *his* own eyes, fell short. To me, both were holy. The distance is infinity, and position is relative. Even I perhaps may have seemed holy to somebody. Some penitent villain.

And Davy one night, having contemplated holiness, said she was restless and would sleep in the guestroom. But she did not sleep: she prayed. All night, like the saints, she wrestled in prayer. Some say that prayer, even prayer for what God desires, releases power by the operation of a deep spiritual law; and to offer up what one loves may release still more. However that may be, Davy that night offered up her *life*. For me—that my soul might be fulfilled, almost the prayer of that Oxford Advent. Now, as I fixed my eyes on the Island in the West and looked not Eastward, she humbly proposed holy exchange. It was between her and the Incarnate One. I was not to know then.

The college term began, and the Christian group at once revived with even more interest and enthusiasm than before. We talked of Christ, and we read Julian's unpublished poems again and again because the students asked for them. The fire glowed on the hearth, and the Lord Messiah, in whose Name we gathered, was in the room.

Many of the students came to talk to us about their problems, and we tried, Davy especially, to be always available. Before the term was a month old we were confronted with a major problem: homosexuality. A girl came to talk to Davy alone; a boy to talk to us both. They came because we were Christians. Our pre-Christian view of homosexuality had been tolerant: if that was what people wanted, why not? And one of our dear friends was a pleasant lesbian lady. But now as Christians what did we think? We didn't know. We knew St. Paul was rather stern about it; but maybe he meant just sex, homosex, without love. Sex that came before God. Might there be, perhaps, a Christian love, marriage even, between men or between women that included homosex but was not dominated by it? We did not know. Our Rector thought not. Eventually I wrote to C. S. Lewis about that matter as well as about prayer—whether holy prayers, like those of Julian and Davy, would be more efficacious because of their merit. Lewis's reference to my spine has to do with my slipping a disc climbing Snowdon in Wales, an injury which still bothered me. His letter:

I have seen less than you but more than I wanted of this terrible problem. I will discuss your letter with those whom I think wise in Christ. This is only an *interim* report. First, to map out the boundaries within which all discussion must go on, I take it for certain that the *physical* satisfaction of homosexual desires is sin. This leaves the homo. no worse off than any normal person who is, for whatever reason, prevented from marrying. Second, our speculations on the cause of the abnormality are not what matters and we must be content with ignorance. The disciples were not told *why* (in terms of efficient cause) the man was born blind (Jn. IX 1–3): only the final cause, that the works of God shd. be made manifest in him. This suggests that in homosexuality, as in every other tribulation, those works can be made manifest: i.e. that every disability conceals a vocation, if only we can find it, wh. will "turn the necessity to glorious gain." Of course, the first step must be to accept any privations wh., if so disabled, we can't lawfully get. The homo. has to accept sexual abstinence just as the poor man has to forego otherwise lawful pleasures because he wd. be unjust to his wife and children if he took them. That is merely a negative condition. What shd. the positive life of the homo. be? I wish I had a letter wh. a pious male homo., now dead, once wrote to me—but of course it was the sort of letter one takes cares to destroy. He believed that his necessity *could* be turned to spiritual gain: that there were certain kinds of sympathy and understanding, a certain social rôle which mere *men* and mere *women* cd. not give. But it is all horribly vague—too long ago. Perhaps any homo. who humbly accepts his cross and puts himself under Divine guidance will, however, be shown the way. I am sure that any attempt to evade it (e.g. by mock- or quasi-marriage with a member of one's own sex *even* if this does not lead to any carnal act) is the wrong way. Jealousy (this another homo. admitted to me) is far more rampant and deadly among them than among us. And I don't think little concessions like wearing the clothes of the other sex in private is the right line either. It is the duties, the burdens, the characteristic virtues of the other sex, I expect, which the patient must try to cultivate. I have mentioned humility because male homos. (I don't know about women) are rather apt, the moment they find you don't treat them with horror and contempt, to rush to the opposite pole and start implying that they are somehow superior to the normal type. I wish I could be more definite. All I have really said is that, like all other tribulations, it must be offered to God and His guidance how to use it must be sought.

I heard you had been troubled with the old spine again. I hope the silence on this topic in your letter does not merely result from selflessness but means that you are now well. Remember me to your very nice wife. You both keep your place in my daily prayers. It is a sweet duty, praying for our friends. I always feel as if I had had a brief meeting with you when I do so: perhaps it *is* a meeting, and the best kind. Pray for me to be made more charitable: we're in the middle of a Faculty crisis wh. tempts me to hatred many times a day.

P.S. I'd nearly forgotten your other point. I presume God grants prayers when granting wd. be good for the petitioner & others and denies them when it wd. not. Might there be cases where

a. The worthiness of the petitioner made it *bad* for him to have his prayers granted: i.e. might lead him to think there was an element of *bargain* about it.

b. The unworthiness made it *bad*: i.e. might lead him to think that God did not demand righteousness.

c. The worthiness made it *good*: i.e. might free him from scruples, show him that his conduct had been right after all.

d. The unworthiness made it *good*: i.e. produced humbled compunction—*unde hoc mihi?*

All v. crude. The point is that worthiness might easily be taken into account tho' not in the way of direct *earning* and *reward.*

On Christmas Eve, when Davy was out of the room, I brought forth an immense photograph of the piers and vaulting of Bourges Cathedral that she had never seen, propping it up at eye level with a single lamp upon it and the others out. Looking at it, one was almost there, gazing up at all that soaring splendour. Then I put the Sanctus from the Mozart "Requiem Mass" on the record player, ready to go at full volume. Fetching Davy in with her eyes obediently shut, I stood her in front of the picture and touched the switch. As the music swept into the room with grandeur, I put my arms around her from behind and whispered, "Open your eyes, dearling." It was a moment of astonishing glory, even to me who had staged it; and Davy had tears in her eyes. Glory and love. I knew I loved Davy more than all the world besides. And she knew it, too.

That moment marked the end of a variously troubled year: The year of well-named Li'l Dreary, which we were now to abandon without regrets. The year of shock and adjustment after Oxford. The year when the Appeal was seen to be impossible to use and the Shining Barrier breached. And the year, consequently, when I responded to Jane's pure and innocent love. It was also the year when Davy, a month or so before its end, offered up her life in holy exchange and utter love for me. Tonight, after Bourges and the "Requiem Mass," she told me, to my horror and dread.

Mole End was the name, from *The Wind in the Willows* of course, that we gave to the basement flat that we moved into in the dead of winter. It was in a huge and handsome ante-bellum mansion set among great oaks in spacious grounds .The flat itself had spacious rooms, and it seemed about a mile from the back room to the front. It had a little forecourt, like Mole's Mole End, under the mansion's front steps. The move was complicated by other people's moving; so that, on the last night of the year, we were not in Mole End though our furniture was, but were rather perched in an upper-storey flat in the same mansion. There we went wearily to earth, my back about done in by lifting boxes of books. I went to bed on a sort of many-windowed sun porch that night, while Davy played gleefully with the wheeled tea trolley —something she had always wanted—that we were to inherit.

On New Year's morning I awoke to bright sunshine pouring in the many windows, and out of them I could see only a fantastic maze of oak branches, along which half a dozen squirrels merrily chased each other. It felt like country, and I was transported back to Glenmerle. Then, hearing a clink, I looked round, and in came Davy wheeling the already beloved tea trolley with an eager, shy delight. And on it—most splendid of meals—a glorious breakfast: eggs and bacon and sausage and country ham —all—and English muffins, hot, and toast, cold, and Oxford vintage marmalade. And of course the teapot under its cosy. We kissed each other and murmured a prayer and ate the lot, laughing now and then at the squirrels and feeding titbits to Flurry. I told her of my being carried back to Glenmerle, and then we remembered that other New Year's Day, shortly after we met, when I brought her first to Glenmerle. We laughed, recalling the old tale of Don and his wreck, and we smiled when we spoke of how young we were then. For a moment we were silent, remembering. I said, "Davy?" She looked at me with bright, remembering eyes—her long lovely eyes—and I said, "I love you." "I know," she said. "And I love you." We looked at each other with that look of perfect understanding that, more than any other single thing, was the essence of our love. I raised my teacup and said, "If it's half as good as the half we've known . . ." and she, lifting hers, said, "Here's *Hail*! to the rest of the road." We drank to that in Darjeeling.

She knew without my saying that I was hers, that I was full of happiness that we were deeply together again, wherever the road led. And I knew without her saying that she had, somehow, come to a new understanding that God in His ample love embraced our love with, it may be, a sort of tenderness, and we must tread the Way to Him hand in hand. We understood without words that we must hold the co-inherence of lovers *and* be Companions of the Co-inherence of the Incarnate Lord: she in me and I in her; Christ in us and we in Him. "Everyone who loves is the child of God," says John (I John IV 7). Perhaps that morning she came back for me and then perhaps, astonishingly, found herself further along the Way. At all events, joy flowered between us, the joy that I had thought to be pagan joy. After all, for Christian and unbeliever, there is but one spring of joy.

Certainly, as we moved into the new year, we held the reality of each other and were lovers and comrades again, as we had been at Oxford and Glenmerle and aboard *Grey Goose*. Mole End, therefore, with its spray of English heather on the wall of the big living-room, was a happy place. We were happy, and for Davy it was in several ways a very fulfilling time. The Christian group, coming every week, sitting on the floor in front of the fire, flourished; and Davy very blithely made all sorts of goodies to put on her dear tea trolley and wheel in to make the meetings gayer. At other times during the week the students of the group and others, as well as faculty friends, dropped in for tea and talk. Many of the students—Bill, Joan, Sandra, Rosie, Anne—became friends. Others told us their deepest problems, coming particularly to Davy because of her warmth of kindness. Belle Hill came by often, brisk and cheerful. We had long Christian conversations with physicist Shirley Rosser, Shirley with his warm grin and prematurely snowy hair. In fact, Mole End, though far less cramped, took on something of the quality of the Studio, with the odd little forecourt in place of the cobbled lane. There was a large opaque glass-brick window, where our wooden cross stood, and it was our "skylight." And of course the coal fire on the hearth and hundreds of books. Now, though, some fine furniture and oriental rugs, Glenmerle things.

At night Davy and I would often go up to Grace Church, to which we had a key. We would pray there at the white altar that had the words "Holy, Holy, Holy" engraved on it—sometimes I would speak the words aloud because of the coming together of purity of vowel sounds and purity of meaning. Then Davy would play for me on the organ, and the little church would be filled with the thunder of the Toccata-and-Fugue or the Little G Minor or "Thou Art the King of Glory." These evenings in the church, dark but for the sanctuary lights and the organ console, swept with the mighty music, were very dear to me and a joyous fulfilment for Davy. Sometimes we would go from the splendours of the music to Mole End and the splendours of poetry. I was writing poetry, too; and she eagerly entered into the process as always, so that the poems were truly ours.

Even more important for her than the music perhaps was her painting. She had not, because of working and tiredness, done any painting since Oxford; but I brought her home a new easel as a surprise, and she began to paint. First she finished a painting, very Blakean, begun at Oxford, after we had spent hours at a great Blake show at the Tate in London. The Oxford painting that she completed—after which it went over the mantelpiece— showed in muted colours a nude female form lying prone, eyes shut, while a great wave—the wave of God—crested above her, ready to thunder down upon her.

Then she began a painting, all in blues and rusty reds, even more Blakean, that revealed something of her soul. And perhaps mine. Set against a background of high, rusty red cliffs in which were two caves or openings filled with blue light, there were six figures. But in reality there were only two, she and I. The caves of blue light were doorways, I think, one very lofty, one low. In front of the low door lay a female figure in an attitude of surrender. A little distance away an angelic figure motioned towards the low door; and from the recumbent form, which was Davy, her soul was shooting off towards the door. The obedient soul—it touched me deeply. On the other side of the picture, a figure sat on a log with praying hands and straight back. A very lordly and Blakean angel gestured imperiously to the high door. But my soul lay on the ground, head propped up on hand and elbow, gesturing back at the lordly angel, clearly arguing with it. This earned my wry smile of recognition. The painting had humour as well as beauty, at least my stiff-backed praying figure and arguing soul were funny in an awful sort of way. And the painting with its combination of deep seeing, seriousness-and-humour, and beauty portrayed the nice balance of Davy's mind. But what made it ultimately so moving and revealing was that Davy, in her divine humility, saw me called to a high destiny—the high door—and herself called to a low one. Making cookies for the students. Not counting the love poured out. That low door probably leads to a throne.

The Christian group and our friends, the organ at Grace, the painting, the poems, Davy herself really rested and full of energy, and our restored closeness and sharing: these were the elements of our content as winter moved on towards spring. We of course continued our little "family prayers," hand in hand, in front of the plain wooden cross on the sill of the glass-brick window; and we alternated between Grace and St. Stephen's, though Davy continued to teach her Sunday class at Grace.

In March we had a great happiness. Julian was able to come down from his monastery for a short visit, bringing Oxford with him and, it seemed, holiness as well. We took him out to our beloved St. Stephen's and showed him where we sometimes prayed at night by the old stone cross in the churchyard, and we all three knelt and prayed there. And we had long hours of talk by the fire of England, where he was born, and Oxford and, always, running through all, the Incarnate Lord. Then on the last morning I took him to the train in the Trout, top down despite a rare "English" fog. Davy in her dressing-gown came gaily out to wave goodbye; and as we circled out the driveway we looked back at her, standing at the entrance to the forecourt, and waved to her. For some reason that departure in the mist with Davy waving so gaily remained with extraordinary vividness in both my and Julian's memories, perhaps because she looked so little in front of the mansion in the grey swirling fog. Julian wrote of his "memory of her standing small and alone in her nightclothes by the steps." But I remember her eager love and gay waves.

April and May were lovely that year. One unusual event was that our Rector by our special request celebrated Holy Communion for us and for Shirley, who had been ill, at Mole End. And Flurry soon after was in heat, with dozens of dogs growling and fighting at our low basement windows and she very pleased within. One day during this period I was walking from the back bedroom through the kitchen where Davy was preparing to bake. I was suddenly impelled to sweep her up in a great hug and kiss, flour going everywhere, holding her as though against the world. She said, in a small, astonished, happy voice, "Why, dearling . . ." And then we both started laughing at ourselves all floury.

But Maytime, above all, was drives in the country in the MG. April and May—Judas trees and dogwood and lilacs. We crept along the winding country roads looking at the flowers and the birds and the newly turned red earth. We went up in the Blue Mountains where it was still early spring. We stopped again and again at St. Stephen's at night, saying our prayers at the old stone cross, and then sitting under the great oaks in the starlight. Once we drove out to Horsebite, where Flurry was born, and contemplated the black walnut in the meadow and talked about the "Sin Picture" and all that had come to pass. Sometimes we went out to the little house we called "Ladywood," where we would sit in its fine doorway and talk of how in another year we might live there.

On the last day of May—I remember the date because we talked of that other last day of May when, in destroyer and motor launch, we met so dramatically at sea in the far Pacific—we drove in the Blue Mountains and then proceeded homewards in the evening along back roads. The sun had set but the mountains glowed an incredible blue as though they were actually made of translucent sapphire, and we were feeling very peaceful and unhurried. The blue faded out of the mountains and the darkness came on, though I could still just see the road in the twilight. Then, as we passed a wood, I heard a whistle and stopped and switched off. It was a whip-poor-will whistling his liquid song, another one answering in the distance. We sat there a long time, holding hands, as the stars came out. This was the Virginia we

loved. At last I started the engine again, and we drove on,
past St. Stephen's, to Mole End.

If May was the month of peace and beauty, June was
the month of excitement and decisions. It began with the
ring of the telephone: the Dean of Wabash, a fine college
in the north, where Lew and Mary Ann were. I knew
the Dean and liked him immensely. Would I like to join
their faculty in English next year? Would I come up
and talk it over? Good, they would be expecting me then.
In the next week or so Davy and I talked intensely about
it—and prayed. Academically a better college, more pay,
the Dean himself, Lew and Mary Ann. But—lovely
Virginia, the Christian group, our own fine Dean John
Turner. But, above all, the group that we had felt to be
a vocation. Still, things have their time. Perhaps we should
now move on, join forces with Lew and Mary Ann?

After commencement, just as it was time to journey
north, Davy came down with a virus. She wasn't very
ill, but she shouldn't go travelling. So I went alone,
making her promise to call Dr. Craddock.

Briefly, we decided to accept the Wabash post, and I
resigned from Lynchburg College. There were moans
from our student group, who said we were abandoning
them. The college president was reported to have said,
"There goes my best teacher." We looked sadly at Mole
End and Grace Church and St. Stephen's. It was a painful decision.

Davy recovered from her virus but felt dragged out.
Dr. Craddock decided that she should go into the University Hospital at Charlottesville, sixty miles away, where
they could run complete tests. "Maybe," he said, "maybe
we'll have to use a wonder drug on this dern thing."
Davy said it wasn't necessary but went. We talked gaily
on the telephone every night, and she said she was feeling better. Still, I arranged an appointment with one of
the doctors to be told what the tests had shown, if
anything.

It was mid-July and hot when I went up in the MG
with Flurry, and I thought I would see the doctor first.
He said: "She's a very sick girl. I'd say no more than one

chance in ten. Maybe six months." He didn't cushion it, but then, how could anyone cushion a thing like that?

The world had changed for ever by the time I replied, an instant later. Quietly I asked him—so quietly that perhaps he thought I didn't care—what it was. It was her liver, he said: it had passed the point of no return. They did not know why. She would die in coma or in bleeding internally and from her eyeballs.

I will say here that, although Dr. Craddock struggled in the dark, as it were, with subtlety and devotion, she did die. And even after a post-mortem no one could say why. We were only in our thirties and didn't drink much. It was, it was thought, a subclinical virus, possibly a tropical one harboured in her body from Island days or possibly picked up in June or possibly the year before. That is all that can be said.

I will also say that I asked Lynchburg College to re-hire me, and, though they had already employed someone else, they did so, breaking the budget. I accordingly resigned my brief post at Wabash College, and, though they renewed the offer in later years, I did not ever go there because of gratitude to Lynchburg College.

As I left the doctor's cool, air-conditioned office for the hot ward, I had to walk all the way down a corridor that seemed to stretch, white and antiseptic, for miles. A very long corridor with Davy at the end of it. Shock vibrated through me with the impact of my heels. What was I to say to her? A resolution was building in me—to sustain her, to hold her through what lay ahead. I must be strong when I told her, but I was not strong now. I might break. I must not break. Tomorrow I would be strong and then I would tell her and sustain her in her hour of knowing.

I went in to her with a cheery greeting. I said the tests were not fully in; and I told her the small news from home. I started to say that I was missing her, but decided I couldn't manage it, and said something else. Finally I said goodbye until tomorrow. But she knew—knew there was something dark in my eyes. We could not hide from each other.

Then I went away, down to the MG. The Trout we had called it. Flurry frisked to see me but became subdued when I put my hand on her head. I drove out of town, still dry-eyed, praying "Thy will be done" over and over—all I could pray. I remembered her offering up her life for me. Tears came in the country, but they were blown away in the wind.

—◄{ VII }►—

The Deathly Snows

On Sunday, one day before the doctor's fatal word, Julian in his New England priory, knowing nothing of Davy's illness or the hospital, offered mass for her and me because of "a far-off intimation" that we needed help. An intimation through eternity.

Monday, walking down the days and years along that hospital corridor with Davy at the end of it, driving down the Virginian counties homeward alone, Monday may have been the worst day of my life. There were to be grim days ahead, but we faced them together in the coinherence of our love. Today, in shock and grief, I walked down the corridor alone, for I had not told her. The world had turned over in one sudden minute.

When I reached Mole End, I began to act. Telegrams and telephone calls went forth to friends, particularly Christian friends, including C. S. Lewis and Maurice Wood, our St. Ebbe's rector. And local friends, too, Shirley and Belle and Preston and Rector Jeffrey. Within minutes and hours a mighty prayer was building. I talked to Dean John Turner and other college officials as well as Dr. Craddock. Non-Christian friends urged me not to tell Davy of what lay ahead; the Christians with one voice, then and later, said she must know. C. S. Lewis said that he was praying steadily and that she must be told. And Julian, saying that he was praying incessantly, wrote: "She should know if she is going to her Calvary." He added, speaking of her by her Christian name: "Poor

Jean, so humble, so good, so eager and affectionate, so holy. God keep her in His hand."

Above all, that Monday, I tried to face what lay ahead. I cleared for action like a frigate going into battle, throwing out of my life everything not relevant to Davy or to my job at the college. I stood and looked a long time at each of Davy's paintings in the light of my perilous awareness. Moved by some obscure impulse, I read the first poem I had ever written to Davy, "Maytime" (p. 31) at Glenmerle, whence comes the name of this chapter: "For ever Maytime, sweet and gay,—/Until the lilacs close/Beneath the deathly snows." An iron resolution built up in me, perhaps the most powerful and unswerving of all my life, that in the months ahead I would do all and be all for her; I would sustain her and hold her up with my love. All I was came into focus in my fierce and almost terrible will to do this, to let nothing impede me from doing this. Then, grimly resolute, I drove to St. Stephen's to kneel in the night by the old stone cross where we together had knelt so often, and I asked God to sustain us both.

Then I was ready to tell her. As I drove in the morning sunshine to Charlottesville, I thought of her offering-up her life for me in the previous autumn. Was this the result? Then I thought with a kind of awe of her belief in July a year ago that she might be going to die, and her asking God then for "one more year" for the sake of the student group; now it was another July—one more year, indeed—and I was on my way to tell her of her death. Any recovery is but a stay of the death that is our common doom: she had had what she asked for. One more year. Was it right for me to ask for more? Was it right for me to ask when she had offered-up her life? How should I approach God? What should I say to the Incarnate God who made the world and suffered it to crucify Him? I thought of *Grey Goose*, never again to sail the waters of this world; I thought of poetry, including my own, and of all dear things, I thought of Islands in the West. Then I rolled it all together into a ball. If she died, I might— since, under God, I must not act to follow her—I might live for years. Those years and all of beauty they might contain I put into the ball. And then I offered-up all of it to the King: take all I have ever dreamed, all I may ever long for including the death I shall certainly long for: I offer it up, oh Christ, for her, for her best good, death or life. This was my offering-up. I asked God to take all, all that was or would ever be, in holy exchange, not for her spared life which would be my good but not perhaps hers, but for *her* good, whatever it might be. Later I would pray that she might recover but only if it were for her good. That offering-up was perhaps the most purely holy and purely loving act of my life.

This was done in the MG, the Trout swimming through the bright morning to Charlottesville. And then, to the westward, over against the Blue Mountains, I saw a rainbow for a shimmering few minutes. Chance or Promise? But God would know from the beginning of what we call time that I should be making my prayer and seeing the rainbow.

With me in the car were yellow roses for her. I do not know why I chose them, except that they were lovely, and I could not bring lilacs. Lilactime was over, for ever now. But the roses had their own beauty; and this was our time of roses. From now on, through the months, there would always be yellow roses with her.

When the nurse had brought a vase and gone again, I sat beside her bed and took her hand. Then I said, "Davy . . ." She looked at me, and I smiled at her. She smiled back. "Dearling," I said. "This—this illness—is maybe going to mean our parting—for awhile." Her hand tightened its grip, but she still smiled. "The doctors say that it means that. But a hundred people are praying for you. C. S. Lewis and Maurice. Peter and Bee, Lew and Mary Ann, Thad, Julian. You are in God's hand, dearling." Despite my will, my eyes filled with tears, but I smiled at her.

She too smiled through tears, and said in a husky voice: "Let all be—" Her voice wavered and she gave a little sob. "—according to His perfect will," she said in a stronger voice. "Yesterday, when you were here, I thought—I thought it might be, well, something bad. Your eyes were unhappy . . ."

I stood up and leaned over her and put my arms around her. "I love you," I said, "whatever it is to be, for ever." I kissed her wet cheeks, and we just held each other for a little. There were tears on my cheeks, too.

Then I told her exactly what the doctor had said. And all that I had done. I told her of my offering-up and of the rainbow. She would be wrapped in prayer, I said; indeed, she was already. Then I said that the clean Christ, who must abhor disease, would heal her if it were God's will, if we prayed steadfastly—she, too. I told her of Julian's mass Sunday and she was awed. Then I gave her my dearest possession: the little gold cross she had given me in Oxford. I put it round her neck.

Hope rose between us, hope rising out of love. We became cheerful. She got up and went over to the window to look down on Flurry in the MG. She called, and Flurry leaped out and ran wildly around looking for her and then attempted to climb the wall of the hospital. Davy laughed and told her to go back to the car, which she did.

From this day forward we never quite lost hope. We didn't doubt the medical findings of course, but there are too many inexplicable "miraculous" cures for anyone, including doctors, to suppose that medicine has the last word. Even this doctor had said one chance in ten. So I prayed, as did many, yet I never wavered on my deeper prayer for her best good.

Davy's sister came and they wept a little together and laughed together, too. Many people journeyed to Charlottesville to see her, coming away moved and strengthened by her courage and love. A bishop laid his hands upon her and anointed her for healing, if it were the will of God.

In due course we brought her home. Shirley Rosser made a bed for her in his big car. On the way up, he offered me all his savings when I should need them. Then Davy made it a merry drive home.

She was very glad to be home in Mole End where it

was cool and quiet, with our books all about and us together. I had moved her big bed into the living-room, and she entertained there like a queen all during the month of August. I cooked for her and rubbed her back and gave her injections; and I got a servant to do the cleaning. I also hunted mosquitoes. That was the summer when everyone complained about them; and of course one mosquito could ruin Davy's precarious sleep. So every night with a torch I hunted them down. Sleep and food were life perhaps, and I took infinite pains to try to make a salt-free diet attractive. Although I controlled visitors to some extent, there were many who came, then and later when she was in hospital. I cannot touch upon a fraction of them, nor can I begin to describe people's great goodness. There were all sorts of gifts of money, often an anonymous envelope found in the mailbox with perhaps half a hundred dollars, all in ones and silver— a collection in some hall—and sometimes bigger gifts. And later students queueing up to offer her the blood—some twenty or thirty pints—she needed. One of my griefs was that my blood was the wrong type, though I gave blood to others to make up.

The incredible thing about the stream of callers, at Mole End and later, was that they came with love to cheer her and they went away cheered and strengthened. Her love and strength flowed out to them. One of the students, later, did a painting of Davy, smiling in the light, leading a darkly silhouetted student towards a tree —the Tree.

Davy and I, facing what must be faced with as much courage and hope and love as there was in us, prayed together that month, the old lovely prayers from the Book of Common Prayer, I kneeling beside her bed. The Rector came to give us Holy Communion. Since Dr. Craddock had said that I might take her out on to the wide laws of the mansion, I borrowed a chaise-longue for her, and every afternoon we sat out there in the shade of a giant oak. We were reminded of Glenmerle, there under the tree, with Flurry lying beside us instead of Laddie. We read together a lot that month. One thing we read and talked about was Thomas Merton's *Seeds of Contemplation*. And of course the old dear poems that were part of the very texture of our life. It seemed to us that now was the time to read our Journal: and out there under the oaks we did so, beginning with happy Glenmerle days—"when we were so happy in May" and our love was young. It was almost all Glenmerle that month: Glenmerle and wandering there by the lily pond, the club and the fire, the dawn flight and the canoe drifting under the stars. And the building of the Shining Barrier. Sometimes, though, we were reminded of later days and would turn ahead to read of the schooner or of Oxford. It gave us an awareness of the whole of our life—and of a sort of unified wholeness that marked it.

Davy was not in pain. She didn't, to my occasional moments of despair, have much appetite for the salt-free diet, despite my efforts. The immediate problem was the build-up of fluid in her abdomen. Nothing could stop it building-up, we knew—up to the point where it would have to be drained by tapping—but the more slowly it built-up the more hopeful we could be. And, in fact, it was not until early September that she had to go in hospital, locally, for a few days for the tap. The doctor said that I might take her in the MG if I would go slowly, so we had a merry little creep in what was essentially a merry little car, our books at Mole End open to mark our place for when she came back.

But she was not to come back. For one reason and another the days in hospital drew out. For weeks it was always next week that she would be coming home; but she never did. Perhaps it was best that we had that month of August at Mole End without the pressure of knowing it to be the last.

From September through November she felt quite good. The doctor said, and I said to inquirers: "She's holding her own." The watchword of those months. She was on cortisone much of that time, a drug that has a rather euphoric effect. At first she was troubled by heat; and I was agonised for her, remembering the summer before when she began to feel good with the advent of the blessed coolness. By an irony of fate the heat hung on this year until October and Hurricane Hazel which, though not striking Lynchburg directly, ended the heat wave in a big wind that brought down tree branches and cut off the hospital's electricity for a bit. But Davy exulted in the wind and encouraged other patients who were afraid.

During the months in hospital I was not to miss even one day in coming to her, almost always twice. Otherwise I taught my classes and that was all. Everything that was not Davy was a blur. Except that I looked at her paintings at home. And I always watched the dawn, the dawn we loved, and *she* watched it. We knew we were both seeing it.

In September there arrived in the post an old shoebox. It was Julian's priceless, fragile, medieval crucifix. Carved in wood, it had not only the Crucified One but, at the top, God the Father looked down from a cloud and the Dove descended, and, at the bottom, Mary stood with a sword through her heart. This was by Davy always. Julian himself could not come, though both he and I begged his prior to let him. But Julian, saying masses for us, praying long hours before the Sacrament, was peculiarly with us all the same in spirit. His cross, his letters made him near, and, even more, his poems. One of his poems, in particular, was pinned up beside Davy and often on her lips:

> If everything is lost, thanks be to God
> If I must see it go, watch it go,
> Watch it fade away, die
> Thanks be to God that He is all I have
> And if I have Him not, I have nothing at all
> Nothing at all, only a farewell to the wind
> Farewell to the grey sky
> Goodbye, God be with you evening October sky.
> If all is lost, thanks be to God,
> For He is He, and I, I am only I.

Davy, too, was saying farewell to the wind, farewell to the wind and sky, watching it all go, fade away, die—and thanking God. And yet she was human, heartbreakingly human, and she did not want to die.

She obediently did everything the doctors and the nurses told her to do: everything except to stay in bed when someone else was in need. Over and over again she was discovered out of bed in the night, sitting beside some other patient who was suffering, soothing her, holding her hand, praying for her. The doctor told me to persuade her to stay in bed; and Davy would look guilty and grin and promise—and then she would hear a sob or a cry in the night. Later, I was to get dozens of letters, some almost illiterate, from people who had been in hospital with her, saying that she had helped and sustained them. One said she was like an angel of God.

The nurses loved her and the hospital servants, too. She enlisted my help to make a grand medal "for faithful service" for one of the black maids, who wore it proudly. Many of the nurses were praying for her. There was one nurse, especially, named Joan, whom we called St. Joan, who loved Davy and was loved. St. Joan was young and swift and valiant, and the name fitted her. Davy never lost her gaiety and sense of humour. People laughed to be around her. Someone gave her a floppy-eared creature which she always spoke of as "St.-Paul-the-dog-or-rabbit"; and she used it to speak "aside" to about how kind people were. It is simply true, without exaggeration, to say that she was a tower of strength to everyone—nurses, doctors, ministers no less than friends—all drew strength from her cheerful, brave, deeply loving spirit. Love shone forth from her; and love not only begets love, it transmits strength.

It might be appropriate to say here, although I was not to know it until the end, that the hospital—the Virginia Baptist Hospital—would not take a penny for all their care of her over months, not even for the meals they occasionally brought me. They said that Davy had done more for them, for their nurses and other patients, than they had ever been able to do for her. And Dr. Craddock, in my opinion a deeply skilled doctor as well as a deeply Christian gentleman, who with his partner saw her daily during all those months, also refused all payment. I didn't ask either doctors or hospital for help and didn't expect it; I had made arrangements to borrow. Goodness and love are as real as their terrible opposites, and, in truth, far more real, though I say this mindful of the enormous evils like Nazi Germany. But love is the final reality; and anyone who does not understand this, be he writer or sage, is a man flawed in wisdom.

Davy strove to do God's will. More important, she strove to make her own will conform to God's will: to will what He willed. Her prayer—and mine, too, often—was the prayer from one of Charles Williams's novels: "Do—or do not." She wanted, humanly, to live; and she, humanly, feared death: yet she was surrendered to God. Her watchword, the phrase always on her lips, was: "All shall be most well." And: "All manner of thing shall be well." She worked on her "maxims" of the Christian life, the first of which was: "Thou shalt *love* the Lord thy God; and if thou canst not yet love Him, thou shalt *trust* Him with all thy mind, soul, and heart." Another one was: "Thou shalt not do anything contrary to love."

But if Davy was a tower of strength to everybody else, I was allowed to be, a little, her strength. This is an exaggeration, for her real source of strength was her crucified Lord, and yet, humanly, she leaned on me. Perhaps it was her divine courtesy; and, indeed, there was a courtesy between us and, sometimes, a sort of supernatural justice. At all events, she did not, perhaps could not, conceal from me her human longing to live and her human fear of death. In Charles Williams's *Descent into Hell* he sets forth his Doctrine of Substituted Love: carrying one another's burdens is *not* just a figure of speech or something meaningful only in terms of physical burdens like a trunk. Davy's burden was not death but the fear of death. I asked her to give me that burden, a real handing over, like surrendering a trunk to a porter.

An act of handing over. And I *took* it—also act. I then entered into the fear, *her* fear, with all my heart and mind and imagination, felt it, carried it along with my own fear, which was also real but other. And her burden grew lighter.

Her room was at the end of a corridor and beyond was a veranda. Every day in a wheelchair I took her, warmly bundled up, out on to that veranda. The MG would be parked where Davy could look down and say hello to Flurry. When I wheeled her out of the room and along the corridor, Davy always cried out gaily to everybody she saw: "This is the high moment of my day!" And everybody would smile. Out there on the veranda we talked and read poems and kissed each other and held hands. How much happiness we had, even under the sentence of death! Usually I brought the yellow roses out there, too. Sometimes a nurse would bring us tea or I would have brought a thermos flask of "proper tea" from home. If there was a letter from Julian or some other friend, we would read it there together; and we would talk about the dawn we had both watched. Usually this time out of doors would be on my earlier call at the hospital, but sometimes I would take her out in the late afternoon or evening, too.

One mild late-October evening, Hallowe'en, in fact, I took her out there, bringing along some fresh yellow roses. I told her, jokingly, that I had made a special trip to Glenmerle for these particular roses, and she chuckled, pretending it was so. We talked that evening of Glenmerle days, feeling them to be but yesterday. We pretended that we had just been in the rose-garden and then, still carrying roses, had walked down to the bridge. The veranda in the twilight, we pretended, was the bridge, and Davy would look over the veranda railing and say, "Oh, look! I see a fish!" And I would say, gesturing towards the lights on the distant avenue, "Lots of fireflies tonight." Once Davy said in a low voice, "Maybe we'll be allowed to meet again at Glenmerle, if . . ." And I put my arm around her and said, "A heavenly Glenmerle. If there's anything I'm sure of, it is that heaven is a coming home. And, for us, Glenmerle." And she said, "The waiting won't be long." Then she said, as a car came in the hospital drive, "Look, there's your father coming home." It was a particularly happy and loving evening, there in the clean cold autumn air with the faint scent of the roses.

That night when I left her, blinking the MG's instrument lights as always as I drove out and seeing the answering blink of her bed lamp, I went home and wrote a poem:

ALL HALLOWS EVE

Tonight, while weighing wild winged hope with fears
Of loss, again the girl's voice crying gay
And sweet—O playmate of lost pagan years!—
Comes ringing in the glory of the May.

O singing beauty! singing though there nears
The moment of all finding and all loss:
Together in our laughter and our tears,
Wind-driven to the centre where ways cross.

Rose garden in blue night, where souls embraced
In holy silence, timeless ecstasy:
Truth grew between us, final beauty laced
The stars, and awed we knew eternity.

A secret sharing passed from eye to eye:
In death the singing beauty does not die.

I brought it to her next day. I whistled our recognition signal under her window, as I always did, and she whistled the second part back. This time I added, "Thou Art the King of Glory." Then, out on the veranda, I read her the poem. A few tears rolled down her cheeks, but they were tears of joy, and she smiled through them at me.

That night, too—All Souls' Eve—I wrote a poem for her. This one, also, moved her deeply; and she kept them both pinned up beside her, along with Julian's poem. My poems and his, together, say how it was:

DYING

Bright with God's spirit
  Awed at that beauty
—You who are near it—
  Unafraid at that footstep
Now that you hear it

Reckless in pity
  Eager in loving
—High in the City—
  Wearing in beauty
Holy simplicity.

T. S. Eliot in the *Four Quartets* says what it is to be a Christian: "A condition of complete simplicity/(Costing not less than everything)." I might not altogether understand those lines but for Davy: it was the condition she had attained.

In November came a worried letter from C. S. Lewis, whom I had had no time to write to since the July letter telling him the position. I did take time to reply to this letter:

It is a long time since you wrote and told me of your wife's grave illness. You asked my prayers and of course have had them: not only daily, for I never wake in the night without remembering you both before God. I have sometimes tried, by sophistical arguments, to persuade myself that your silence might somehow be interpreted as a good omen . . . but how could it? If you can bear, will you tell me your news. If she has gone where we can feel no anxiety about her, then I must feel anxious about you. I liked you both so well: never two young people more. And to like is to fear. Whatever has happened and in whatever state you are (I have horrid pictures in my mind) all blessings on you.

One day in December it was a bit too cold for the veranda, so I wheeled her into our alternative place, a sort of many-windowed sunroom. We talked about Hawaii— the blue sea and the tradewind clouds—and how she had gone into the sea from the yacht after my uniform cap.

She chuckled at the incident and was her usual gay self, but it seemed to me that she was a bit fuzzy and confused.

The following day when I came and whistled the recognition signal under her window, there was no reply. Of course she might be talking to the doctor. But when I entered the room, I saw that they had put bed-railings up to keep her from falling out. The nurse told me that she was going into coma. The nurse spoke to her, but there was no reply. I spoke to her and said I had come. She smiled angelically, but did not open her eyes. I said, "Open your eyes, dearling." She smiled again, but that was all. I said, "Your eyes are still shut. I can't see you if your eyes are shut, can I?" She gave a faint giggle, but nothing more. I sat there beside her for an hour or two, holding her hand; and then I had to leave.

That night when I returned she had sunk deeper into the coma. The doctor came and spoke to her, but there was no response. He thought that she would never come out of it. I had prayed that she would not die in coma and so had she, that she would die, if die she must, clear-eyed and aware. But now it seemed that it must be in coma. Perhaps it would be better so. I took the bars down so that I could hold her hand. I leaned over and kissed her, and, for some reason, I thought of the line in my early poem to her: "One April kiss as dark comes flooding." Darkness for her, and a sort of poignant sorrow flooding through me. I kissed her cheek again, and she said in a small, far-away voice: "Oh, love . . ." I spoke to her, but she was silent; so I just sat there, holding her hand. After a few minutes she again said in that little voice: "Oh, love . . ." All that evening, at intervals of about thirty seconds, came the murmur: "Oh, love . . ." Twice nurses came in to give her injections. Each time as the needle pricked her, she said—as though it were she hurting another: "Oh, I'm so sorry." Then, after a few minutes of silence, the little voice would begin again, saying: "Oh, love . . ." She was saying it to me, I knew. Wherever she was, whatever remote land she was wandering in, she was reaching to me. The slow hours passed, and every minute or half-minute the gentle little remote voice. If it isn't just a meaningless form of words, I suppose my heart broke that night. It really means, though, loving past all measure.

The next day they began intra-venous feeding. She was totally unresponsive to doctors or nurses. Then I found that I could reach her. If I spoke of Laddie or Glenmerle, she would murmur. I told her about Laddie having hold of the pig's tail, and she gave a delighted giggle—to the amazement of a nurse who came in just then. I asked the nurse to bring me something for her to eat. The nurse said it wouldn't work but brought it. I told Davy to open her mouth, and she did, and I put the spoon in it, telling her to swallow, and she did that. I fed her the whole dishful, as though she were a baby. The nurse tried it, but Davy could not hear any voice but mine. After that the hospital forgot visiting hours and I forgot classes: I fed her all her meals.

And I talked her out of that coma. Maybe she would have come out of it by herself. But, beginning with that meal and extending over the next few days, I talked to her, and she heard me. I hummed the Humoresque, and she murmured happily. She laughed gaily when I spoke of amusing things we both remembered, and she squirmed happily when I said loving things. I gently whistled the recognition signal, and she puckered up her lips and tried to respond. She would even try to speak. When I said, "Sweetheart," she would utter a pathetic little, "Sweee . . ." But the next day she was able to say "Sweetheart." Finally I tried the "Alert" whistle, and her eyes fluttered open for a moment. Gradually she came out of it.

It seems strange to say it, but these were the most purely happy days since the dreadful announcement had been made, months before. For this one brief period, the *awareness* of death was lifted from her. And I was filled with a wild hope that, somehow, God might make me His instrument to save her, pour His strength through me into her. There was a sort of joy between us. I was not just loving her, I was as wildly in love as I had ever been, and so was she. We talked of Glenmerle, because it was immediate to our minds through our reading of the Journal under the oak and our pretending on the veranda. So for a few days in the dead of winter, we wandered about Glenmerle in springtime together, down by the old lily pond and in the orchard, and we were young and in love.

She came wholly out of the coma—against all predictions—came out of it with a memory of happiness. But then of course the awareness of death looming over her returned. Yet, still, we felt a sort of hope springing out of the overcoming of the coma. And I reminded her constantly that she had *given* me the fear of death, and that I was bearing it. I was bearing it, for both of us.

Christmas Day was a good day. She felt livelier and even had a bit of an appetite. The kind hospital invited me to stay, and they brought me a tray of Christmas dinner, too. Because of the hope that was in us, it was a merry little dinner. My Christmas present to her was a poem, in my pocket. It was a poem that I had started long before, but then it had been altogether different, about an imaginary person. Even then she had loved it. Now I had rewritten it completely, making it a song about us—as well as a prayer and a hope: and it was my gift to her. Now, as we finished dinner, I said: "Davy—here is my Christmas present to you." And I read it gaily:

SONG OF TWO LOVERS

In England over the endless sea
(I dream, my dearling, for you and me:
   Tomorrow if not today)

There stands in Dorset by the sea,
In the gentle airs of the West Country,
   A house that is tall and grey,

An old grey house beside the sea,
And there two lovers live merrily,
   Most merrily and gay.

Two willows near and a great beech tree
Trace starlit patterns of fantasy,
   And spring in the breeze by day.

These lovers go walking by the sea,
Their hair in the wind blows light and free,
   And their lips are kissed by the spray,

They stroll in the lane and follow the bee,
They lie in the grass beneath a tree,
   And they sing as they wander away.

At dusk they turn to the house by the sea,
Lightly and gaily come home to tea,
   She carries a bright bouquet.

They stop at the church quite faithfully
And sweetly together they bend the knee—
   Oh it's thanks they give as they pray!

Sometimes they dress most handsomely:
Go up to London Town to see
   Some books and a friend and a play.

And twice, O Oxford town, to thee:
First for the joyful ecstasy
   Of the dreaming spires and the may;

And then in soft winter dusk to be
In cold empty streets without a key
   Yet never alone or astray.

Then home to the tall grey house by the sea
To sit close by the fire and read poetry
   As long as the night will stay.

Just so in England right merrily
Two lovers so lightly live and, see!
   Hands linked as they go their way.

One lover, oh dearling! looks like thee;
The other lover, dear one, is me—
   And to dream can be to pray.

So it was a song for Christmas Day, too; and it was
too happy to admit of anything but hope. She listened
with tears in her eyes, tears and smiles; but I think that
she never in her life loved a Christmas gift so much,
just because she so loved that song. But her Christmas
was not done. I excused myself on some pretext to go
and fetch her final gift, with the collusion of the hospital: Flurry. It is difficult to say who was the more

ecstatic: both dog and mistress yelped in joy. Davy embraced Flurry and Flurry, moaning with pleasure, licked her hand. A second later she leaped up on the high bed for one quarter of a second before I whisked her off again.

It was a lovely Christmas. When that night, I drove happily homeward with our happy collie, my thoughts were all of love, of love overcoming death: the love of God and our dear love, triumphant after the years. What we had resolved to do a decade and a half before—to keep the springtime magic of inloveness—we had done. If last year had been a wavering, almost a forgetfulness, now the love was pure as fire. We had had what we had chosen, not business success or scholarly acclaim but a great love. And, under God, perhaps that love would save us.

But it was not to be. After those few good days, she began to go swiftly down hill; and pain came. We knew she was going to die. Once in a confusion of pain, she said pitifully: "Please let me go home." But after tortured days, the pain diminished, though she was not actually better. One day—though I didn't know it until afterwards—she told the Rector: "It will be one more week—maybe a little longer." That same night I jotted down about my time with her: "She was dear and sweet, wanting to be kissed."

A night or two later, she said to me: "You must hold on to your promise not to follow me, not to die by your own hand." She was, of course, thinking of our old high resolution to go together—even as I had been thinking of it, haunted by it. The resolution to take *Grey Goose* to sea and sink her. Even now we could still do it.

But I said, "I will keep my promise. I will."

"Maybe God will take you," she said, a little hopefully. "Maybe He will take you at the same moment: that would be sweet."

"I pray He does," I said. "But it will not seem long, if He doesn't."

One evening—it was just past the middle of January—I was with her, as always. We prayed together and talked a bit, and I read her one or two short things from C. S.

Lewis and George MacDonald. Then she asked me to read the "Song of the Two Lovers." I read it, and she said, "Oh, I love it!" No one said anything for a moment. I sat there holding the poem, and she looked at me, her eyes still bright and beautiful in her somewhat ravaged face. She smiled a little and whispered: "My golden one!" Her eyes closed, and we remembered together that flight in the dawn, with the lilac petals streaming out.

Then she seemed drowsy, and I said perhaps I should go soon and let her get a good night's sleep. She said she thought that would be nice. Then she said sleepily, "When you come tomorrow, bring some 'proper tea.'" "I'll do it," I said. "Go to sleep now, dearling." I held her a little while, warm and drowsy, and kissed her; and she snuggled in my arms. Then I stroked her brow and hair until she was asleep, and went quietly out. I blinked the instrument lights as usual, even though I knew she was asleep. After all, she might have awakened.

At three in the morning, the telephone. I think I knew before my eyes were open. It was the hospital. Davy was dying. Her pulse was slowing. There could be no rally. I asked how long. They thought several hours. It had come at last. I took the time to wash and shave, wondering if it was right to use those few minutes that I might have with her. But I had to come to her—I had to face what must be faced—clean.

It was a bitter winter night. The MG's top was down, but I left it so, and with Flurry raced towards the hospital through deserted streets. Now would be the time for God to cause the steering to give way and take me, too. I felt an immense temptation to swerve into a wall; but I had promised.

Davy said to the nurse that I had come. The nurse thought her mind was wandering. Then I walked in. Davy had heard our recognition signal, whistled in the night. The nurse departed and the hospital staff left us alone. Once St. Joan just put her head in and looked lovingly towards the bed. I nodded, and she went away again.

Davy was perfectly aware and rational. I thought flickeringly that, at least, our prayer that she should not die in coma but aware had been granted. She was not in pain; she was simply slowing to a stop.

After we had greeted each other and I had kissed her, she said she was thirsty, and I reached past the yellow roses for the carafe and glass. And I gave her a cup of water in the night—our old symbol of courtesy. Then I prayed one of the prayers we always prayed:

Lighten our darkness, we beseech thee, O Lord; and by thy great mercy defend us from all perils and dangers of this night; for the love of thy only Son, our Saviour, Jesus Christ. Amen.

Then Davy prayed. She prayed aloud for the hospital and the doctors by name and the nurses, including St. Joan, asking God's blessing on them all, in Jesus's name. I stroked her hand, looking at her face. I said another prayer; and at the end of it I said: "Davy—I love you for ever." She whispered: "Oh my dearest!"

There was a long silence, I still stroking her hand. Then she said in a stronger voice: "Oh God, take me." I knew then with certainty that she understood that she was dying. I said: "Go under the Love, dearling. Go under the Mercy." She murmured: "Amen." And then she said: "Thank you, blessed dearling." I kissed her very lightly, so as not to interfere with her breathing.

Then we were silent. Her lips were slightly parted and her eyes were half-open. Every now and then I dipped a swab into the water and moistened her lips. There was no response. I knew with tearless clarity that she was going. I continued to hold her hand.

St. Joan came quietly in and gave me Davy's wedding ring, taken off when her fingers became so thin. I took Joan's hand for a minute, and then she went quietly out. I looked at the ring with its ten tiny diamonds—the ten months we had known each other before we were secretly wed in the thunderstorm. Then I put it on Davy's third finger, saying in a low voice: "With this ring I thee wed . . . for all eternity." I do not know whether she heard; but I think she did, for her fingers tightened the least bit.

Time passed, a long time; and there was no change. Each time she breathed there was a faint moan. The sky was beginning to lighten a bit in the east. I thought she might be unconscious.

Suddenly her fingers tightened on mine. She said in a clear weak voice: "Oh, dearling, look . . ." She didn't go on, if there was more. I *knew* that if I said, "What is it?" she would make an effort and go on; but I did not do so. I don't know why I didn't. She might have been saying "look" as one who suddenly understands something, or as one who beholds—what? Her voice was so frail, I could not tell which it was. I wished very much to know; I could have asked her; I did not. And I shall not know this side of eternity, for they were her last words: "Oh, dearling, look."

More time passed. The sky was becoming bright. I was now nearly certain that she was unconscious. I still held her hand, her left hand with the ring on it. I did not wish to hold her to life; I merely wished to be *with* her. Every now and then I said in a low voice: "I am here, Davy; I am with you." But there was no response.

Then she stirred. There was no change at all in her half-parted lips or eyes or the hand I held. But then her other hand and arm came slowly up from her side. I could not think what she was doing. The hand moved slowly across her. It found my face. She touched my brow and hair, then each eye in turn. Then my mouth. Her fingers moved to each corner of my mouth, as we had always done. And I gave her fingers little corner-of-the-mouth kisses, as we had always done. Then her arm fell slowly back. Past seeing and past speaking, with the last of her failing strength, she had said goodbye.

In one of her earliest letters, when we were first in love, she had spoken of "the gentle awkward yearning I feel for you, just to touch your face." And touching my face, in the old way, was her last act in this world.

The dawn, the dawn we loved so well, was radiant in

the sky. The most glorious dawn for weeks. As the light had grown stronger, she had grown weaker. Perhaps she was taken up into the light, for now the faint moan in her breathing ceased. Then her breathing slowed. My face was close to hers. Then each of three breaths was lighter than the one before. There were no more. I knew on the instant of her dying that she was dead. A little dribble came out of her mouth. I wiped it away, and I shut her mouth and her eyes.

She could not say it to me, so I said it, whispered it, to her: "All shall be most well, my dearling." Then I kissed her lightly and stood up.

As I stood there in that suddenly empty room, I was suddenly swept with a tide of absolute *knowing* that Davy still was. I do not mean that I thought her body might still live; I knew it didn't. But past faith and belief, I *knew* quite overwhelmingly that she herself—her soul—still was.

The door opened and the head nurse came in, and I formed the words, "She's gone," without speaking. The nurse took her wrist for a moment, nodded, and went away.

I began to pack her things. Nurses offered to do it, but I did it. An orderly came and took the box down to the car. Dr. Craddock came in, his face kind. I told him that I was quite certain that no doctor could have fought more skilfully for a patient's life, and we shook hands. Just for one second my control broke, and I was nearly torn in two by an enormous sob. I said I was sorry, and he went away.

I looked at Davy, lying there, a last time. She looked as though she were asleep, and I had always especially loved her, warm and relaxed and asleep. I kissed her still-warm lips. Then I took one of the yellow roses and drove away with Flurry in that bright morning. I did not know it, but St. Joan, off duty and not allowed to stay, was keeping vigil by her window in the nurses' house to see my car go.

The next day a small box, very light, was brought to me: it contained her ashes. I looked at them that night,

clean and white. All I could think of was: Of her bones
are coral made.

Late in the night, I went out to the MG with the box,
leaving Flurry at home. The top was still down, and I
left it so because that was the way it was when we drove
in May. I headed for St. Stephen's under an almost star-
less sky. Once, long before, we had had an argument over
Browning's poem, "The Last Ride Together," and I had
finally convinced her, over stubborn resistance, that a
"ride" meant horses, not a carriage. I smiled faintly, there
in the MG, at the memory: she *liked* the carriage. But
now we were having a sort of a last ride together, and
it was a carriage, after all, or at least the MG. As we
turned into the St. Stephen's road, I said lightly: "You
win, dearling."

At St. Stephen's I turned in, under the oaks. I could
see only one or two dim stars through the bare twisting
branches. I got out and picked up the box. There was
something else, dimly, on the seat. It was the rose, so I
took that, too, and walked into the graveyard. Still holding the box, I knelt a moment by the old stone cross and
prayed. Something cold touched my neck: snowflakes
were drifting down. I stood up. It was cold—the dead of
winter. I opened the box and began to scatter the ashes,
using a sower's motion. When I had done, the flakes were
coming down hard. I left the rose on the old cross. I said
aloud: "Go under the Mercy." Then I went away, and
her ashes were covered with the blanket of the snow.
The deathly snows.

⸫ VIII ⸫

The Way of Grief

DEATHS

My dearest died at dawn: to some far strand
A lonely soul sailed down the long bright seas.
Alone I sowed her ashes under trees,
Cold, starlit-bare, and sad—where hand in hand,
When moonlight haloed churchyard oaks in May,
We'd knelt beneath an old stone cross to pray.

The grim and almost fierce will to do all and be all for
Davy that I had held before me like a sword for half a
year became now, upon her death, tired though I was, a
no less resolute will to face the whole meaning of loss,
to drink the cup of grief to the lees. I came, thereby, to
see something of the nature of loss and grief.

First there were the immediate duties. Davy and I had
done it our way: the night drive to St. Stephen's—our
last "ride" together—and, as I said in my poem, the sow-
ing of the ashes. And I would face the grief alone; I
would not show it before others. I felt I must allow the
sorrowing Rector a small service for her at Grace Church,
and another with both Rectors at St. Stephen's. But Davy
and I, outdoors alone in the night, had had our service.

The next day I taught my classes. By then I had
written some sixty letters, each one ending: "And in
Davy's words: 'All shall be most well.'" I caused it to
be known that I did not want condolence calls, and I
believe some people thought me callous. I ordered tract
racks for both churches in her name, as she had asked

me to do. I went through her things like a storm—a sorrowing storm—giving to friends what she had told me to give them. And I set about keeping another promise to her: transferring her hundreds of marginal notes from the pages of her father's crumbling old Bible to our newer one.

The Christian student group came again, week by week, to Mole End. I saw a letter written by one of the boys, Bill, in the group to a friend, describing his reaction to the news of Davy's death. He wandered blindly, half-stunned, into the college library, thinking: "She no longer exists in the world. I can't ever again drop in on a rainy afternoon and sip tea with her and talk. The question kept beating through my mind—'Why did she have to die? She was so young and so good—why?' " In the library he saw two girls of the group and they smiled at him. How could they? he wondered. Then he found himself smiling, understanding suddenly what their smiles meant: "Davy IS." And then: "We all three clasped hands and smiled at each other. And I think Davy smiled at us that day."

I could smile, too. And I was conscious of a sort of amazement that the sky was still blue and a steak still tasted good. How could things go *on* when the world had come to an end? How could things—how could *I*—go on in this void? How could one person, not very big, leave an emptiness that was galaxy-wide? Everything—every object—was pervaded by the void. I could teach my classes smilingly, even to calmly reading a poem about loss; and I perceived that in teaching one part of the mind—the subjective part—is cut off. But that first day of teaching after the St. Stephen's night, when I left the class to go home, I saw the MG, small and somehow forlorn, invaded by that void, and I was barely able to get off campus before the tears came. But I observed next day that the MG did not have that effect again. There were, though, thousands of other things and memories, *each* of which must be seen once in that piercingly bleak emptiness.

Along with the emptiness, which is what I mean by loss, and along with the grief—loss and grief are not the same thing—I kept wanting to *tell* her about it. We always told each other—that was what sharing was—and now this huge thing was happening to me, and I couldn't tell her. Someone speaking of the pain of stopping smoking remarked: If only I could have a cigarette while I suffer! I sometimes thought I could bear the loss and grief if only I could tell her about it. So I did. I wrote to her in the quiet evenings—I did not go out at all—and told her. Writing a letter is a real form of conversation in which the image of a distant person is held in one's mind. I could not have spoken aloud to thin air with any sense of reality, nor could I now write to her, but then I could really speak to her in letters. I did not save them or reread them, those long letters of our companionship, but I could write them—to her. Whether she read them, over my shoulder perhaps, is of course a different matter.

I dreamt of her, not ever as much as I wished to do, but about once a month for over a year. The first dream was in the first fortnight. In it she was ill as she had been in hospital, but across the mountains there was a doctor who could heal her. And I was carrying her in my arms over mountain passes. It was dark and raining, but I did not mind. She was light in my arms and, beneath her hood, she was—we both were—merry. That was all. A purely happy dream. The warm reality of Davy. Of course I wept when I woke—and all but prayed to dream again. But three or four weeks—never more or less—must pass. All the dreams were joyous, or a mixture of joy and pain. Ordinary dreamlike dreams. Full of love and tenderness and comradeship but never sexual. In one dream she was well and we were going gaily off in the MG when, sickeningly, her illness returned; and we held each other in desperate love. Joy and pain. In another dream we were merely running hand in hand across the great sweep of the Glenmerle lawn.

In a letter to Davy I contemplated loss and grief. The death of any familiar person—the death, even, of a dog or cat—whether loved or not leaves an emptiness. The great tree goes down and leaves an empty place against the sky. If the person is deeply loved and deeply familiar the void seems greater than all the world remaining. Under the surface of the visible world, there is an echoing hollowness, an aching void—and it cuts one off from the beloved. She is as remote as the stars. But grief is a form of love—the longing for the dear face, the warm hand. It is the remembered reality of the beloved that calls it forth. For an instant she is *there*, and the void denied. It is not the grief, involving that momentary reality, that cuts one off from the beloved but the void that is loss. In the end one can no longer summon forth that reality, and then one's tears dry up. But while it lasts, it is a shield against the void; and by the time the grief wanes, the terrible emptiness of loss has given way to a new world that does not contain the shape of the beloved figure.

But that waning was far into the future. In my first letter to Davy I wrote of the blanket of snow at St. Stephen's and added, a bit sentimentally: "May it keep you warm, my darling." A fortnight after her death, I wrote, "It seems impossible that two weeks ago you were alive: it seems infinitely longer. It also seems impossible that you are dead. This is an act I am going through. Later we shall laugh about it, you and I." Although it brought tears to my eyes, I sometimes sang our Oxford song about the Lady sweet and kind and how "I did but see her passing by/And yet I love her till I die." The tears came freely, and I did not attempt to refrain them when I was alone. Indeed, for over a year, there was no day I did not weep, and I did not find that tears cut me off from her. It was the tearless void that severed us at times.

Mostly, though, we were, in some way, together. She was not (to my knowledge or perception) with me in ghostly form, although I later came to think she had been perhaps. But in a not-at-all mystical sense she lived, she was vivid and alive, in me. Our love continued. The final severance was not yet.

One of the letters I wrote the day after her death was to C. S. Lewis. I told him how she died and how I meant to scatter her ashes at St. Stephen's, as she and I had planned. But we had also thought it might be fitting for a handful of those ashes to be scattered at little Binsey church near Oxford. Would he—Lewis—do it? There was no reply to my letter, and I decided he must be away from Oxford.

I, therefore, entrusted the tiny packet to my friend, Edmund Dews, who, indeed, had first taken us to Binsey-by-the-well. Edmund had already written of Davy's "valiant and painful struggle, too far away for her to comfort me." And then of his grief at her death, ending his letter: "And I grip your hand." Now on a mild and misty winter day Edmund walked across the meadows to Binsey and scattered the ashes, saying "Under the Mercy," as I had asked, and "watched by a dozen brown-and-white cows, waiting by the gate to be admitted into the farmyard."

But Lewis was not away: he was waiting for the ashes. His letter had been lost in the post. Now he heard from Edmund. In my letter to Lewis I had spoken of my moment by Davy's body of absolute knowing that she still was, and of my curiously consoling thought that nothing now could mar our love: the manuscript had now gone to the Printer.

Lewis replied to a further letter from me, replied from Magdalene, Cambridge:

I heard from your friend about 2 days ago, and today I have got yr. letter of Feb. 5. I am most distressed to find that my answer to your previous letter has never reached you; particularly since its miscarriage has left you in doubt whether I wd. have accepted the v. sacred office of scattering the ashes. I wd. have liked to do (if you can understand) for the v. reason that I wd. not have liked doing it, since a deep spiritual *gaucherie* makes [me] uneasy in any ceremonial act; and I wd. have wished in that way to be honoured with a share, however tiny, in this Cross. All you told me in your previous letter & all you tell me in this moves me deeply and it is a high privilege to be admitted to such a beautiful

death, an *act* wh. consummates (not, as so often, an
event wh. merely stops) the earthly life. And how you
re-assure me when, to describe your own state, you use
the simple, obvious, yet now so rare, word *sad*. Neither
more nor less nor other than sad. It suggests a clean
wound—much here for tears, but "nothing but good
and fair." And I am sure it is never sadness—a proper,
straight natural response to loss—that does people harm,
but all the other things, all the resentment, dismay,
doubt and self-pity with wh. it is usually complicated.
I feel (indeed I tried to say something about it in that
lost letter) v. strongly what you say about the "curious
consolation" that "nothing now can mar" your joint
lives. I sometimes wonder whether bereavement is not,
at bottom, the easiest and least perilous of the ways in
wh. men lose the happiness of youthful love. For I
believe it must *always* be lost in some way: every merely
natural love has to be crucified before it can achieve
resurrection and the happy *old* couples have come
through a difficult death and re-birth. But far more have
missed the re-birth. Your MS, as you well say, has now
gone safe to the Printer.

It is remarkable (I have experienced it), that sense
that the dead person *is*. And also, I have felt, is active:
can sometimes do more for you now than before—as if
God gave them, as a kind of birthday present on arrival,
some great blessing to the beloved they have left behind.

Be careful of your own bodily health. You must be,
physically, v. tired, much more tired than you know.
Above all, don't yield to the feeling that such things
"don't matter *now*." You must remain, as she wishes, a
good *instrument* for all heavenly impulses to work on,
and the body is part of the instrument.

I shall be nervous about all letters now that one (and
at such a moment) has gone astray. If this reaches you,
a line in answer will re-assure me.

You are always in my prayers, even whenever I wake
in the night. Keep me in yours.

Under the Omnipotence

It had never occurred to me that I was having a right
response to death by being merely, though of course
immensely, sad. Grief unalloyed. But the radical proposition in that letter was that death might be the "easiest

and least perilous of the ways" to lose one's love. The easiest! But loves "must *always* be lost." The proposition contained a sort of comfort, though I was far from accepting it. Still, I thought about it. The rebirth of love he spoke of, wouldn't we as Christians achieve that, even in life? But he said *death* and rebirth. Yes, but what about dying to self? Look at Davy. Look at—um, well, look, at least, at how devoted I was to love. And at the hospital —no lovers could have loved more. Yet could it be that death looming had brought about the rebirth? What if she had not died? It must be thought about.

C. S. Lewis was to be *the* friend in my loss and grief, the one hand in mine as I walked through a dark and desolate night. Other friends gave me love, and it was a fire to warm me. But Lewis was the friend I needed, the friend who would go with me down to the bedrock of meaning. I told him the insights that came to me through my grief observed—the title of the book he would write on his own future bereavement—and he gave me not only love but wisdom and understanding and, when necessary, severity.

One of the greatest occurrences of my own grief was the strange thing that began to happen within a day or two of her death. It was the flooding back to me of all the other Davys I had known. She had been in this year of her dying the Davy she had become—the Christian Davy of Oxford and since. Even when we had read about Glenmerle days under the oaks, she had been the Davy she had become. But now the young girl of Glenmerle, the blithe spirit of the Islands, the helmsman of the schooner—all were equally present. They had been gone—except perhaps for those fragile days of heartbreaking young love during the coma. Now they were all with me—for ever. The *wholeness* of Davy. That wholeness can *only* be gained by death, I believe. In writing to Lewis of my understanding of this astonishing phenomenon, I used the analogy of reading a novel like *David Copperfield* that covers many years. In that book one follows the boy David running away to his Aunt Betsey Trotwood, the youth David loving Dora, the mature

David with Agnes. While one reads, chapter by chapter, even as one lives one's own life week by week, David is what he is at that particular point in the book's time. But then, when one shuts the book at the end, *all* the Davids—small boy, youth, man—are equally close: and, indeed, are *one*. The *whole* David. One is then, with reference to the book's created time, in an eternity, seeing it all in one's own Now, even as God in His eternal Now sees the whole of history that was and is and will be. But if, as the result of death, I was now seeing the whole Davy at once, I was having a heavenly or eternal vision of her. Only, in heaven I would have not vision only but *her*—whole.

All this, which seemed to me a major insight into the nature of bereavement, I put to Lewis, along with some ironic comments on the change in my once-famous "luck." Long before, friends had thought me lucky: my First Honours in college (because I had been lucky enough to get the right questions), my happy marriage (because I had been lucky enough to find the right girl). But, since Christianity, several things had not been so fortunate, culminating in Davy's death. I sent him a photograph of Davy, perhaps in hospital; and asked him about Cambridge.

Lewis replied:

I was v. glad to get your letter of Feb. 14. And here "luck" worked the other way. It had come unstuck and the envelope was open, but the letter inside, intact.— Your real or supposed change of luck since your conversion (whatever it may really mean) is an old story: read Jeremiah XLIV 15–18. And I have seen it laid down by a modern spiritual author (whose name I forget) that the experience is to be expected. You remember the vision of Our Lord that said to St. Theresa on some frightful occasion "This is how I always treat my friends." (I must not conceal her answer, "Then, Lord, it is not surprising that You have so few.")—What you say about the total Jean being apprehensible since the moment-by-moment Jean has been withdrawn (backed by the v. good analogy of the novel page-by-page and the novel after you've read it) is most true and important. I see no reason why we shd. not regard it as what St. Paul calls an *arrabon* or earnest of the mode in wh. all can reveal themselves to all in heaven.—Oh, and thanks v. much for the photo, tho' to me (you see it with other eyes) it appears not v. like, far from flattering.—Do you know Coventry Patmore's *Angel in the House* and (still more, but the first is to be read as a prelude) *Love's Victory*. They deal superbly with some of the experiences you are having.—About letters, someone told me that surface mail, tho' slower, was safer than air & more reliable. Is this untrue? Yes, I have gone to a newly created Chair of Med. and Renaissance English at Cambridge. The atmosphere here is slightly more Christian and far more kindly and gentle & less hard boiled than at Oxford.—An R.C. tells me that they in general forbid cremation because, tho' it by no means logically implies, yet in uneducated minds it tends to *go with*, disbelief in the resurrection of the body. But they allow it when there is any special reason—e.g. a plague. I don't think, myself, it matters one way or the other. God bless you. Do drop the "Mr." before my name.

Accordingly, I called him Lewis thenceforth, until, later, he said to call him Jack.

The loss of Davy, after the intense sharing and closeness of the years, the loss and grief was, quite simply, the most immense thing I had ever known. Long before, when we were raising the Shining Barrier, we had been haunted by the thought of parting through death. If we became so close, how should one of us bear the death of the other? So we had planned the last long dive—going together—and thus completed the Barrier. But God had breached the Shining Barrier: and I was having to bear the unbearable. If I must bear it, though, I *would* bear it —find the whole meaning of it, taste the whole of it. I was driven by an unswerving determination to plumb the depths as well as to know the Davy I loved: to understand why she had lived and died, to learn from sorrow

whatever it had to teach. It was a kind of faithfulness to
her. I would *not* run away from grief; I would *not* try
to hold on to it when—if, unbelievably—it passed.

As a way of understanding, I planned a study of our
years together, a study that I later came to call the
Illumination of the Past. In preparation for it I wrote to
many people asking to be given or lent Davy's letters to
them. Meanwhile, I was finishing up the notes in her
old Bible—learning much about her in the process—and
doing other tasks I had set myself, often working with
tears blurring my eyes. I was also rereading the books
that had meant the most to us. While I worked and
wept, I thought about our life together and the meaning
of it, the meaning in relation to God.

In March I was thinking a good deal about her offering-
up her life for me, and then my offering-up as I drove
to Charlottesville to tell her of her death—and the rainbow over towards the Blue Mountains just afterward.
That offering-up, in its pure submission to God's will
and its selfless love for Davy, was perhaps my nearest
approach to holiness—and then the rainbow. It's hard,
since Noah, not to see a rainbow as a sign of hope. And
at such a moment. But she had died. Did it mean, then,
that she was to have what would be her best good—her
death? Or was it meaningless?

I wrote to Lewis about it. I also sent him a letter I'd
found written by Davy to Lewis but never sent, presumably because I had written to him about the same
thing, the matter of homosexual students. I also spoke of
perhaps publishing my thesis as by her as well as me,
because Davy would have liked that.

Lewis replied in early April with a meaningful com-
ment on the rainbow sign:

> It was a strange experience to get a letter from Jean
> this morning. I return it. You will see that it deals with
> a problem on which you also wrote to me, probably at
> about the same time. Indeed her reason for not sending
> it might be the discovery that you had done, or were
> about to do, the same.

I can't now remember what I said in my lost letter about the "Signs." My general view is that, once we have accepted an omniscient & providential God, the distinction we used to draw between the significant and the fortuitous must either break down or be restated in some v. much subtler form. If an event coming about in the ordinary course of nature becomes to me the occasion of hope and faith and love or increased efforts after virtue, do we suppose that this result was unforeseen by, or is indifferent to, God? Obviously not. What we should have called its fortuitous effects must have been present to Him for all eternity. And indeed, we can't suppose God saying (as a human artist might) "That effect, though it has turned out rather well, was, I must admit, no part of my original design." Then the total act of creation, including *our own* creation (wh. is going on all the time) meets us, doesn't it? in every event at every moment: the act of a Person dealing with persons and knowing what He does. Thus I wouldn't now be bothered by a man who said to me "This, which you mistake for grace, is really the good functioning of your digestion." Does my digestion fall outside God's act? He made and allowed to me my colon as much as my guardian angel.

I guess (I don't know) that Trevelyan is a temperamentally pious Agnostic-with-hopes of the best, old liberal kind. He's certainly not a churchman; I have heard him say so.

I give no advice about the thesis, and I think you ought to be guided by ordinary academic considerations. Forgive me for suggesting that the form "what Jean would have liked" could come to have its dangers. The real question is what she wills *now*; and you may be sure her will is now one with God's. A "sovereignty in the pluperfect subjunctive" is often a snare. The danger is that of confusing your love for her (gradually—as the years pass) with your love for a period in your own past; and of trying to preserve the past in a way in wh. it can't be preserved. Death—corruption—resurrection is the true rhythm: not the pathetic, horrible practice of mummification. Sad you must be at present. You can't develop a false sense of a duty to cling to sadness if—and when, for *nature* will not preserve any psychological state forever—sadness begins to vanish? There is great good in bearing sorrow patiently: I don't know that there is any virtue in sorrow just as such. It is a Christian duty, as you know, for everyone to be as happy as he can. But you know all this already.

All love.

What Lewis said about the breaking down of the distinction between the significant and the fortuitous struck deeply into my mind. If he was right—and in reason he was—then *nothing*, nothing at all, was without meaning. The world was charged with meaning. The rainbow's significance—since Davy *had* died—could only be, I thought, that her death had been, in some way as yet unknown to me, her best good. At the time of the rainbow, though, I could not have known its meaning beyond a sense of indefinite assurance. Signs must be read with caution. The history of Christendom is replete with instances of people who misread the signs.

If I may glance ahead, almost a year ahead from this point in the chronological narrative, there occurred then such a misreading of God's meaning, and it is not without significance concerning my relationship to God in this whole period of loss and grief. At that time, a year later, I was considering my own future, and praying about it. Should I stick to my "tent-making" at the College, or make tents at Wabash, or, so to speak, make sails by cutting all ties and going back to *Grey Goose*? I wanted God to tell me. One evening in the country, a calm and peaceful evening with the sun going down behind clouds and a golden sky, I was praying for that guidance, asking Him to tell me, somehow, what He wanted me to do. In that instant a sudden sharp wind came out of nowhere, a tremendous gust, and was gone again.

I remembered what Lewis had said about the significant and the fortuitous. Did this wind mean God's promise to give me the guidance? I thought it did. I suppose I might have interpreted it as meaning a schooner under the wind—or God's saying that if I did go to sea He would blow the sticks out of the yacht. But I took it to be a promise of guidance.

But no guidance came, and God seemed remote. The world was still empty without Davy, and now God seemed to have withdrawn, too. My sense of desolation increased. God could not be as loving as He was supposed to be, or—the other alternative. One sleepless night, drawing on to morning, I was overwhelmed with a sense of cosmos empty of God as well as Davy. "All right," I muttered to myself. "To hell with God. I'm not going to believe this damned rubbish any more. Lies, all lies. I've been had." Up I sprang and rushed out to the country. This was the end of God. Ha!

And then I found I *could not* reject God. I could not. I cannot explain this. One discovers one cannot move a boulder by trying with all one's strength to do it. I discovered—without any sudden influx of love or faith—that I could not reject Christianity. Why I don't know. There it was. I could not. That was an end to it.

An hour later I recalled that I had *chosen* to believe, pledged my fealty to the King. That was another reason why I couldn't reject God, not without being forsworn.

I wrote to Lewis about the gust of wind and its aftermath. I also told him of remembering what now seemed to me a wrong I had done someone in the past, and what I had now done to make amends. And I spoke of coming to England.

Lewis replied:

I am v. glad to hear of the righted wrong and still more to hear that you are re-visiting England. We must have some good, long talks together and perhaps we shall both get high. At the moment the really important thing seems to be that you were brought to realize the impossibility (strict sense) of rejecting Christ. Of course He *must* often seem to us to be playing fast and loose with us. The adult must seem to mislead the child, and the Master the dog. They misread the signs. Their ignorance and their wishes twist everything. You are so sure you know what the promise promised! And the danger is that when what He means by "wind" appears you will ignore it because it is not what you thought it would be—as He Himself was rejected because He

was not like the Messiah the Jews had in mind. But I
am, I fancy, repeating things I said before. I look forward very much to our meeting again. God bless you.

Apart from leaping to conclusions about "signs," the
significance of this brief aberration of despair, never to
happen again, lay in its indication of how certainly I
belonged in the army of the King. I was not allowed to
resign. But if this was the way of it now, it was the way of
it in that first spring, to which I now return, when I had
no thought of quitting God's camp, which was also
Davy's.

As March moved into April—a quarter of a year since
I had last seen Davy—I was at last ready to begin my
major effort of the bereavement: the Illumination of the
Past, as I came to call it. To begin with it was simply
a study of all our years. The other tasks I had set myself
were done. I had assembled, and put into chronological
order, hundreds of letters Davy had written over the
years. I had the diaries and journals we had kept. I had
her paintings done in their various periods and our photograph album. But I had gone further than these helps:
I had searched out and bought recordings of music we
had liked or merely chanced to listen to a good deal in
some period, knowing how evocative music is, and I had
even bought small flasks of various colognes and scents
she had worn in various periods, including especially
English lavender. I had all our favourite poems of the
years. I had already been reading meaningful books from
our past, but I had saved some of the dearest ones, such
as *Peter Ibbetson*, until now.

Every day after classes, sitting in the great silent living-
room at Mole End, with the appropriate paintings
propped up round me and the record player ready to go
at a touch, I sought the past. The diaries and journals
made the central thread, of course: most years were very
completely recorded. But I would pause to read a letter
she had written or read a poem, perhaps aloud, or to
listen to music. Or to look anew at a painting and study
photographs. I made a few notes as I went along, some-

times of particular insights about the past. Then at night
I would write to Davy about them: I was still writing *to*
her, still with a sense of writing to a real person. I even
hoped—hoped intensely—that she would, somehow, know
what I said.

I travelled through the past at the rate of a month or
two a day. I could not go much faster and still listen to
the music—often whole symphonies—and read the poems.
The books, novels and the like, I read at night, after I
had written to her.

Another reason for not going faster was that what I
was doing was emotionally exhausting. There was no
day, no hour, without tears, as I had known there would
be. The music tore me with longing for her. And yet
there was joy, too. And humour—often I laughed aloud,
only to be crying an instant later.

It came to me quite early on in this study of times past
that she—that Davy—did, in fact, know what I was doing
and approved. And even more strongly I received, or
seemed to receive, an intimation that she, wherever she
was and in whatever state, was missing me, too. I have
no evidence for the truth of this beyond my own growing
conviction that it was so. Naturally, with Davy so vividly
present in my mind, and so loved, I might well be in a
psychic state to receive such intimations, if they do, in
fact, happen—or to persuade myself that I was having
them, of course. But I heard no voices nor saw any beloved ghost (much as I should have welcomed her); and
yet I remain convinced of my two intimations: that she
did, in truth, know and approve of the Illumination of
the Past; and that she was longing for me as well as I
for her.

In a pocket-diary note that survives, I wrote: "I am
up to Davy's visit to Grand Canyon, and I am reading
The Transients. Then comes *Peter Ibbetson*. And I love
you so much I could die. How I hope you know!"

In my letters to her I accepted that these intimations
were true. Also in those letters were the insights that
came to me from our past, seen in the light of all that
was to be. I saw where we had made mistakes and where

we seemed sometimes to have chosen so rightly that it was as though we had some dim inkling from the God we were yet to discover.

One insight from the past, which I might have closed my mind to but for Christianity was not quite so shocking as it would have been if Davy in that last year or so had not seemed increasingly to accept St. Paul's dictum on the relationship of husband and wife: that the man is head of the wife *as* Christ is head of the Church. Although we should fiercely have denied it, except perhaps for Davy in that last year, I saw that I *had* exercised a sort of headship—in the sense of the initiatory or leadership rôle—that was accepted, even *desired*, by Davy without either of us being aware of it. It had been loving and gentle, all decisions were discussed, there was never a hint of command, and yet, despite mutual tenderness and deference, it was, I now saw, *there*: that veiled and loving headship. We had eschewed husbandly authority from the first, Davy was combative and intelligent, we believed everything a modern feminist could have urged: yet something of headship had all along been there. Having known one woman deeply, having myself made every effort to see with a woman's eyes, I could not now believe that my subtle headship or Davy's acceptance of it was merely conditioning. Now I wrote to her about it, wondering without decision whether, despite all feminist denial, such a relationship were not inbuilt in the creation and *effectively* denied—which, after all, we, loving so deeply, had not been able to do—only at heavy cost to love.

The Illumination of the Past was a quite incredible experience. An analogy might be something like this: one is seated in a dark room around the walls of which is a complex mural—the past—and in one's hand is a tiny, brilliant spotlight. As the spotlight touches the mural, one scene leaps into vivid colour and illumination. Foot by foot the spotlight creeps about the walls, down the vista of the years.

As I travelled through the past, month by month, year by year, so it leaped into life. I remembered not only that which was written down but a hundred things besides. Most astonishing of all, I found myself *thinking* as I had thought then. I was a pagan again; I could hardly believe I should become Christian—nor did I like the prospect. Everything—the written word, the music, the scents, the pictures—carried me into the particular period I was illuminating. I was not merely looking at it: *we*, Davy and I, were living there again. Without exaggeration, it was one of the two or three most amazing experiences of my life. Even though I had planned it, I had not had the faintest idea that the past could be recreated with such extraordinary brilliance and reality.

Apart from what I learned of the past, the Illumination was, despite all the tears, worth doing for the joy. I spoke earlier of being desolated by the MG, little and lonely, as I came out to it on the day following the St. Stephen's night, adding that *it* never called forth the tears again. And of course going through her clothes, as well as that old Bible, brought forth tears often. Now I learned a great principle of the way that grief operates. As I went through the past, day by day, ten thousand forgotten or half-forgotten memories of Davy came to me with all the colour and vividness of life. For one instant *that* particular Davy—gay or mocking or inquisitive or adventurous or loving—stands before me, warm and real and alive. I respond to her with a surge of love and pure joy. That is followed an instant later by the awful awareness that *this* Davy, too, is dead. Then, irresistibly, come the tears—the tears for this particular Davy. Until now *she* has not been touched by death—and she, too, must die. On the day following, if I reread that bit in the Journal, she will not stand before me: there will be no tears. Each memory calls forth warm living reality *once*: it is followed by another little death and the tears.

One day, for example, we were living again in the Virginian farmhouse, Horsebite Hall, with Gypsy and her puppies. Down on the Eastern Shore the schooner was a-building. On this particular day, at this particular moment, I looked out of the kitchen window, and there was Davy coming along the fence with a small basket.

She had gone to fetch the eggs from the henhouse. I went out to meet her in the mild spring weather. She smiles at me. I catch her in my arms and hold her close and kiss the top of her head: her hair is sunny and warm and sweet. I have not thought of this moment since her death or, indeed, for years. Now for one lovely moment she is alive and warm in my arms, and I smell and feel her hair. Then the little death and the tears. I shall always love the memory, but I shall never again be able to evoke this Davy. But tomorrow, perhaps, I shall be summoning up memories on the decks of *Grey Goose*.

Some people run away from grief, go on world cruises or move to another town. But they do not escape, I think. The memories, unbidden, spring into their minds, scattered perhaps over the years. There is, maybe, something to be said for facing them all deliberately and straightaway. At all events, it is what I did in the Illumination of the Past.

Davy and I, after a journey in which we had seen some old friends that we hadn't seen for a decade or longer, observed and discussed a curious thing. On first remeeting someone not seen for years, one may feel: Who is this stranger, grown so fat, so cynical, so something? But in a few minutes, whatever the changes, one finds the person one knew. The unique person abides. Always. The peculiar quality of "John-ness" in John or "Mary-ness" in Mary. And we decided that that unchanging "John-ness" was the soul.

Now I was discovering it anew in Davy, going through the years: I was touching her soul, the very essence of her being. I described earlier how *all* the Davys began to flow back to me shortly after her death, and I recovered the wholeness of her. Now with the Illumination of the Past the process was completed. It is sometimes said that the fourth dimension is time or duration: one does not see a person or thing in any one instant of seeing. And I was seeing Davy in all her years—I even had her baby and childhood pictures and scribblings. As nearly as a lover can do, I was seeing the whole of her—a wholeness I would never lose—and knowing her soul.

It is often said that both Heaven and Hell are retro-active, that *all* of one's life will eventually be known to have been one or the other. In the co-inherence of lovers I had seen in hospital the Christ in her—*the* Co-inherence. Did she see Him in me, I wonder? More dimly perhaps. At all events, I was now seeing in the Illumination of the Past the Christ in her, even in that "playmate of lost pagan years" of my poem, the *Heaven* in her, from the beginning. The pain of the thousand deaths of past Davys in earthly flesh was worthwhile, not only because the joy outweighed the pain, but because I touched her soul. I knew her, at least partially, as her—and my—Incarnate Lord must do.

As the gentle heartbreaking spring—April and our magic Maytime—came on, I went more and more out into the flowering country to walk or just sit and think, alone with her. The Illumination of the Past was still going forward, though approaching its end, but, still, I spent hundreds of hours in the country, going especially to the deserted house we had called Ladywood. I developed a fancy that Davy was in the wind—perhaps she was—and the light touch of the breeze on my face seemed her touch. But there were no tears, ever, in the country: there were too many intimations of heaven. I thought, as I walked along country roads or sat in the doorway of Ladywood, of how full our years, brief as they were, had been of love and joy and beauty. Although we should never have even a silver anniversary, it seemed to me that we perhaps had known more of adventure and all the loveliness and play of life than many who reach golden anniversaries. And it seemed to me that we were bound each to each, she in me and I in her, through all eternity, both of us Companions of the Co-inherence. Although the tears would be with me for many a day to come, I was content.

One afternoon at Ladywood I went to sleep in the grass and dreamt of Davy. The dream harked back to a sum-mer afternoon in England when she and I, travelling to a nearby village on a doubledecker bus, had yielded to a shared and wordless impulse to get off the bus and walk.

But the dream seemed to me so much future and present as well as past that I wrote a poem of it:

SUMMER

O love! do you remember? country bus
    And England, meadows and blue sky?
The drowsy-sweet lost summer calling us
      To walk there, you and I?

And how you drew my eyes to yours, still gazing
    Till quietly between us two,
Across the bus, our eyes grown soft and praising,
      A summer sweetness grew.

A country stop. A glance. And out we went
    With joy to walk knee-deep in heather,
To drink with summer, holiness: content
      To be in Christ together.

The red bus ambled off. Larks sang, "Dear one,"
    I murmured. "On that hill, the tree."
The moment, underneath that long-gone sun,
      Became eternity.

I woke. It was a dream at dusk, but this—
    A heaven on an English hill,
The sweet surrendering glory of the kiss
      We gave—is with me still.

Yet was it but a dream? Or my dream only?
    Somewhere are you remembering, too?
Or is it only I, remembering, lonely,
      And waiting still for you?

⸻❈{ IX }❈⸻

The Severe Mercy

May at Ladywood was a month of thought. A month of searching after the meaning of things. At Mole End the Illumination of the Past was still going forward, with many tears that marked the death of the successive brief realities, almost in the flesh, of the images of Davy from the past; and her mortal body had perished four months before. A third of a year since I had seen her in the flesh, longer now than we had ever been apart. But the final separation still lay ahead, although I was not clearly aware that it must be. Davy was still with me, not only in my letters to her but, I half-believed, in the wind. I was strangely happy amidst my sorrow that May, sitting often in the doorway of Ladywood with the birds singing round me and the Blue Mountains hanging in the sky.

There were two main strands, one growing out of the other, in my Maytime thinking. One of them, the earlier of the two, was about time and eternity: its roots stretched back to Glenmerle and it had been pushed into the forefront of my thoughts by the Illumination of the Past. The other strand of my thinking, which was related to it, was concerned with God's eternal mercy and was brought to a focus by a letter from C. S. Lewis in early May. But the thoughts on time and eternity should come first.

In a golden summer when our love was young Davy and I had sat on a stone wall near Glenmerle and talked about unpressured time—time to sit on stone walls, time to see beauty, time to stare as long as sheep and cows. At

my father's club, sitting before the fire, we had spoken
of "moments made eternity," meaning what are called
timeless moments, moments precisely without the pressure
of time—moments that might be called, indeed, *timeful*
moments. Or *time-free* moments. And we had clearly
understood that the pressure of time was our nearly in-
escapable awareness of an approaching terminus—the bell
about to ring, the holiday about to end, the going down
from Oxford foreseen. We had dreamed of *Grey Goose*
as a way to escape the pressure of time, though no one
escapes entirely. Life itself is pressured by death, the final
terminus. Socrates refused to delay his own death for a
few more hours: perhaps he knew that those few hours
under the pressure of time would be worth little. When
we speak of *Now*, we seem to mean the timeless: there
is no duration. Awareness of duration, of terminus, spoils
Now.

Immediately after Davy's death I had experienced the
amazing phenomenon, made complete by the Illumination of the Past, of the flowing back to me of all the
Davys of all the years, the whole Davy, the eternal Davy,
even as we hold all the David Copperfields when we
have closed the book. We are in an eternity with reference to the book's created time, but *we* live and have our
being in time: God's created time. If, indeed, that is so,
if God is eternity and time is a created thing, then Davy
must now be divorced from time and in eternity. But I
was not: I was in time. The college bell still summoned
me to eight o'clocks. And yet I was being given an eternal
view of Davy. Therefore I was, in some sense, looking
into eternity. What did that mean? That the barriers
between time and eternity were not so impassable as one
had supposed? Might one see still deeper into eternity?
Or, at least, into the meaning of time and eternity?

Reflecting upon my perception of the total or eternal
Davy, so much more *completely* to be known and loved,
I realised that without conscious awareness of it I had
had—we all have had—other glimpses of the eternal. I
could recall our Glenmerle dog, Laddie, as stubborn
puppy and the gay powerful wolf later as one dog. Or

England: the name summons up more than the England of Oxford days, especially to a reader of history: it is at once the England of Drake and the defiant lion that was Churchill. Or Athens: all it was and still is, though buried beneath the centuries. Perhaps, apart from our historical memory, there is an Athens in eternity, for Athens would be Athenians. And Davy and I had talked in hospital of meeting again in an eternal Glenmerle.

If the recovery of all the Davys focused my attention upon eternity, the Illumination of the Past focused my mind upon time: the harrying of time. I saw with immense clarity that we had always been harried by time. All our dreams back there in Glenmerle had come true: the schooner *Grey Goose* under the wind, the far islands of Hawaii in the dark-blue rolling Pacific, the spires of Oxford. But all the fulfilments were somehow, it seemed to me, incomplete, temporary, *hurried*. We wished to know, to savour, to sink in—into the heart of the experience—to possess it wholly. But there was never enough time; something still eluded us.

When we were in France with Edmund and Lore, we drove into Paris on a lovely spring day on our way to the Channel. We were not going to "do" Paris this trip, we were just passing through. But as we drove, top down, the buildings were noble against the sky, the parks were full of merry lovers, the river sparkled and Notre Dame was mellow in the sun. In one of the letters to Davy— the only one that survives—in this time of my grief, I said: "We were in our beloved Oxford for three years and Paris for not that many hours; and yet I wonder if Paris were not more *complete* or eternal an experience than Oxford?" We were not hurrying to "see" Paris. It was for us like the Lady sweet and kind passing by: a timeless impression. Of course, in reality, there were timeless impressions, time-free moments, in Oxford, too. But there we did feel that despite all that became part of us —bells and spires, C. S. Lewis and a host of friends, the face of the Warden of All Souls and the River Cherwell on a sunny day—there was something more, something still deeper, that we hadn't time enough—world and time enough—to reach. We didn't at all feel that we were *unable* to reach it, only that there wasn't time enough.

We shall come back, we said, and find it. We shall go back to the Islands and grasp the essence. We shall have the ultimate *Grey Goose* on a blue and timeless ocean. But there wasn't time enough to go back, way leading on to way. And if we had gone back, there wouldn't have been time enough then, either, for ahead there would be a terminus. Always.

Keats, I think, sensed man's need for the timeless. His grecian urn is a "foster-child of Silence and slow Time," and it "tease[s] us out of thought/As doth eternity." He consoles the young lover on the vase with the words: "For ever wilt thou love, and she be fair." It is, surely, the eternal that Keats aches for. And I see the same longing in Shelley and many another poet.

I saw it so clearly that May: how we had been harried by time. Always we were transients. Except perhaps at Glenmerle. Glenmerle had always been, would always be. That's why as a symbol it was so important to us. Of course it was not really immune to time: it passed and is, indeed, destroyed by our barbaric progress towards ever huger, sicker cities. All the same Glenmerle remains, ghostly and eternal.

The timelessness that seems to reside in the future or the past is an illusion. We dreamt of *Grey Goose* by the pool at Glenmerle, dreaming of the schooner sailing into a quiet lagoon of some far island, and the dream was charming because the *image* was without time, or time-free. In reality, the log to write, the meal to get, the topsail to be mended. The holiday trip to England is full of timeless images—the moments in Wells or Coventry Cathedral, the long talks with Peter or Jane, the hours in the peaceful countryside. In reality, even without the fearfully time-pressured guided tour, there are trains to catch, shirts to wash, sleep to get, rooms to book before it's too late. The future dream charms us because of its timelessness; and I think most of the charm we see in the "good old days" is no less an illusion of timelessness.

In the reality of Now the clock is always ticking. One

might suppose, looking at the glossier advertisements of watches—ever more exact, ever more spectacular flashings of the passing second—that modern man considers time a lovesome thing or, possibly, has a watch fetish. We might be better advised to hurl the lot into already-polluted Lake Erie.

And yet, after all, the clock is not always ticking. Sometimes it stops and then we are happiest. Sometimes—more precisely, some-not-times—we find "the still point of the turning world." All our most lovely moments perhaps are timeless. Certainly it was so for Davy and me. That very day when we sat on the wall and talked of time. Slow summer days at Glenmerle. The yacht ghosting at half a knot over calm waters, no one caring whether she arrived anywhere. Dreaming along the Cherwell and the skylark singing. I think we sought the timeless by a kind of intuition. Timeless moments—that "still point." Whether long or short makes no difference, for time is stopped. When I came aboard *Gull* and looked down the hatch at Davy's head bent over her seashells in the light of the cabin lamp with all the vast, mysterious night around me, the moment of perceiving might have been ten seconds or ten minutes—to someone else. Time had stopped for me.

In the Illumination of the Past I came in due course to the most purely timeless moment of all the years: the night in *Grey Goose* of the sea-fire. One's response to the description of that night may suggest whether, as I believe, the longing for eternity is built-in to us all. We had come up on deck some time in the night, wakened by the swing of the yacht at her anchor. A cool north breeze. A million brilliant stars above the dark slender masts. And every little wave crested with cold sea-fire. Without a word, Davy snuggled close and my arm about her, we had remained, the beauty pouring into us, remained for—what? An hour? Three hours? We never knew or cared. Finally, with wordless consent, we had gone below to sleep to the lift and stir of the yacht. A foretaste of eternity.

If, indeed, we all have a kind of appetite for eternity,

we have allowed ourselves to be caught up in a society that frustrates our longing at every turn. Half our inventions are advertised to save time—the washing machine, the fast car, the jet flight—but for what? Never were people more harried by time: by watches, by buzzers, by time clocks, by precise schedules, by the beginning of the programme. There is, in fact, *some* truth in "the good old days": no other civilisation of the past was ever so harried by time.

And yet, why not? Time is our natural environment. We live in time as we live in the air we breathe. And we love the air—who has not taken deep breaths of pure, fresh country air, just for the pleasure of it? How strange that we cannot love time. It spoils our loveliest moments. Nothing quite comes up to expectations because of it. We alone: animals, so far as we can see, are unaware of time, untroubled. Time *is* their natural environment. Why do we sense that it is not ours?

C. S. Lewis, in his second letter to me at Oxford, asked how it was that I, as a product of a materialistic universe, was not at home there. "Do fish complain of the sea for being wet? Or if they did, would that fact itself not strongly suggest that they had not always been, or wd. not always be, purely aquatic creatures?" Then, if we complain of time and take such joy in the seemingly timeless moment, what does that suggest?

It suggests that we have not always been or will not always be purely temporal creatures. It suggests that we were created for eternity. Not only are we harried by time, we seem unable, despite a thousand generations, even to get used to it. We are always amazed at it—how fast it goes, how slowly it goes, how much of it is gone. Where, we cry, has the time gone? We aren't adapted to it, not at home in it. If that is so, it may appear as a proof, or at least a powerful suggestion, that eternity exists and is our home.

So it appeared to me. It appeared to me that Davy and I had longed for timelessness—eternity—all our days; and the longing coupled with my post-mortem vision of the

total Davy whetted my appetite for heaven. Golden streets
and compulsory harp lessons may lack appeal—but timelessness? And total persons? Heaven is, indeed, *home*.

I attempted that spring something impossible: a sort
of picture of what heaven might be. I could only describe
it, though, in temporal terms. We haven't the words for
eternity. It is perhaps worth noticing how many words
—italicised—suggest time and are, therefore, quite inadequate. Still, this is what I wrote:

It is a heavenly *afternoon*. Davy and I have *just* had
a timeless luncheon (I am assuming that God will not
waste so joyous an invention as taste). I *then* say to her
that I *shall* wander down to sit beneath the beech tree
and contemplate the valley for *awhile*, but I *shall* be
back *soon*. I do so. I contemplate the valley for some
hours or some *years*—the words are meaningless here
where foreverness is in the air. At all events, I contemplate it *just as long* as I feel like doing. *Then* I get
up and start back, but I meet someone, C. S. Lewis,
perhaps, and we sit on a bench and maybe have a pint
of bitter and talk for *an hour* or *several hours*—*until*
we have said all we have to say *for now*. And *then*
I got gladly back to Davy. She, *meanwhile*, has played
the celestial organ, an organ on which perhaps every
note of a song can be heard *at the same time*: that is,
the song not played in time with half of it gone and
half yet to be heard. She has played the organ for *a
few minutes* and is *just* turning to greet me *when* I
come in. Whether I was away for *an hour* or *a hundred
years*, whether she has played for *ten minutes* or *thirty*,
neither of us has waited or could wait for the other.
For there simply is no time, no hours, no minutes, no
sense of time passing. The ticking has stopped. It is
eternity.

Of course it will not be like that. What it will be is
quite beyond anything we can imagine. And yet it will
be home. Of that we may be sure. I am as certain of
timelessness to come as I am that time was the worst of
the evils in Pandora's box.

Although I must live long years in time beyond Davy, somehow I felt certain that we should go on to the Eternal Majesty together, nor would she be conscious of delay. The idea is hinted at in this poem, looking ahead to another death:

DOORWAY

Now from my chains I flee,
Fair is the way I see,
   Heather and wind and you.

Dearling, O wait for me!
Evermore light and free,
   Running uphill to you.

Beauty shines down on me,
Love and eternity,
   Heather and wind and you.

Glory, O Christ, to Thee!
Joy like a flame for me,
   Running uphill with you.

With the eternal Davy in my consciousness, with the perception that our choicest moments had been the timeless ones, with the recognition of time as a hostile environment, I had looked as deeply into eternity as I could. Yet I also perceived that the past tends to appear to us as rather more timeless than it, in fact, was. If heaven and hell, are, indeed, retroactive—all our lives the one or the other—might not eternity be retroactive, too?

In late May in my rather minuscule hand I wrote of my thinking to Lewis. I spoke also of the closeness of Davy and me and of that aspect of it that was an effort to develop feminine understanding in me, masculine in her. I had just had an important letter from Lewis, but I shall give his reply to my thoughts on time and eternity first:

> I have your letter of May 20. My own hand is now so bad that it ill becomes me to blame yours; but cd. you make it a bit *larger*? I shall need a microscope else.

What you say about time is what I've long thought. It is inadequate to, and partially transcended by, v. simple experiences. E.g. *when* do we hear a musical air? Until the last note is sounded it is incomplete; as soon as that sounds it's already over. And I'm pretty sure eternal life doesn't mean this width-less line of moments endlessly prolonged (as if by prolongation it cd. "catch up with" that wh. it so obviously cd. never hold) but getting off that line onto its plane or even the solid. Read von Hügel's *Eternal Life*, Boethius *Consolations* (nice 16th c. English version on the right hand page of the Loeb edn.) About the nature of the relation between spouses in eternity, I base my idea on S. Paul's dictum that "he that is joined with a harlot is one flesh." If the lowest, most corrupt form of sexual union has some mystical "oneness" involved in it (and by the way what an argument *against* "casual practice!") *a fortiori* the married & lawful form must have it *par excellence.* That is, I think the union between the risen spouses will be as close as that between the soul and its own risen body. But (and this, as you see, is the snag) the risen body is the body that has died. ("*If* we share this death, we shall also share this resurrection"). And so—as you say in one of your postscripts—your love for Jean must, in one sense, be "killed" and "God must do it." You'd better read the *Paradiso* hadn't you? Note the moment at wh. Beatrice turns her eyes away from Dante "to the eternal Fountain," and D. is quite content. But of course it's all in the text "Seek ye first the Kingdom . . . and all these other things shall be added unto you." Infinite comfort in the second part; inexorable demand in the first. Hopeless if it were to be done by your own endeavours at some particular moment. But "God must do it." Your part is what you are already doing: "Take me—no conditions." After that, through the daily duty, through the increasing effort after holiness—well, like the seed growing secretly . . . What you say about the *she* in you & the *he* in her certainly does *not* seem to me the plains of Gomorrah and is in some sense (*what* I don't well know) probably true. There might be an element of delusion in the form it took: I don't know. But it did occur to me when reading it that my doctor friend once rebuked me for the v. exact attempts at precision I made in describing a pain to him. He said

"All that about just how it felt, its unique quality, is generally useless & unreliable to us as doctors. Tell me where it is & how long you've had it. If I need anything more, I'll ask." Possibly all those fine points wh. distinguish your loss from all the other losses suffered by other lovers are less important than they (v. naturally) seem to you. These sonnets, written about 10 years ago, are not in every way addressed to your condition, but they put some things perhaps a little better than I cd. put them here. I am in great trouble about my dear brother's dipsomania: pray for him and me. God bless you.

[P.S.] Let me have the sonnets back sometime: but no hurry.

The "Five Sonnets" he sent were later to appear under that heading in his *Poems*. They spoke to me very powerfully, indeed; and I should send them, in my turn, to any lover bereaved. In them Lewis warns the bereaved against anger at heaven, though "Anger's the anaesthetic of the mind," and against despair, which contains a hint "Of something like revenge," and against any seeking from the beloved an earthly comfort. Instead, as Dante learned, seek God first: "Ask for the Morning Star and take (thrown in)/Your earthly love."

Lewis, as he has said in *Surprised by Joy*, was brought to the Incarnate God by his longing for joy, a joy that does not reside in any earthly object that seems to promise it. In *Pilgrim's Regress* he describes this joy, the very longing for which is itself sweetness and joy: quite possibly, indeed, the purest joy that we can ever know on earth. At first the longing is for an "unnameable something, desire for which pierces us like a rapier at the smell of a bonfire, the sound of wild ducks flying overhead . . ." But, then, we fix that sweet and poignant longing for joy upon some earthly object. We shall, we believe, find that joy if only we can climb the blue mountains, find the Blue Flower, win the love of some particular lady in blue, or sail beyond the blue horizon in our schooner to our own new-found-land. Secretly we are all perhaps the Questing Knight. And yet, whatever the object of our quest, we learn when we find it that it does not ever contain *the* joy that broke our heart with longing. Thus, Lewis says, "if a man diligently followed this desire [for joy], pursuing the false objects until their falsity appeared and then resolutely abandoning them, he must come out at last into the clear knowledge that the human soul was made to enjoy some object that is never fully given—nay, cannot even be imagined as given —in our present mode of subjective and spatio-temporal experience." This, I think, is what C. S. Lewis's life and writings are *about*; and mine, too. Davy and I, having each other, longed for unpressured time—time-free existence—for thus we should find joy. We dimly glimpsed eternity, but what we, like Lewis, longed for was joy. But, though we never quite forgot the timelessness that was originally the end to which the boat was to be the means, we sometimes in those early years saw the schooner-to-be as an end in itself, an object containing joy.

Pondering Lewis's words about joy and my own think-ing upon time and eternity, recalling the tendency of Davy and me to substitute the means for the end, not only the yacht for the time-free existence it was to make possible but also other glimpses of heavenly joy—joy through love and beauty—that we were allowed and what we made of them, especially the Shining Barrier, I came to wonder whether *all* objects that men and women set their hearts upon, even the darkest and most obsessive desires, do not begin as intimations of joy from the sole spring of joy, God. One man's intimation of joy through beauty and his longing to be, somehow, one with that beauty may lead him to painting and thence, the beauty half-forgotten, to advocacy of nothing more than an artistic fashion; or that same desire to be one with beauty may lead another man to cut-throat art-collecting or to flamboyant, Wildean excesses in his personal life. Some-one else may link the joy with a glimpse of heavenly justice and then be led into law or perhaps communism, justice in the end forgotten. A boy growing up in a crowded, squalid flat may associate the joy with clean spaciousness which then becomes affluence, the desire for which causes him to become a crook, believing vaguely that the world owes him his heart's desire. An inkling of joy through human love might lead to lust and orgiastic cruelty. The priest's vocation may spring from his glimpse of God as joy, but that vocation may become episcopal politics, God mouthed and forgotten. Even a Hitler may begin with a longing for joy through peace and order. Davy and I had our glimpse of joy, joy eternal not limited by time, and sought *Grey Goose* as a way to it. If we sometimes made the schooner an end in itself, still it did, in truth, give us much of unpressured time in which, to use Lewis's brilliant analogy, we did sometimes escape from the endless line of minutes on to the plane, supremely so on the night of the cold sea-fire when all our inklings of eternity and love and beauty became one.

I said earlier that there were two intertwined strands in my Maytime thinking, the earlier one, beginning with the Illumination of the Past, having to do with time and eternity, and the later one, begun by Lewis's early May letter, having to do with the death of love and with mercy.

I had written to Lewis in April, a long letter, telling him the story of the Shining Barrier quite completely, including the completion of the Barrier by the last long dive. I told him its purpose—to keep inloveness. I told him why we had not had children—lest they should come between us by lessening our sharing.

Lewis's reply led perhaps to this book and gave it its title:

> Your letter is a wonderfully clear and beautiful expression of an experience often desired but not often achieved to the degree you and Jean achieved it. My reason for sending it back is my belief that if you re-read it often, till you can look at it as if it were someone else's story, you will in the end think as I do (but of course far more deeply & fruitfully than I can, because it will cost you so much more) about a life so wholly (at first) devoted to US. Not only as I do, but as the whole "sense" of the human family wd. on their various levels. Begin at the bottom. What wd. the

grosser Pagans think? They'd say there was excess in it, that it wd. provoke the Nemesis of the gods; they wd. "see the red light." Go up one: the finer Pagans wd. blame each withdrawal from the claims of common humanity as unmanly, uncitizenly, uxorious. If Stoics they wd. say that to try to wrest part of the Whole (US) into a self-sufficing Whole on its own was "contrary to nature." Then come to Christians. They wd. of course agree that man & wife are "one flesh"; they wd. perhaps admit that this was most admirably realised by Jean and you. But surely they wd. add that this One Flesh must not (and in the long run cannot) "live to itself" any more than the single individual. It was not made, any more than he, to be its Own End. It was made for God and (in Him) for its neighbours—first and foremost among them the children it ought to have produced. (The idea behind your voluntary sterility, that an experience, e.g. maternity, wh. cannot be shared shd. on that account be avoided, is surely v. unsound. For *a.* (forgive me) the conjugal act itself depends on opposite, reciprocal and therefore unshare-able experiences. Did you want her to feel she had a *woman* in bed with her? *b.* The experience of a woman denied maternity is one you *did not* & *could not* share with her. To be denied paternity is different, trivial in comparison.)

One way or another the thing had to die. Perpetual springtime is not allowed. You were not cutting the wood of life according to the grain. There are various possible ways in wh. it cd. have died tho' both the parties went on living. You have been treated with a severe mercy. You have been brought to see (how true & how v. frequent this is!) that you were jealous of God. So from US you have been led back to US AND GOD; it remains to go on to GOD AND US. She was further on than you, and she can help you more where she now is than she could have done on earth. You must go on. That is one of the many reasons why suicide is out of the question. (Another is the absence of any ground for believing that death *by that route* wd. re-unite you with her. Why should it? You might be digging an eternally unbridgeable chasm. Disobedience is not the way to get nearer to the obedient.)

There's no other man, in such affliction as yours, to whom I'd dare write so plainly. And that, if you can believe me, is the strongest proof of my belief in you and love for you. To fools and weaklings one writes soft things. You spared her (v. wrongly) the pains of childbirth: do not evade your own, the travail you must undergo while Christ is being born in you. Do you imagine she herself can now have any greater care about you than that this spiritual maternity of yours shd. be patiently suffered & joyfully delivered?

God bless you. Pray for me.

After this severe and splendid letter I loved Lewis like a brother. A brother and father combined.

If I had been at all tempted to break my promise to Davy about following her by my own act, the temptation vanished after one horrified look at Lewis's "eternally unbridgeable chasm." In the margin by it there's a small "*Ugh!!*" in my hand.

In my reply I told Lewis of these reactions and thanked him for his clarity and honesty and trust. I said that Davy and I, in fact, *had* kept springtime—Oxford had been June perhaps—and then it was all over. I said that perhaps she and I *had* shared the experience of a woman denied maternity through our closeness and empathy. And I promised to think deeply about all he had said. His subsequent letter on eternity has been given.

My thinking on time and eternity had prepared me— by showing me that God was what we had always longed for, longed for as "timelessness"—for the more rigorous thinking that must follow this "severe mercy" letter. If God is to be, in truth, sought *first*, He must be seen as heart's desire.

The central thrust of the Severe Mercy Letter came in the next-to-last paragraph, beginning: "One way or another the thing had to die." *Had* to die. But it might have died in a different way. Lewis had said something like this before, in his first letter after Davy's death. There he had said: "I feel . . . v. strongly what you say about the 'curious consolation' that 'nothing now can mar' your joint lives. I sometimes wonder whether bereavement is not, at bottom, the easiest and least perilous of the ways in wh. men lose the happiness of youthful love. For I believe it must *always* be lost in some way: every merely natural love has to be crucified before it can achieve resurrection and the happy *old* couples have come through a difficult death and re-birth. But far more have missed the re-birth. Your MS, as you well say, has now gone safe to the Printer." Again the same note: our love *had* to die, but there are many ways of dying.

It was death—Davy's death—that was the severe mercy. There is no doubt at all that Lewis is saying precisely that. That death, so full of suffering for us both, suffering that still overwhelmed my life, was yet a severe mercy. A mercy as severe as death, a severity as merciful as love.

This is not a concept that will have an immediate appeal to everyone, not in a society that celebrates both romantic and sexual love as the great goods and hates death as the great evil. And, indeed, apart from death as a release from frightful pain for those already doomed, how can death be called a mercy? Here were two young people in their thirties who loved each other and longed for her to live: how can her death be seen as a *mercy?*

If, indeed, we had broken the Law—by attempting perpetual springtime, by being "us-sufficient," by rejecting the children we might have had—then, no doubt, her death might be seen by some of the grimmer sort of religious folk as a richly deserved divine punishment. But had we not become Christians? Might we not through that faith have achieved the "difficult death and re-birth" in life and in the end become one of the "happy *old* couples?" Why did she, so humble and so holy, have to die? Was not her death, if decreed by God, severity without mercy?

It is with the Law I must begin. The Law of God. But not, though, all the Law that we may have violated. If somebody expects a *mea culpa* for our rejection of children, she will not get it. I do not know whether it is licit to refuse children; it is for the theologians to decide, whether anyone listens or not. The question became irrelevant for us when Davy went in hospital.

Equally I cannot speak with any theological assurance upon Lewis's dictum that "Perpetual springtime is not allowed." The question was resolved by her death. What we had was perhaps merely a prolonged "northern" springtime of inloveness. In terms of the seasonal analogy, there are many variations: lush girls becoming mothers— summer and fruiting—in their teens, virtually missing springtime altogether; worldly-wise, burnt-out youths leaping straight into autumn or winter. We, in attempting to keep the April inloveness, were perhaps blindly seeking eternity. And it was so gay and lovely that I cannot, being uncertain of the Law, feel very penitent.

And yet I can say this about the Law: we as creatures —we as created by God—existed for Him. Not for ourselves. That, at least, is certain.

Davy and I, in Lewis's words, "admirably realised" the Christian ideal of man and wife as One Flesh. That was the Shining Barrier: and in so far as the Shining Barrier meant closeness, dearness, sharing, and, in a word, love, it must, surely, have been sanctified by God. To avoid creeping separateness in the name of love was simply being true to the sacrament of marriage.

But the Shining Barrier was more than that. In its Appeal to Love—what is best for our love—as the sole criterion of all decisions, it was in violation of the Law; for what was best for our love might not be in accordance with our love and duty to our neighbour. And the Shining Barrier contained an ultimate defiance of God in our resolute intention to die together in the last long dive.

But the Shining Barrier had been breached by God's assault troops, including C. S. Lewis in the van; and we had bent the knee. The Appeal had been broken, to my dismay; and the last long dive had been forbidden, to our haunting sorrow in hospital. We had thought our love invulnerable; and so perhaps it was to the world, as long as the Barrier stood. But God had breached it, after which our love was vulnerable to any menace.

In the Severe Mercy Letter, Lewis said: "You have been brought to see . . . that you were jealous of God." So I had said to him: it had been one of the sharp and shattering insights of my agonised grief. Jealous of my God! Or jealous of my lover's Divine Lover. This was precisely what it had been when I moped about Li'l Dreary and wouldn't read my Bible and played with Jane. *Mea culpa* in truth. Of course I hadn't known I was jealous of God. It was an almost unthinkable thought, and it remained unthought—and even more unthinkable—while I was pleading for Davy's life in the hospital months and pouring my strength into my total commitment to her. But the jealousy was there. And God knew.

Neither the fact that our love had become vulnerable through the breach in the Shining Barrier nor the fact that I was, almost latently, jealous of God affected us in those last months in hospital when I was living for her and she was dying for God.

Still, the Barrier was breached and the jealousy was there. What would have resulted from them if she had recovered? That is the question I must ask. How if at the last minute—after, perhaps the gay young love of her coming out of the coma and our happy and hopeful Christmas with the "Song of the Two Lovers"—she had begun to mend? How if she had gone on mending until she was quite well? The doctors would have been astonished; they would have said, "Almost a miracle." We, being so hopeful, might have been less astonished. But very grateful to Christ the Healer.

And we would have been joyful. I should have loved her the more dearly, because I had feared to lose her and because, like Persephone, she had come back from the gates of death. And she would have loved me the more dearly, because I had not failed her ever in those terrible months.

But the immediate joy and gratitude could not have gone on for ever. She, after her naked knowing of God, would have been even more overwhelmed by His glory and even more surrendered to His will. She might, indeed, have believed herself returned to life for a holy purpose. And I would still be jealous of God and would again remember that the Appeal to Love could not be used.

Or would my jealousy have been overcome, once and for all, by the miracle of her healing? But it *wouldn't* have been the miracle. It would have been "almost a miracle." It would have been, as perhaps any miracle must be, subject to other explanations—her will to live, the doctors' skill. Perhaps the prognosis had been wrong to begin with. If my jealousy, unknown and unsuspected, had endured in the terrible crisis of her dying and her holy and beautiful submission to the will of God, it would not have disappeared because of something "almost miraculous." It would, for a long time, have been dormant, with even less chance of being detected; but it would have been there still.

The question, therefore, remains: what would have happened, not immediately but in the long run, if she had got well? How would it have been with us in three years? Ten? How remote the crisis and recovery would seem ten years later!

If my judgment of myself—that the jealousy would survive—is correct, there are, I think, three possibilities to be examined:

(1) I should, somehow, have become as wholly committed—mind and heart—as she. It had not happened while she was in hospital. My moment of selfless offering-up had been for *her* best good, which may come to the same thing as the Kingdom's good, but is not the same in intention. My commitment was to *her*. If, unimaginably, my duty to God had seemed to require my leaving her there in hospital to cope alone, I would not have done it. Never. As Lewis rightly saw, I had moved from "us" to "us-and-God" but was still light-years from "God-and-us" in my pagan heart. I, therefore, conclude that—unless God had compelled me by grace—I should not have become as wholly committed as she.

(2) I should have attempted, with some success, to damage or lessen *her* commitment to God, not admitting of course, even to myself, that I was doing it. She would have been full of love and gratitude to me. I should have spoken of balances, a balance between love for each other and love for God. Was there not excess in her service to

God if our love was hurt thereby? I might, in fact, have succeeded in reducing her devotion to a "comfortable" level. By thus arguing, I should really have been reintroducing the old Appeal in a slightly changed form. Davy was human—intensely human—and she loved me. It may be that the closeness at Mole End, beginning with that New Year's breakfast, was a very human and slight weakening of her allegiance to God owing to a sort of mute appeal from me. I might have weakened her faith. Or driven it underground to burst forth later. But I think I should have failed. She was too far gone in God's service, especially in her naked surrender to the Majesty there in hospital. It cannot be supposed that God would have looked kindly upon my effort or refrained from supporting her.

(3) I should have come to hate God—or Davy. If I have not become as committed as she and cannot weaken her faith, what remains? My jealousy of God remains: it will revive. The Appeal is still broken. It would begin by my drifting away from God, only a little at first. But it is not how far; it is which direction. Away or towards. And in three years? Or ten? Time enough. And in the end, I should have come to hatred of God who had stolen my love though she still lived. The hatred of course would have been concealed as ceasing to believe. Nobody admits to hating God. But, then, with Davy quite lost to me—would I not come to hate her, too? Her holiness would, more and more, appear to me as hypocrisy. Or fanaticism. We have so many useful words. And, above all, she would be a traitor to our love. Then, soon or late, a new Jane, without the innocency. And all the Shining Barrier would be down.

These possibilities—the last two—are almost too frightful to contemplate. But if I am to be honest, I must face them. If (1) doesn't happen, if I attempt (2) and fail, then (3). I come to hate God. Or Davy. Or, most likely, both. In this terrible judgment, I take into account what I know of myself. I am not one to plod along day by day or quietly to accept contracted horizons. And, necessarily, I should have had to move towards God or away. If see-

ing Davy's most lovely love of her Incarnate Lord in
hospital had not brought me to seek Him *first*, would
anything else have done it—except her death? Contemplating these dreadful possibilities—coming to hate my
God! coming to hate my dear love!—I cry, even as I
write: "No, no! My God! It could not have happened!
Never!" But the I that cries out is the man who knew
her death in that winter dawn and all that followed.

If my reasoning—my judgment—is correct, then her
death in the dearness of our love had these results: It
brought me as nothing else could do to know and end
my jealousy of God. It saved her faith from assault. It
brought me, if Lewis is right, her far greater help from
eternity. And it saved our love from perishing in one of
the other ways that love could perish. Would I not rather
our love go through death than hate?

If her death did, in truth, have these results, it was,
precisely, a severe mercy.

Our love *had* to perish, Lewis says. Perish in its earthly
form, at least, or perish utterly in hate or indifference.
Perish unless it could be redeemed. But must we assume
that God decreed her death? Or let her die when He
could have healed her, because of the good results? Either
question, it seems to me, is too simple. Creation is a con-
tinuing act, I believe, and, although God allows us choice,
His eternal will is acting upon the consequences. Our
love, to be redeemed, would have had to die to its old
self in both of us, both of us seeking *first* the Kingdom,
both of us turning our eyes to Dante's "eternal Fountain,"
and each of us content in the other's doing so. *She* would
have been content. It took her death, ironical as it must
seem, to make *me* content in her turning her gaze from
me to the eternal Fountain.

But then—did I doom her to death? How if I had
turned towards the eternal Fountain with adoration?
There would have been no jealousy then. Only the
laughter of the Great Dance. "Ask for the Morning Star
and take (thrown in)/Your earthly love." If I had, would
she have begun to heal? Of course I do not know. I
must not presume to answer, for God may have had

purposes beyond my imagining. But I am at peace with the question.

C. S. Lewis said in the Severe Mercy Letter that I would in the end come to think as he was thinking about our love but that I would think "far more deeply & fruitfully" than he could because it would cost me so much more. This book is, in fact, the fruit of the thinking that my friend and my father-in-Christ, all those years ago, gave me to do. I said to him three years after that May letter, although my thinking was not yet done, that I felt a rightness and harmony in Davy's death.

A year before her death, Davy offered-up her life for me, for the fulfilment of my soul. If I could cease to be jealous of God only through her death, if the love we both loved could only be saved through her death, if I would turn my eyes towards the eternal Fountain only through her death, is it unlikely that her offering-up was accepted?

And if I offered-up all I was to God, whatever I thought I meant by that at the time, was I not, in fact, offering-up *myself* to God, pledging, as it were, to turn to the eternal Fountain? And would that not *be* her best good after the God in whom she had her being? It is awesomely mysterious: if she gave that which she offered, it would *be* the fulfilment of my soul; and if I gave that which I offered, it would *be* her best good after God. The Great Dance.

There were other prayers besides the offerings-up. One year before she went into hospital, Davy, half-sick and with an intimation of death, prayed for one more year. Her symptoms were the same as those which were to be her death. After her prayer, she then got well and lively. C. S. Lewis was to say, years later, about someone else facing death and healed for awhile: "There can be miraculous reprieve as well as miraculous pardon." Davy prayed for the year. One year later, almost to the day, she was pronounced dying.

The specialists' prognosis was that she would die in coma or of bleeding. I prayed very hard that she not die in either of those ways but die, if she must die, clear-eyed and aware. She died improbably clear-eyed and fully aware. No horrors. As Lewis said, "a beautiful death, an *act* wh. consummates (not, as so often, an event wh. merely stops) the earthly life."

I prayed to be allowed to take her fear of death. She, understanding this kind of substitution or carrying another's burden, *gave* me the fear. And I took it, knowing it to be altogether different to my own fear of loss; and with all my strength and imagination entered in to *her* fear. She seemed to be improbably free of it. That, too, was an intimation of the Great Dance.

Long years before I even knew Davy, my dog, Polly, was struck by a car. The vet said no hope, paralysed hind quarters, and wanted to put her out. But I thought that I, who loved her, must do it. I went back to Glenmerle and took Polly and my rifle and a piece of steak into the woods. She ate a bit of the steak to please me. And I stroked her and called her good dog till she went to sleep. Then I fired.

There was something about Davy's death that was, very remotely, like that. Considering the prayers and their answers and considering the events—her coming out of the coma, the merry little celebration of Christ's birthday, and the way she died, taken up into the light—I cannot escape the impression that Somebody was being very gentle with us. Perhaps she had to die—for me, for our dear love, for God. And I had to live with grief, for God. But He was, perhaps, as gentle with us both as He could be.

Our Shining Barrier love, however much we did not know of the meanings of God, was in many ways both innocent and good. Our subordination of self to the love was, at least, a step towards the dying to self that is the inexorable demand of Christ. We sought the beautiful and perhaps the good, and we came at last to Messiah. Our love was troubled for awhile by my heart's paganism, but still we loved and neither of us was consumed by the cruel passions of self. In the end, all we asked of God, even the reprieve, was given us—all except the final healing. But our prayer for that was always conditional, mine by her best good, hers by the Kingdom's good. Our love—under the aweful shadow—was deep and clear. If God saved our love—and, indeed, transformed it into its real and eternal self—in the only way possible, her death, it was for me, despite grief and aloneness, worth it. How much more worth it she, who has me to forgive in the Great Dance, may count it. We ended as we began—in love. We even ended as we began in another way, for, at the time of the coma, we were for a few fragile days young lovers wandering in the misty spring of vanished Glenmerle.

Only Love Himself with a severe mercy could breach the Shining Barrier and, by breaching it, save that guarded love for the eternity it longed for; and the Love and the Law are one.

Soon after that Ladywood May was over, with thoughts of eternity and the beginnings, at least, of thoughts on the severe mercy in my mind and with my grief in my heart, I went travelling. And on a moonlit June night I walked in between the gateposts of Glenmerle and down through the park by the old lily pond, now dried-up, to the bridge.

Epilogue: The Second Death

DEAD COLLIE

I'll not catch such a flurry of living and grace,
  To chase down the wind is sheer folly:
Just say that my life has a void lifeless place
  For a little dead collie.

Still I muse on your goodness—so glad to be good—
  Free courtesy ruled your brief living,
Never thinking you could disobey if you would,
  And purely forgiving.

A whistle from me and you whirled from your play,
  Up ears and eager paws drumming,
Your duty and wishes all one in the gay
  Swift rush of your coming.

Even now a clear whistle might reach and surpass
  All limits and bring back the rushing
Of printless gay paws running over the grass,
  And the silky head brushing.

Two years have passed since Davy's death—it is again
the dead of winter—and in those years grief has remained
the salient fact of my existence. The Second Death is
not yet, but one more link with Davy is broken when
Flurry goes. She had been with us since pagan days in
Grey Goose and at Horsebite, and she had charmed the
student group. Flurry and Davy had had a delighted
reunion on that last Christmas Day, and she had been
the companion of my grief. Always I had been touched

222

by her goodness. Sometimes at night when I went out to call her, I would know by distant barks that she was playing with other dogs, and I would wonder whether perhaps she might choose not to come to my whistle. But then in a moment there would be the swift patter of paws and a joyous whirlwind would arrive. There was an emptiness when she went, I hope, to join her mistress. My poem is really about them both.

At this time, two years, almost to the day, after Davy's death, I had the most remarkable dream—if it was a dream—of my whole life. I dream as most people do in fragmentary and half-remembered scenes. My dreams of Davy, however treasured, had been ordinary dream-like dreams. But now I had a dream—the "Oxford-Vision Dream"—so detailed, so significant, so completely unlike anything I ever dreamt before or after, that the great question was whether to believe that it represented a reality. I was as aware of its significance during the dream as I was afterwards. When I dreamed it, there at Mole End, I was about to sail for England; but in the dream I was already there, in Oxford. If the dream did represent truth—if I was dreaming true—then it was of God.

THE OXFORD-VISION DREAM

It was morning. I had come back to Oxford two years after Davy's death and found digs, a ground-floor room with its own door opening onto a large garden with paths angling across it. I was just dressed to go out to an early lecture at the Schools. Morning sunlight was slanting in the windows. I heard a small sound and turned: it was Davy. I was fully aware that she was dead and, instantly and overwhelmingly, aware that something miraculous was happening. I was, I told myself, full awake.

"Davy!" I cried.

She smiled broadly. I felt a pure joy as I took a step towards her, but I also felt a little tentative, hesitant.

"It's all right, dearling," she said, and held out her arms. I went into them, and we hugged each other and kissed—the kiss was heaven. But even in the joy, I was conscious, with a sort of amazement, that she was warm

and solid. Weren't ghosts supposed to be . . . But I
could feel her shoulder blades under my hands. I stood
back and looked at her. She looked just as she had
always done, even to the slight dark circles under her
eyes. I felt an immense gratitude to her, and to God for
letting her come. There was, also, just a hint of shy-
ness, tentativeness—not knowing quite what the rules
were, so to speak, for this sort of thing. I, standing
back, looked at her face, her clothes, all in a second
or two.

"Davy, Davy!" I said.

"Oh, my dear!" she said. Then she added, "I can't
stay long."

We went over and sat on the edge of the bed with
our arms around each other, and I said something
about being grateful for ever that she was there at all.
Then I couldn't resist asking her how she, in heaven,
could have dark shadows under her eyes.

She grinned, knowing me, and then said seriously,
"I can't tell you that. I can't tell you very much at all."

I grinned back at her. "That's reasonable," I said.
Then, after a little silence, I said, "Can you tell me one
thing, dearling? Are you—well, *with* me sometimes?
I've sometimes thought you might be."

"Yes, I am," she said. "I know all your doings."

"Thank God!" I said. Then I said, very casually,
"And my letters to you—have you, um, read them?
Over my shoulder, maybe?"

She knew—we always knew—that it was important
to me. Her arms around me tightened, and she said in
a low voice, "Yes, dearling. I've read them all."

And then our eyes met in that look of perfect understanding—that look of *knowing*—that I had missed more
than any other thing. After that, we just sat there on
the edge of the bed, holding each other, cheek to cheek.
There was more said, and there was laughter. And I
was pervaded with bliss. I don't recall her exact words,
but she gave me to understand that she had wanted
this meeting as much as I could have done; and I remember thinking that God had allowed it because He
loved her.

Finally, she said that she must go, and I accepted her
going peacefully. She left by the door, and I leaned in

the doorway, watching her go across the garden and through the alleyway. Then she was gone.

I turned back into the room, thinking, "How I've been blessed!" It was, of course, too late for the lecture. I would, I thought, go up to the High and get some breakfast. I put on my tie and jacket, thinking very happily about this wonder that had happened. Then— there she was again. But with a difference. She stood there, merely smiling a little; and now, I realised, I could see through her. Then, even as I watched, she lifted her hand in a little wave and faded and was gone.

I murmured to myself, making a distinction that I don't now fully understand: "This was an apparition and the other was a vision. Dear Davy! she came back again just to show me that she really is with me." And I smiled at the corner where she had been and perhaps still was. Then I went out.

There was a great deal more of the dream, equally real and detailed: I went to breakfast, met friends, the waitress got muddled and forgot the bacon; I started to tell one of the chaps about the vision and then realised after a few words that no one who didn't see it could believe it, so changed the subject. After breakfast I walked down towards the House with him, but left him and took shelter in St. Aldate's porch when rain came on.

Then I awoke in Virginia. What was I to make of this extraordinary dream? Was it just a dream? Or something more? I remembered what C. S. Lewis had said about the relationship between the significant and the fortuitous in the total act of creation. Then how could that dream be merely the accidental effect of whatever I had had for dinner? It must, I decided, on some level contain truth. It was a sort of "All shall be most well." It left me with a serene, peaceful happiness that lasted a long time.

A fortnight later I was on shipboard, sailing for England. One night I came up on deck. It was bitter cold and ice drifted in the dark ocean. In my hand I held Davy's grey-goose ring and her wedding ring with its ten little diamonds, one for each of the months we had

known each other before I put it on her finger. And one
for each chapter of this book, perhaps. Just a few more
diamonds and there would have been one for each of our
years. Now I dropped them quietly overboard into the
deep sea.

Liverpool, and the boat train to London. With me was
a friend who had also been on the ship, and we were
planning a fortnight in London before I went on to
Oxford. But there on the train, rushing through the
night, I was seized by a terrible urgency to get to Oxford.
It was sudden; it was causeless; but it was irresistible.
I've never known anything quite so powerful without
some sort of reason. Still, I told my friend London was
off. A taxi to Paddington, where I rang up a small hotel
on the Banbury Road. Then the Oxford train. Another
taxi—not looking out—to the hotel. I booked in and left
my cases. Then I stepped out into the dark, misty Oxford
night.

Instantly I was overwhelmed—by Oxford. The air itself
—the familiar mixture of coal smoke and mist. Bells ringing somewhere. Never has a place, just as a place—and
only smell and sound at that—had such an impact on me.
Davy!—she and I had left here together, in winter like
this; and now I was coming back alone. This was the
city, for us, of God. And the city of a hundred friends,
though all, except the dons, were gone. I walked that
night like a ghost about the town, hearing the bells,
peering up in the darkness at St. Mary's spire. The Turl
and Jesus. The dark bulk of the Bodleian. Beaumont
Street and, on St. John's, the narrow passageway to Pusey
Lane. I stood again in the cobbled lane in the mist and
the light of the gaslamp. There was the Studio, dark and
empty. The tears mixed with the mist on my face. Then
in the darkness I walked to the village of Binsey and on
to the churchyard where Edmund had scattered a handful
of ashes. I sat there a long time on a mossy headstone, the
song of the Lady sweet and kind humming through my
mind. Coming back into Oxford I thought of the "Song
of Two Lovers"—the line about being in Oxford in dark
empty streets without a key. It could have been written

for this night; but if there were an old grey house by the sea for Davy and me, it must be waiting by the ocean of eternity.

In the next days I found digs in Wellington Square— I was to be in England for half a year—and I called on the few people I knew. I had not exchanged letters with C. S. Lewis for several months—I tried to wait until I had something to say—and now I heard to my astonishment that he was married. He had said nothing of any such prospect in the letter I'd had in September which spoke of the "good, long talks" we must have "and perhaps we shall both get high." As soon as I was settled in I wrote to him at Cambridge, saying that I was in England and was he, in fact, married?

Lewis replied on March 7th:

> Yes. I have married (knowingly) a woman desperately ill, almost certainly dying: Joy Davidman whose *Smoke on the Mountain* you have probably read. She is in the Wingfield and of course I spend all of the week end I possibly can at her bedside. If you cd. meet the 1.15 from Bletchley on Sat. we cd. lunch together at the Royal Oxford before I catch the bus for the hospital.

We did so meet, and he told me of marrying Joy in a civil ceremony, simply as an act of friendship to prevent the Government deporting her to America as a communist, despite her being a lapsed communist and, in fact, a Jewish Christian. He and she had even drawn up a paper stating that the marriage was not a real one. But in less than a fortnight from our luncheon Lewis was to marry her sacramentally with a priest at the hospital bedside. Lewis told me that he had come to love her, and he wanted to take her home to the Kilns to die. But he quite certainly said that he was in love with her.

He and I met a good many times for lunch in the months to come, and I went several times to the Kilns, in Headington, Oxford, to talk to Joy or to both of them. She was of course in bed—support straps hanging from the ceiling. She was not expected to live more than a year or, of course, ever to be again out of bed. Despite pain— she would wince now and then as we talked—she was cheerful and interested in everything.

Then one day I took the train to Cambridge. It was a fine spring day, and I had the compartment to myself with all the windows open. The train meandered slowly and rather delightfully across England, stopping often to rest, perhaps, or to admire flower beds, while birds sang round about. Lewis said later that he and his friends called the train the Cantab Crawler.

At Magdalene I had Pepys's old room. After dinner at the high table, at which there was good-natured banter about Oxford men coming to Cambridge, Lewis and I talked until very late in his rooms. It was, in fact, one of the finest evenings of talk I can remember; and it was now that I began, at his invitation, to call him Jack, at least in talk. We spoke, I remember, of love and grief— the grief I was still undergoing and he was so soon to face. He said he was praying for Joy's recovery and asked me to pray for that, which I of course did. He said that because of Joy, he had come to see certain things I had said about my love for Davy in a new light. I told him about my thinking on the relationship of grief to the presence of the beloved, how the latter calls forth the former. I told him of my belief that Davy, too, had under-gone bereavement and sorrow and, in that connection, told him of the "Oxford-Vision Dream." He was thought-ful about the idea of the dead undergoing bereavement, and then said he could see no reason why it might not be so. I said that I had feared losing the reality of Davy but that the Illumination of the Past, now long since over, had seemed to impress her reality on my mind. One of us suggested, then or later, that if the dead do stay with us for a time, it might be allowed partly so that we may hold on to something of their reality. Lewis, who had evidently thought further about the idea of the dead also experiencing sorrow, brought it up again, saying that the soul's progress towards the Eternal Being might necessitate the experience of bereavement, either in life or after-wards.

There was to be another journey to Cambridge, and that night we talked about poetry, including his five sonnets, which I had virtually memorised; and about Greek myth. In some letter I had expressed the idea that Jane in *That Hideous Strength* was sort of a stereotype, and in his reply, now regrettably lost, he said that I should have a look at the woman in his next book. She was Orual and the book, one of the greatest novels of the century, I think, was *Till We Have Faces*. Now I took it all back: Orual was no stereotype; she was, indeed, a great character. Again, it was a grand evening of talk.

C. S. Lewis was a strong, genial, stimulating, loving presence in my life from Oxford days through Davy's death and the immensity of grief that followed. He was, above all, a friend. Although my book is nearing its end, its main theme completed or nearly so, I propose to carry on the theme of Lewis and Joy, briefly, through excerpts from his later letters to me. My reason for doing so is, at least partly, some curious parallels between my experience, recounted in this book, and his.

When I received the note from him in March, and when we were together in Cambridge and at the Kilns, Joy was a dying woman, but Lewis and, no doubt, Joy was praying, as I was, for her recovery. In the autumn, when I had returned to Virginia, the excerpts begin. (The ellipses here are mine.)

Lewis wrote:

[27 November 1957] My own news continues better than we ever dared to hope. The cancerous bones have rebuilt themselves in a way quite unusual and Joy can now *walk*: on a stick and with a limp, it is true, but it is a walk—and far less than a year ago it took 3 people to move her in bed and we often hurt her. Her general health, and spirits, seem excellent. Of course the sword of Damocles hangs over us. Or shd. I say that circumstances have opened our eyes to see the sword which really hangs always over everyone.

I forget if I had begun my own bone disease (*osteo-porosis*) when you were with us. Anyway, it is much better now and I am no longer in pain. I wear a surgi-cal belt and shall probably never be able to take a real walk again, but it doesn't somehow worry me. The intriguing thing is that while I (for no discoverable reason) was losing chalcium [calcium?] from my bones, Joy, who needed it much more, was gaining it in hers. One dreams of a Charles Williams substitution! Well, never was a gift more gladly given; but one must not be fanciful.

It is nice being in love with Hellas, I expect. My brother is well. Write from time to time. *Of course* you are in my prayers as I am in yours.

[26 April 1958] A letter from you is always a refresh-ment. First as to your question. Joy's improvement con-tinues. Indeed except that she is a cripple with a limp (the doctors, rather than the disease, shortened one leg) she is in full health. She had an x-ray examination last week wh. shows that the bones have re-built them-selves "firm as a rock." The Doctor, doubtless without what a Christian wd. regard as true seriousness, used the word *miraculous*. I am also, by the way, nearly quite restored myself. I sometimes tremble when I think how good Joy and I ought to be: how good we would have *promised* to be if God had offered us these mercies at that price. . . . All blessings. I wish we lived nearer.

[15 Dec. 1958] My wife's recovery is really more like resurrection. We have been to Ireland together. She walks (with a stick and a limp) about the wood shoot-ing—or anyway shooting *at*—pigeons; we walk together to the Ampleforth Arms. My brother is also well, and my own bone disease is as good as cured—anyway, quiescent. . . . I have lately passed my 60th birthday. I pray for you nightly and wd. much like to meet. Very good wishes, and warm love from us all.

[The next letter (or letters) is missing.]
[16 April 1960] You *must* pray for me now. Joy's cancer has returned and the doctors hold out no hope. Of course this is irrelevant to the question whether the previous recovery was miraculous. There can be miracu-

lous reprieve as well as miraculous pardon, and Lazarus was raised from the dead to die again. I can't write much else; you can well imagine why.

[Upon receiving the above letter, I immediately sent them the sculptural reproduction of a 12th-century Norman Christ that hung above my bed, telling him not to write. Joy died on July 13th. In July or August Lewis wrote about his grief, a letter I did not retain, except for an excerpt on the Norman Christ, which he hadn't at first liked though Joy did: "but it has grown on me gradually . . . I believe it will come to mean a great deal to me."]

[23 Sept. 1960] We are . . . much at one in our re-action to grief and I find much wisdom in your poem. [Possibly "Shining Barrier."] My great recent discovery is that when I mourn Joy least I feel nearest to her. Passionate sorrow *cuts us off* from the dead (there are ballads & folk-tales wh. hint this). Do you think that much of the traditional ritual of mourning had, un-consciously, that very purpose? For of course the primi-tive mind is v. anxious to *keep them away*.

Like you, I can't imagine real Eros coming twice. I still feel married to Joy.

[30 June 1962] I am now as convalescent as (appar-ently) I am ever likely to be. Loneliness increases as health returns. One must have the *capacity* for hap-piness in order to be fully aware of its absence. We must talk of 1000 things when you come.

In these letters and a number of later ones and in my letters to him, we talked, of course, of a hundred other things. I joked mysteriously about a drastic step I was contemplating for awhile, a secession from academe to the schooner life; and we spoke of literary and theological subjects. I was to see him once more, in 1963, in the fortnight before his death. We made tea there in the Kilns and talked about prayer and books, including my booklet "Encounter with Light" (written two or three years earlier) which he had liked. He was his usual in-cisive self; though, because of his illness, he would doze momentarily during the talk. We set a date for a future

meeting. When the day came, he was dead. I learned
later that the Norman Christ I had given him was over
the head of his bed when he died. In connection with my
earlier thoughts on time, Lewis and I in our friendship
were somewhat harried by time: in my 1957 journey to
England he was just marrying a seemingly dying woman,
and when I came again, he was dying.

Davy, ill and believing herself to be dying, prayed for
one more year, and recovered—for one year. Lewis and
Joy, when she seemed certainly dying, prayed, and she
was healed—for a couple of years. In both illnesses there
may have been a Charles Williams substitution. When
Lewis and I talked of the loss and grief that I was experiencing, he, improbably, was only a few years away
from a similar experience of grief. When he was undergoing it, he must have remembered all we had said about
the nature of grief. Indeed, in the letter two months after
Joy's death, he wrote: "We are much at one in our reaction to grief." And we were at one, also, in the belief that
genuine inloveness is, as I put it in my Shining Barrier
poem, a "once-given grace," for he wrote: "Like you, I
can't imagine real Eros coming twice."

When he died, I remembered his great shout across
the Oxford High Street: "Christians NEVER say goodbye!" In eternity there will be "time enough." And as
Jack said, "We must talk of 1000 things when you come."

To return to my 1957 stay in England, my time there,
after the second journey to Magdalene in the Cantab
Crawler, was drawing to a close.

Only a fortnight before I was to sail, I went to see a
friend in Lincoln. He had told me how to find his rooms
in the Cathedral Square, saying that he would be along a
bit later. The train arrived about sunset, and, as I walked
up the ascending streets, past old houses, towards the
cathedral above, the air was full of golden light. Davy and
I had never been in Lincoln, yet now, when I had walked
but a short way, I became aware of an extraordinary sense
of her presence. It was very peaceful, having her there,
if she was. There was no catch in my throat or tear in my
eye, just the sense of her presence. And as I walked up

that hill, Davy seemed to walk lightly beside me. The sun was setting now. The gold turned to red. Rooks circled, flying home to their nests in the cathedral towers. The great bell boomed for the half hour. The cathedral was rose-red in the sunset. And Davy was beside me. I was tranquilly happy. All was most well.

I did not think of that lovely walk up to the rose-red towers as a farewell, yet perhaps it was. In later times I was to think of it as the last thing *we* did.

In Virginia again, no longer living at Mole End, I found that my tears were dried. The grief had passed. When I drove out to Ladywood, there was no sense of Davy's being there with me, nor any sense that she was in the wind. If I wrote to her—I attempted it but once—I found myself saying "she" instead of "you"; the feeling of its being a real letter had vanished. There were no more dreams. It may be that through the evocative power of music, I might have felt a stab of grief, but I had no wish to force it or prolong it beyond its natural term.

This—the disappearance of the sense of the beloved's presence and, therefore, the end of tears—this is the Second Death.

I could not escape the impression that the Second Death was a *withdrawal*—that Davy had withdrawn herself from me. It seemed something more or other than merely a changing psychological state in me. It seemed to correspond to some actuality, some real spiritual event. If, indeed, grief is a *response* to the presence—seeming or real—of the dead, then the end of grief might correspond to some necessary turning away on *their* part. That walk up to the cathedral might have been, in truth, a farewell.

The disappearance of the grief is not followed by happiness. It is followed by emptiness. C. S. Lewis in his letter on eternity quoted me as saying that my love for Davy must, in some sense, be killed—and "God must do it." Now perhaps God *was* doing it. And it was, precisely, my earthly love for her—an earthly love that would endure as long as she seemed near—that was being killed. That love had not died when she died—had not died perhaps in *either* of us—and it sustained me in the grief that may have been *our* grief. She had been near me, it seemed, waking and in dreams—especially in that one incredible dream. I had felt her in the wind. I had rushed from London to Oxford to find her in the misty night. I had walked up the streets of Lincoln with her.

Now all that was gone, leaving emptiness. I wanted the grief again, not for itself but for its corollary: the presence that calls it forth. But it is not allowed. There was only emptiness. I was drained of all emotion. My mother, whom I loved, died, and I could not feel anything. Life had no savour. The Second Death, in many ways, is a harder thing than the first, only of course one has no tears for it.

I wrote to Lewis about it in November, and in the first half of the November 27th letter already given (the letter, though divided, is complete) he replied:

> It hardly seems a quarter of a year since you were such a welcome visitor in Oxford.
>
> I note what you say, that you are now in your second bereavement; that which bereaves one of the bereavement itself. And, as you unflinchingly see, it is "according to the Law." I feel you are probably right in thinking that the fading of the beloved as-she-was is a necessary condition of the trans-mortal and eternal relation. May we not conjecture (am I repeating myself?) that when Our Lord said "It is expedient that I go away" he stated something true *par excellence* of Himself, but also true, in their degree, of all his followers?

The Second Death and Davy's withdrawal towards the Mountains of Eternity—whatever it means—does not of course mean that I love her any the less, though it is a love without the immediacy of the flesh. Because of the dream that raised the Shining Barrier, because of the intense sharing of love and beauty, Christ and death and grief, we were perhaps as close as human beings can be. And the union thus created will, I believe, transcend death: it endures and will endure.

In her dying I was, as intensely as I could be, *with* her. Her last words were to me. Her blindly reaching hand found my face, as she knew it would. When I myself come to cross that boundary that she has crossed, I think I shall find her hand and hear her voice first of all. Perhaps by the old lily pond at Glenmerle.

But in my thoughts of her I come back again and again to that foretaste of eternity on the decks of *Grey Goose*: the timeless beauty and closeness of the night of the sea-fire. An image, not of the past but of what is to be.

Under the Mercy.

The End

DATES OF THE C. S. LEWIS LETTERS

* Certainly 16 April; postmark 18 April.

INDEX OF POEMS BY TITLE AND FIRST LINE

ABOUT THE AUTHOR

Sheldon Vanauken is a professor at Lynchburg College, Lynchburg, Virginia.

INSPIRATIONAL FAVORITES

EUGENIA PRICE

St. Simon's Trilogy

☐ 12712	Beloved Invader	$1.95
☐ 12835	New Moon Rising	$1.95
☐ 12717	Lighthouse	$1.95
	and	
☐ 6485	Don Juan McQueen	$1.75
☐ 8878	Woman To Woman	$1.50

HAL LINDSEY

☐ 11545	The Liberation of Planet Earth	$1.95
☐ 11132	Satan Is Alive And Well On Planet Earth	$1.95
☐ 11259	The Terminal Generation	$1.95
☐ 10382	There's A New World Coming	$1.95

The MS READ-a-thon needs young readers!

Boys and girls between 6 and 14 can join the MS READ-a-thon and help find a cure for Multiple Sclerosis by reading books. And they get two rewards—the enjoyment of reading, and the great feeling that comes from helping others.

Parents and educators: For complete information call your local MS chapter, or call toll-free (800) 243-6000. Or mail the coupon below.

Kids can help, too!

Bantam Book Catalog

Here's your up-to-the-minute listing of over 1,400 titles by your favorite authors.

This illustrated, large format catalog gives a description of each title. For your convenience, it is divided into categories in fiction and non-fiction—gothics, science fiction, westerns, mysteries, cookbooks, mysticism and occult, biographies, history, family living, health, psychology, art.

So don't delay—take advantage of this special opportunity to increase your reading pleasure.

Just send us your name and address and 50¢ (to help defray postage and handling costs).

BANTAM BOOKS, INC.
Dept. FC, 414 East Golf Road, Des Plaines, Ill. 60016

Mr./Mrs./Miss_____
(please print)

Address_____

City_____State_____Zip_____

Do you know someone who enjoys books? Just give us their names and addresses and we'll send them a catalog too!

_____

Mr./Mrs./Miss_____

Address_____

City_____State_____Zip_____

Mr./Mrs./Miss_____

Address_____

City_____State_____Zip_____

FC—9/76